RELIGION KILLED JESUS

Religion didn't save Jesus , it crucified him

Printed in the United States of America

First Printing, 2025

ISBN 979-8-9939940-0-0

Heartwinners Publishing
10861 Hamilton Club Dr. Suite 206
Raleigh, N.C. 27617

Religionkilledjesus.com

Table of Contents

powerful reminder that redemption comes not through systems or traditions, but through a relationship with the living Christ.

When Truth Threatens Power

In every generation, truth's defenders rise again. And in our own time, we have witnessed this pattern repeat itself in the life and death of Charlie Kirk, a modern voice who refused to trade truth for acceptance.

The church at the crossroads

Centuries after the Cross, religion found new ways to silence its prophets through councils, prisons, and flames. The Church, now clothed in Roman power, turned its judgment outward, branding those who questioned authority as heretics.

The Living Christ
The author's testimony of ministry and transformation, discovering the power of God at work through sharing the Gospel, calling believers to action, and urging the Church to be doers of the Word, not hearers only.

Introduction

There are moments in history when truth and religion part ways. *Religion Killed Jesus* was born out of my search to understand how something meant to bring humanity closer to God could become the very system that condemned, silenced, and destroyed His messengers. I did not write this book to attack faith, nor to cast stones at believers, but to uncover the profound contradiction between the teachings of Christ and the machinery of organized religion that arose in His name.

Throughout history, the Church has stood as both a light and a shadow. It preserved sacred knowledge, yet it also burned saints and prophets who challenged its authority. It taught forgiveness, yet it executed Joan of Arc. It preached humility, yet it amassed power and wealth in the name of heaven. The heart of this book beats with one question: how could religion, a structure built around the story of Jesus, become the instrument of His death?

This book is a journey through scripture, history, and conscience. It is a search for the truth behind the crucifixion, not just as a historical event, but as a spiritual symbol of how human pride, fear, and control often crucify what is divine in the world. My purpose is not to condemn the Catholic Church or any denomination, but to awaken thought, invite reflection, and challenge blind tradition.

I wrote *Religion Killed Jesus* for those who still hunger for truth over ceremony, for those who have been hurt by hypocrisy yet still believe in love, and for those who sense that the real Jesus, the one who walked among the poor, forgave the sinner, and challenged the religious elite, is still calling us to follow Him, not a system.

As I write this book from my home in Raleigh, North Carolina, I often find myself retreating to the mountains or the quiet solitude of the beach. Those places where the noise of the world fades, and creation seems to breathe, help me feel closer to God's presence. Away from the rush of the city, my mind clears, and the Holy Spirit works in ways that words can barely describe. It's in those still moments that I hear the truth most clearly: religion may shape our beliefs, but only a personal encounter with God transforms the soul.

These moments have fed my spirit far more than any worship service.
They have become my altar.
They are the reason I wrote this book.

Those are the moments when I listen, really listen for His voice.
Not the voice of a preacher or a program,
But the living voice of the Holy Spirit.

That's where this book began, not in a study, not in a pulpit, but in the sacred stillness where God finally had my full attention.
This book is my testimony not of perfection, but of pursuit.
It's about the God who still walks the streets, who still speaks to broken hearts,
And who still turns the ashes of religion into the fire of revival.

"He healeth the broken in heart, and bindeth up their wounds." **Psalm 147:3**

The hum of the city is never too far away, yet my heart always longs for quiet. That's why I often escape to the mountains or the ocean, two places where the noise of life fades, and the presence of God feels near enough to touch. In the mountains, there's a sacred stillness, a whispering peace that feels ancient, eternal. At the beach, I watch the waves come and go, and I'm reminded that God's grace moves the same way: endless, steady, and always reaching the shore of the human heart.

I genuinely listen for the voice of the Holy Spirit in quiet moments, not from preachers or tradition. This book started there, when I finally gave God my full attention.

Each experience in life, in its own way, added something to my understanding of God. But even with all my years of learning, listening, discovering, and experiencing setbacks and triumphs, the truest lessons come when it's just the Word and me. In the quiet hours, alone with Scripture, I found what no sermon could give: the presence of God Himself.

That's where my faith deepened. That's where the questions began. And that's where I realized that religion, the very thing meant to bring us closer to God, can sometimes pull us away from Him.

I was baptized as a youth, long before I truly understood the meaning of the Bible or the depth of faith it calls us to. Like many others, I learned the stories of Scripture in Sunday school, told like fairy tales, filled with heroes and miracles, but often stripped of their more profound truth. It wasn't until adulthood that I began to study the Word of God with seriousness, thoughtfulness, and hunger. I would read and meditate on specific passages for hours, letting them settle into my heart and challenge what I had been taught.

My walk with God has not been shaped solely by formal religion, but by a combination of personal study, mentors, and the guidance of the Holy Spirit. Much of what I know came from being self-taught, studying scripture late into the night, cross-referencing passages, and searching for the heart of God through prayer. I also owe much to the voices who have helped illuminate the path: my late friend

Archie Morris from Chesterfield, Virginia, whose faith and insight profoundly influenced me; teachers like **Jerry Falwell** and my time as an undergraduate student at **Liberty University**; and influential preachers and evangelists such as **John Hagee, Charles Spurgeon, Billy Graham**, and **Dr. Mark Chironna**. Each one offered a piece of the puzzle, but I discovered that the most profound understanding of God doesn't come from pulpits or classrooms; it comes from solitude, from being alone with His Word.

Over the years, through both study and life experience, I've come to see that religion and God are not the same. Religion can point us toward Him, but it can also stand in His way. The rituals, traditions, and systems meant to glorify Christ have too often crucified the very truth He came to reveal. *Religion Killed Jesus* was born out of that realization, the painful yet liberating understanding that the greatest enemy of faith is not disbelief, but the misuse of belief.

This book is not written to condemn any denomination or to cast judgment on the Church. Instead, it is written to expose how easily human pride, politics, and power can distort what was meant to be pure and divine. It is a call to return to the essence of Christ's message, a message of love, forgiveness, and truth that has too often been buried beneath centuries of religious tradition.

I believe that the power of God is best felt when a person seeks Him sincerely, without pretense or performance. Salvation is not earned; it is a gift freely given by grace through faith. That truth alone should humble every human heart. My hope in writing this book is that readers will not only question the structures that have distorted the Gospel but rediscover the living Christ who still calls us beyond religion into relationship.

Religion Killed Jesus is not just a critique of history; it is a search for truth, a journey of faith, and a testimony of what I have come to believe: that knowing God begins when we strip away everything man has added and listen once more to the voice of Jesus Himself.

Chapter One

The Reason I Wrote This Book

There was a moment during a church service when it felt more like a concert than a sanctuary.
The music was perfect, the lights divine, but something was missing.
I looked around and saw lifted hands, but empty eyes, emotion without transformation.
Noise without anointing.

And I realized: it's not the church that needs fixing. It's the altar.
When the altar is restored, the fire will fall again.

Over the years, I've felt God's presence most not under chandeliers or in choirs but on sidewalks, in hospitals, in nursing homes, and in broken conversations with souls the church often overlooks.
I've seen God move most powerfully **outside** the walls that claim to contain Him.

When I visit a nursing home and hold the hands of the elderly who have no one left, I feel Heaven closer than in any cathedral.
When I sit beside a young man who's lost his parents, or a

teenage girl crying because she feels unseen, I think the Holy Spirit speaks through my silence more than through any sermon.

When I kneel beside a homeless man, not only giving him a meal, but giving him time, presence, and dignity, I sense the pleasure of God fill the air like holy incense.

"Inasmuch as ye have done it unto one of the least of these My brethren, ye have done it unto Me." **Matthew 25:40**

When Church Wounds

Yet, even as I poured my heart out for others, I faced my own fire.
There was the heartbreak of being betrayed by those closest to me.
my wife, who mocked the very ministry God had given me, and my pastor, who turned a cold shoulder when I needed spiritual refuge the most.

Their rejection cut deeper than words,
Because it came from the people who should have offered grace.
Those wounds became my wilderness.
They taught me that only God can fill the human heart with true love,
For human hearts, even in the Church, are easily poisoned by jealousy, pride, and bitterness.

"The heart is deceitful above all things, and desperately wicked: who can know it?" Jeremiah 17:9

But those same experiences also refined me.
They stripped away my dependence on approval, titles, and platforms.
They forced me to find God not in religion, but in

relationship.
Not in applause, but in anointing.

There is no wound deeper than one that comes from the house of a friend.
David knew this pain well when he cried,

**"For it was not an enemy who reproached me; then I could have borne it.
But it was you, a man my equal, my companion, and my acquaintance." Psalm 55:12–13**

Betrayal in the Church feels different because it's a wound wrapped in Scripture.
It comes not from the hand of an unbeliever, but from someone who claims to know the truth.
It is the Judas kiss that confuses the soul.
A reminder that not everyone who walks beside you is walking with God.

But even in that heartbreak, God had a purpose.
He allowed those betrayals not to break me, but to birth something within me.
A deeper hunger for His presence, a clearer understanding of His mercy.
What I thought was rejection was actually redirection.
The silence of man drove me into the sanctuary of God.

In that lonely place, I learned that the same Jesus who His own disciple betrayed.
is the same Jesus who walks beside the brokenhearted.
He was betrayed by His inner circle, denied by Peter, and deserted by His followers.
yet He still prayed, **"Father, forgive them."**
The Church may wound, but Christ still heals.

Those wounds became the proof of my calling.
They taught me that love must endure beyond offense,

And that forgiveness is not weakness; it is the power of the cross alive within us.

Now I can say, as Joseph said to his brothers,

"You meant evil against me, but God meant it for good." Genesis 50:20

For every betrayal, God birthed a blessing.
For every rejection, He gave a revelation.
For every tear, He gave testimony.

I learned that ministry is not about being loved by man.
it's about being known by God.
And sometimes, the breaking comes before the blessing.
Because only when the vessel is broken can the oil truly flow.

**"Many are the afflictions of the righteous:
But the Lord delivereth him out of them all." Psalm 34:19**

Prayer for healing church wounds

Heavenly Father, you see every silent tear and every hidden heartache we carry. Today, we bring before you the pain caused by pastors, leaders, and others we once trusted. In this moment, we choose to forgive, just as you forgave on the cross. We ask you to heal our hearts, restore our joy, and lead us back into a place where we can love, serve, and worship with freedom once again.

Remind us, Lord, that the Church is not a building but your people, with you as our Head. May your Spirit renew all that has been broken within us and let your presence become our refuge and our healing.

Thank you for transforming our wounds into strength and turning harm into holiness. We trust you to use even our deepest hurts for your glory.

In Jesus' name, Amen.

Writing from the Fire

There are moments in life when your heart becomes so full that silence no longer feels right.
That's what led me to write this book.
I didn't set out to write a religious critique or a theological thesis; I set out to write the *truth*.
The kind of truth that's been stirring in my spirit for years, growing stronger every time I opened my Bible and asked, ***"Where did we lose Jesus in the midst of religion?"***

When silence no longer suffices

There are seasons in life when the weight of what we carry inside can no longer be contained. My own heart reached that point of fullness that made continued silence impossible. That moment of overflow is what compelled me to begin writing this book.

I never intended to produce a scholarly critique of religion, nor was I interested in composing a dense theological treatise. My aim has always been to share the truth, the very truth that has quietly but steadily grown within me, intensifying with every page of Scripture I have turned and every question I have whispered in prayer.

Time and again, as I opened my Bible, a single question echoed through my spirit: **"Where did we lose Jesus in the midst of religion?"** This search for the heart of Christ, apart from tradition and ritual, is at the core of every word that follows.

As I write these words, I sit in my home.
The hum of the city lingers outside my window, yet my heart longs for quiet.
That's why I often retreat to the mountains or the sea places where I can hear Him clearly.
In the mountains, there's a stillness that feels like eternity.
At the ocean, the rhythm of the waves reminds me of grace, endless, faithful, and always returning.

A Childhood of Ritual Without Revelation

When I was young, I was baptized, like many others, before I truly understood what it meant. I believed what I was told, sang the songs, and listened to the stories in Sunday school. But if I'm honest, the Bible was taught to me more like a storybook than the living Word of God. The lessons felt distant tales of lions, giants, floods, and miracles, but not in a way that reached my heart or changed how I saw the world.

I don't say that to criticize the people who taught me. They did what they knew. But looking back, I realize I didn't yet know Jesus; I only knew *about* Him. There's a difference between memorizing Scripture and meeting the One it speaks of. That realization didn't come until much later in life, after the world had tested my faith, and I had begun searching for God not through religion, but through relationship.

The Search for Real Understanding

As an adult, something changed in me. I began reading the Bible not as a storybook or a ritual text, but as the **living breath of God** written on paper.
I didn't just read it, I wrestled with it, questioned it, and meditated on it. I could sit with a single verse for hours, even days, turning it over in my spirit until it revealed its depth.
Some verses clung to me for weeks, shaping my thoughts and my prayers until I finally understood what the Spirit was saying.

"The entrance of Thy words giveth light; it giveth understanding unto the simple." *Psalm 119:130*

My study was self-taught, but never solitary; the **Holy Spirit** was my most excellent teacher.
Along the way, God placed people in my path who expanded my perspective. Yet, even with all those teachers, I learned that the most profound truths come not from sermons or seminars but from **silence and Scripture**.
In the quiet hours of study, when it was just the Word and me, I felt something no denomination could give: the **presence of God Himself**.

Seeking Truth Across Religions

In my quest for truth, I studied many faiths. I wanted to understand what people believed and, more importantly, *why*.
I wasn't chasing religion; I was chasing revelation.

"Blessed are they which do hunger and thirst after righteousness, for they shall be filled." *Matthew 5:6*

The Church of Jesus Christ of Latter-day Saints (Mormonism)

When I was young, I spent time with the **Latter-day Saints**. Their discipline impressed me with clean living, family-centered values, and dedication to service. They introduced me to the idea that faith involves community. Yet over time, I saw how their focus shifted from the Bible to *The Book of Mormon*.

Their foundation rested more on the writings of Joseph Smith than on the Gospel of Christ.
While their intentions were sincere, I realized that their religion depended too heavily on an earthly prophet rather than the **living voice of the Holy Spirit**.

"For there is one God, and one mediator between God and men, the man Christ Jesus." *1 Timothy 2:5*

Still, I learned something valuable from them: **devotion must never replace discernment**. Even the most disciplined faith can lose sight of truth when it elevates tradition over transformation.

Jehovah's Witnesses — Knowledge Without Relationship

Later, I studied with the **Jehovah's Witnesses**. They knew Scripture impressively well. Their memorization of the Bible was unmatched; they could quote entire passages effortlessly.

But I also noticed something missing: **the warmth of grace**. Their emphasis on rules, organization, and doctrinal correctness left little room for the tender relationship that God desires with His children.
They taught me facts about God, but not the **feeling** of His presence.

Their rejection of holidays and celebrations struck me as unnecessary, not sinful, but overly cautious. While they sought purity, they often lost joy.
I came to understand that holiness is not about what you avoid, but **who you adore**.

"For the kingdom of God is not meat and drink; but righteousness, and peace, and joy in the Holy Ghost." *Romans 14:17*

It taught me an important truth: when religion becomes more about **rules than relationships**, it creates fear instead of freedom.

Evangelical Teachers — Passion and Presentation

In time, I also learned from well-known Bible teachers.
I listened to **Charles Stanley**, whose calm, steady preaching helped me see God as patient and personal.
I studied the fiery sermons of **John Hagee**, whose passion for Scripture reignited my own hunger for the Word.
I even listened to **Joel Osteen** in my earlier years. His positivity was appealing, but I soon realized that

encouragement without conviction is spiritual sugar. It tastes good, but doesn't nourish.

"For the time will come when they will not endure sound doctrine; but after their own lusts shall they heap to themselves teachers, having itching ears." — *2 Timothy 4:3*

These ministries showed me the broad spectrum of modern Christianity from prosperity preaching to prophetic truth. Yet, through all of them, the Spirit kept whispering the same lesson: **"Know Me for yourself."**

"So then faith cometh by hearing, and hearing by the word of God." *Romans 10:17*

One night, while I was working out of town and staying in a hotel, I turned on the television around **11 o'clock**. Dr. Mark Chironna was preaching from **Joshua chapter 2**, the story of *Rahab and the two spies.*

As he spoke, the Holy Spirit came upon me like a tidal wave. It was not emotion alone; it was revelation. The passage came alive, and for the first time, I understood the deeper meaning of Rahab's story: how God's grace can reach into the darkest corners and bring redemption out of sin.

Rahab and the Two Spies: A Lesson in Grace and Purpose

The story begins with Joshua sending two spies into Jericho to gather information about its walls, water, food supply, and defenses.
They ended up in the house of **Rahab**, a prostitute. To the

world, Rahab's home was a place of shame. But to God, it became a place of salvation.

"And they went, and came into a harlot's house, named Rahab, and lodged there." *Joshua 2:1*

The spies hid there when Jericho's soldiers came looking for them. Rahab, risking her life, concealed them and sent the soldiers another way. Her courage wasn't born from religious piety it came from a spark of faith. She said to them,

"The Lord your God, He is God in heaven above, and in earth beneath." *Joshua 2:11*

That confession changed everything. God used a woman whom society had written off to deliver His messengers and to preserve His plan.
Rahab, a sinner by reputation, became a saint by faith.

"By faith the harlot Rahab perished not with them that believed not, when she had received the spies with peace." *Hebrews 11:31*

In time, Rahab's life was redeemed. She married Salmon, an Israelite, and became part of the lineage of **Jesus Christ Himself,** proof that grace not only forgives but also rewrites history.

"And Salmon begat Boaz of Rahab." *Matthew 1:5*

This truth struck me deeply: God's mercy is not limited by our past, and our flaws do not bind His purpose.
The same God who used Rahab can use anyone, even those the world calls unworthy, to accomplish His divine plan.

The Spirit at Work in the Ordinary

That night in the hotel, I couldn't sleep. The Holy Spirit stirred so powerfully in me that I knew I had to do something with what I had just heard.
The next day, though my job was in **sales**, I felt compelled to **evangelize** instead. I went door-to-door, not selling a product but sharing the story of Rahab from *Joshua 2.*

I told people how God used a woman the world despised to bring deliverance, and how the same God can redeem anyone's story.
Some listened, some didn't, but nearly three-quarters of the people I met that day were open, even moved. I didn't plan that. The Spirit orchestrated it.

"It shall not be you speaking, but the Spirit of your Father speaking through you." *Matthew 10:20*

That day became one of the most powerful experiences of my life.
It reminded me that the Holy Spirit doesn't just inspire sermons; He **commissions ordinary people every day to carry His message**.

God Uses the Imperfect to Reveal the Perfect

The message of Rahab also taught me something about **discernment**.
When I look at modern society and even our political and religious leaders, I see how quickly people are to dismiss those whom God may still be using.

Rahab was a prostitute, yet she became part of Christ's lineage.
David was an adulterer, yet God called him **"a man after My own heart."**
Peter denied Jesus three times, yet was chosen to lead the Church.

"My strength is made perfect in weakness." *2 Corinthians 12:9*

Sometimes God works through unlikely people, even through leaders whom the religious world rejects.
That's why I've often said: Don't be too quick to assume who God can or cannot use.

One modern example I often think of is **Donald Trump**. Whatever one thinks of his personal life, I believe, as many discerning Christians do, that God has used him to uphold certain **biblical principles** in an increasingly anti-Christian culture.
Like Cyrus, the Persian king whom God called His "anointed" to deliver Israel (see *Isaiah 45:1*), Trump's role may not have been one of spiritual perfection, but of spiritual purpose.

"Thus saith the Lord to His anointed, to Cyrus, whose right hand I have holden, to subdue nations before him." *Isaiah 45:1*

This is where **maturity in faith** comes in: discerning what God is doing, even when His vessels are flawed.
Immature believers look only at appearances. Mature believers look for God's hand amid imperfection.

Balancing Conviction with Compassion

Over the years, I've learned that being dogmatic drives people away, but being diplomatic opens the door for conversation.
We can stand on truth without closing our hearts.
We can disagree without despising.

That's what Rahab's story reveals: God doesn't work through condemnation but through **connection**.

She didn't come to faith because someone judged her; she came because she encountered grace.

"For God sent not His Son into the world to condemn the world; but that the world through Him might be saved." *John 3:17*

Our mission, then, is not to argue people into heaven but to **love them toward Christ.**
To be firm in truth but soft in spirit.
To represent Jesus not as a judge behind a pulpit, but as a Savior reaching through the rubble.

The Day Faith Became Fire

That night, watching **Dr. Chironna** changed something in me forever.
It was the moment I realized that the Holy Spirit doesn't wait for perfect conditions; He moves in **obedient hearts.**
He can speak through a sermon on TV, a verse in the Bible, or a voice in the still of the night.

"And it shall come to pass afterward, that I will pour out My Spirit upon all flesh." *Joel 2:28*

The next day's door-to-door experience wasn't planned; it was **Spirit-led.**
And through it, I learned that revelation is not meant to stay in our notebooks; it's meant to move our feet.

Faith without obedience is just thought.
But faith in motion, that's where miracles begin.

"Be ye doers of the word, and not hearers only." *James 1:22*

That was one of the first times I felt the fire of the Holy Spirit consuming me from the inside out.
And it confirmed what all my searching had been leading to:
God is not confined to pulpits, pews, or politics. He moves wherever hearts are willing to listen.

Education and Spiritual Formation

I also studied through **Liberty University**, where I learned theology and how to read Scripture systematically and defend doctrine.
That academic foundation gave me clarity, but it also showed me something deeper: **even education can become an idol if it replaces revelation**.

It's one thing to know about God; it's another to know Him. Knowledge may fill your mind, but only relationship fills your soul.

"Ever learning, and never able to come to the knowledge of the truth." *2 Timothy 3:7*

The Balance Between Truth and Love

Through all these journeys in Mormonism, Jehovah's Witnesses, evangelical ministries, and academic theology, I learned that the closer I came to religion, the further I sometimes drifted from the simplicity of Jesus.

Religion loves to debate doctrine.
Jesus invites you to dine with Him.

Religion teaches *about* God.
Jesus says, *"Follow Me. And you will develop a relationship with God."*

"Come unto Me, all ye that labour and are heavy laden, and I will give you rest." *Matthew 11:28*

The lesson I took from all of this is that truth and love must walk hand in hand.
Being "right" means nothing if it separates you from grace.
God never asked us to win arguments; He asked us to win hearts.

Holidays, Culture, and Conviction

One of the areas where religious divisions often surfaced was in **holidays**.
The Jehovah's Witnesses condemned all of them; the Mormons observed them cautiously; evangelicals embraced them freely.

I came to believe that while some cultural traditions are indeed worldly or vain, others can be redeemed as opportunities to **witness Christ**.
Christmas, for instance, may have cultural elements that stray from biblical accuracy, yet it's also a time when the name of Jesus is spoken aloud in millions of homes. Why waste that?

"To the pure all things are pure." *Titus 1:15*

The key is not whether the holiday is perfect, but whether **Christ remains at the center**.
Faith is not about rejecting everything; it's about redeeming everything that can be used for God's glory.

The Real Lesson of the Search

Looking back, I realized that every religion, denomination, and movement I studied gave me something, but none gave me everything.
Each one carried a piece of the puzzle, yet only the **Holy Spirit** revealed the whole picture.

"But the Comforter, which is the Holy Ghost, whom the Father will send in My name, He shall teach you all things and bring all things to your remembrance." *John 14:26*

My search for fundamental understanding wasn't about joining a religion.
It was about recognizing that no religion can replace revelation.
An institution does not own truth; it is **embodied in the person of Jesus Christ.**

"Jesus saith unto him, I am the way, the truth, and the life: no man cometh unto the Father, but by Me." *John 14:6*

Now, as I reflect on those years of study, I can say with confidence:
The more I learned about religion, the less I needed it.
And the more I learned about Jesus, the more I realized He was all I ever needed.

When Religion Becomes the Barrier

Through study and prayer, I began to see how man has often taken what was meant to be holy and turned it into hierarchy, how Jesus' message of mercy, love, and humility was twisted into systems of control, power, and pride.

The more I read the Gospels, the clearer it became that it wasn't the sinners or the outcasts who killed Jesus; it was the religious leaders. The priests, the scholars, the ones who claimed to represent God. They were so blinded by their traditions and authority that they couldn't recognize the Messiah standing right in front of them. And I couldn't help but wonder: how many times since then has religion repeated the same sin?

That realization disturbed me, and it still does. It's not a comfortable truth, but it's a necessary one. Because once you see it, you can't unsee it. The very structure that was supposed to glorify God had, in many ways, crucified Him repeatedly through hypocrisy, corruption, and pride.

A Calling to Speak

Religion Killed Jesus wasn't written in anger; it reflects my desire to speak truth and guide believers toward what matters. I've witnessed religion's power to divide, but also Christ's ability to forgive and heal. My purpose shifted from preaching to writing, offering hope to those who feel disconnected from church but still seek God. This book is my testimony and a reminder that God's love exceeds all religious boundaries.

The Simple Truth

Through extensive reflection, I have concluded that salvation is not the result of personal merit but rather something received. It does not reside within human rituals, but in what is described as the grace of God. The role of the cross was not to establish a religion, but to foster a connection.

It has become apparent to me that the significance of Jesus's death extends beyond atonement for sin; it represents liberation from the constraints imposed by human systems that separate individuals from God. While religious institutions historically played a role in Jesus's crucifixion, His teachings endured. The resurrection serves as a testament to the enduring nature of love.

This book was composed to illustrate that the presence of God persists beyond institutional frameworks and is accessible to all who sincerely seek. Regardless of location, whether in a cathedral, a remote cabin, or along the shoreline, the opportunity for encounter remains available.

The motivation for writing this work is to document the realization that while religious forces contributed to His death, love prevails and continues to reach individuals universally.

There are moments in life when your heart becomes so full that silence no longer feels right. That's what led me to write this book. I didn't set out to write a religious critique or a history lesson; I set out to write the truth. The truth that had been stirring in my heart for years, quietly growing stronger every time I opened my Bible, looked at the world, and asked myself why the message of Jesus seemed so far removed from the religion that claimed His name.

The Retreat (information on this retreat is at the end of this book): Discovering Peace, Identity, and the Enemy

I attended a spiritual retreat of healing about 15 years ago, and it helped me gain spiritual revelations and healing. I have referred people to this retreat, and it has changed their lives. One of the deepest reasons I want you to attend the retreat is to experience what cannot be taught in a classroom or explained in a sermon. A retreat pulls you out of the noise, out of the chaos, out of the constant demands of life long enough for you to finally hear God again. It is in stillness that you discover a truth Jesus promised:

27

**"My peace I give to you… not as the world gives"
(John 14:27).**

At the retreat, you learn that the peace of God is not the absence of problems; it is the presence of Christ inside you. It is the realization that no matter what storms rage around you, God is on your side, and the Holy Spirit gives you the supernatural ability to walk through life with calmness and clarity. When you encounter this kind of peace, you begin to understand that **the world didn't give it, and the world can't take it away.**

But another revelation unfolds there as well: the unveiling of **the enemy**. You begin to see how the enemy, Satan, works. Still, the spirits that operate through people strategically place specific individuals, situations, and temptations in your life with one goal: **to destroy you.** Jesus warned us plainly,
**"The thief comes only to steal and kill and destroy"
(John 10:10).**

The retreat teaches you to recognize spiritual attacks, manipulation, toxic relationships, and emotional traps *before* they pull you under. The Holy Spirit gives you a conviction deep inside your spirit so you can identify danger, discern motives, and walk away without apology. Protecting your peace becomes a spiritual discipline because that peace is like gold, precious, unbreakable, and not for sale at any price.

When you finally understand your value in Christ, you will **never again put yourself on the auction block, never** again allow your identity, your dignity, or your destiny to be sold, traded, or diminished by the opinions or actions of others. You realize your life is infinite in worth. No earthly scale, no material possession, no bank account can determine your success. You measure yourself only by who you are in Christ.

And this is the greatest empowerment:
You are not just someone who can identify the enemy; you are a **warrior** who can defeat him. Not in your own strength, but because you know who your Father is. You know the authority Jesus gave you **(Luke 10:19)**. You know that the battle belongs to the Lord (2 **Chronicles 20:15**). You know that no weapon formed against you shall prosper **(Isaiah 54:17).**

Once this becomes real in your heart, you carry a quiet confidence that cannot be shaken. Even if you never become everything the world says you "should" be, you already know you have arrived because you walk in the identity and victory of Christ. That truth becomes your anchor, your shield, and your freedom.

Chapter Two

About My Father's Business — The Boy Who Confused Religion

Every year, the people of Israel streamed toward Jerusalem for Passover. The dusty roads filled with caravans, the sound of song and sacrifice rising from every direction. Among them walked a boy of twelve from Nazareth, his parents proud, his heart already stirred by something eternal. His name was Jesus.

Luke tells us that, after the festival, Mary and Joseph began their journey home, only to realize, a day later, that the boy was missing. When they found Him three days later, He wasn't lost; He was exactly where He meant to be.

He was sitting in the temple courts, not playing among the children but reasoning with the rabbis. He was *listening and asking questions* that pierced the armor of religious tradition. The learned men marveled at His understanding. Mary, relieved and confused, asked why He had done this. His reply would echo through eternity:

"Why did you seek Me? Did you not know that I must be about My Father's business?" — Luke 2:49

That sentence was the dividing line between religion and revelation.

Religion Observed, Relationship Revealed

Every Jewish boy of His age was expected to sit at the feet of teachers of the Law, to memorize Torah, and to honor the ritual system. Yet Jesus did more than listen—He taught. He revealed insight far beyond His years, showing that the presence of God is not confined to scrolls or sacrifices.

Even at twelve, He was showing Israel what it had forgotten: that God desired mercy more than offerings (Hosea 6:6). The priests busied themselves with ritual; the boy sought relationship.

In that moment, the Lamb of God was already walking among the lambs that would be slain, foreshadowing the day when His blood would end the need for theirs. He was a child who saw what scholars could not: the temple had become a system, not a sanctuary.

The Temple System: A Kingdom of Control

To understand the weight of His words, we must look at the temple as it was. Herod's temple was a magnificent white stone and gold that gleamed under the Judean sun. It stood as both a monument to God and a monument to man's pride.

The temple courts were divided: Gentiles kept to the outer court, women were restricted to another, and priests occupied the inner sanctum. Access to God was controlled, measured, mediated. Religion had become an empire within an empire: Pharisees, Sadducees, and priests using law as leverage.

To them, holiness was hierarchy.
To Jesus, holiness was humility.

When He told His parents He was about His Father's business, He wasn't rejecting Judaism, He was reclaiming its heart. His Father's business was never to preserve systems, but to pursue souls.

From the Child in the Temple to the Man Who Cleansed It

31

Years later, that boy returned to the same temple, now as a man. The same courts He once filled with wisdom were filled again with merchants, tables, and the stench of greed. The sound of doves and the clink of coins drowned the sound of prayer.

The child who once sat among teachers now stood as Judge.

"It is written, My house shall be called a house of prayer; but ye have made it a den of thieves." — Matthew 21:13

He overturned the tables. Silver scattered across the stones. Merchants ran. Priests stared in outrage. Once again, religion was confusing and contradictory.

The moment foreshadowed in His youth had reached fulfillment: He was about His Father's business, cleansing His Father's house. But this time, it wasn't a lesson, it was a reckoning.

What began with questions ended with confrontation. The boy who amazed teachers now rebuked them. The child who spoke of His Father's business now revealed that business for what it was: redemption, not religion.

The True Meaning of "My Father's Business"

In Hebrew tradition, the "Father's business" referred to a son learning his father's trade. A fisherman's son learned nets, a carpenter's son, wood. Jesus, as the carpenter's son, was building something, but not of stone and timber. He was building a Kingdom of living hearts.

Each interaction, each act of compassion, was part of that work.

- Healing the sick was the Father's business.

- Feeding the hungry was the Father's business.

- Forgiving the sinner was the Father's business.

And when He overturned the tables, He was still doing His Father's work, tearing down the barriers between God and man.

The child's statement at twelve was a glimpse into the eternal: that God's business is people.

The Foreshadowing of the Cross

The religious leaders who first heard of this prodigy likely dismissed Him as a precocious boy. Yet within twenty years, those same religious structures would call for His death. The same temple He cleansed would later pay silver for His betrayal.

From His first visit to Jerusalem to His last, the path was marked by the same resistance—religion defending itself against revelation. His zeal for His Father's house would eventually consume Him, just as Scripture foretold **(Psalm 69:9).**

But it wasn't the merchants who destroyed Him; it was the priests who feared losing their power. The child's conversation in Luke 2 and the man's actions in **Matthew 21** are mirror images of one truth: the system built to reveal God had become the system that killed Him.

Reflections for the Modern Church

The story is more than history; it is prophecy. The same spirit that corrupted the temple still creeps into modern sanctuaries.
We build programs instead of altars.
We sell convenience instead of conviction.
We guard buildings instead of hearts.

But Christ's words echo still: *"I must be about My Father's business."*
The question for us is simple: are we?

"For where your treasure is, there will your heart be also." Matthew 6:21

Committees do not manage the Father's business; they do so by compassion. It is not conducted in boardrooms, but in prayer rooms. It happens when believers take their faith from the pews to the people.

When the Church remembers that the tables will turn again, not in anger, but in awakening.

When Power Trembled The Road to the Cross

The Rise of Resistance

As Jesus grew, so did the opposition. The same religious system that marveled at His wisdom as a child began to despise Him as a man. His words cut deeper than the prophets before Him, for He spoke not of law but of liberty.

The Pharisees, guardians of tradition, prided themselves on obedience to the letter but were blind to the Spirit. The

Sadducees, wealthy and politically allied with Rome, feared that His growing influence would disturb their arrangement with Caesar. And the scribes, experts in Scripture, could quote every prophecy yet failed to recognize the One who fulfilled them.

Each miracle He performed tightened their fear. Each parable exposed their hypocrisy. He healed on the Sabbath, forgave sins without sacrifice, and ate with sinners while refusing their rituals of purity. They saw not a Savior, but a threat.

"If we let Him alone, all men will believe on Him, and the Romans shall come and take away our place and nation." John 11:48

So the Sanhedrin convened, a council not of discernment but of conspiracy. And Caiaphas, the high priest, unknowingly prophesied the divine plan when he said:

"It is expedient for us that one man should die for the people, and that the whole nation perish not." John 11:50

Religion had found its justification. The plot was set.

The Snare of Judas

Among the twelve, Judas Iscariot moved like a shadow. He had heard every sermon, witnessed every healing, and yet his heart remained tethered to silver more than Spirit. When Mary of Bethany broke her alabaster jar to anoint Jesus, Judas grumbled about the waste, a moment when greed betrayed grace long before his kiss would.

"Then one of the twelve, called Judas Iscariot, went unto the chief priests, and said, What will ye give me,

and I will deliver Him unto you? And they covenanted with him for thirty pieces of silver." — Matthew 26:14–15

That sum was the price of a slave, the same cost Zechariah had prophesied centuries before (Zechariah 11:12). The transaction was more than treachery; it was prophecy fulfilled.

And yet, Judas was not alone in his betrayal. While he sold Christ for silver, the rest would sell Him for safety. At the table where love and bread were broken, fear was already eating with them.

"All ye shall be offended because of Me this night." — Matthew 26:31

The Court of Night — The Sanhedrin's Trial

When the moment came, religion met under darkness. The council that claimed to represent God gathered secretly to condemn His Son. Justice was twisted, the law was broken, and false witnesses rehearsed their lies.

The High Priest demanded that Jesus declare His identity. And when He said, *"You will see the Son of Man seated at the right hand of Power,"* Caiaphas tore his robe and shouted, *"Blasphemy!"* the same robe he would have worn entering the Holy of Holies. Holiness itself now stood before him, and he called it heresy.

"The rulers take counsel together, against the Lord, and against His Anointed." — Psalm 2:2

The verdict was not born of truth but of fear. The priests handed Him to Pilate because they lacked the authority to kill, but not the desire. Pilate's basin washed his hands, not his heart. The crowd's cry of "Crucify Him!" drowned out the whisper of conscience.

Religion had chosen its god: **control**. Rome had chosen its peace: **compromise**. And heaven had chosen its path: **the cross.**

The Silent Savior

The Lamb said nothing. When accused, He answered not. When struck, He did not retaliate. In silence, He fulfilled Isaiah's prophecy:

"He was oppressed, and He was afflicted, yet He opened not His mouth: He is brought as a lamb to the slaughter." **— Isaiah 53:7**

The same lips that had spoken storms into calm now held peace in suffering. The same hands that had healed lepers now bore iron and blood. The very priests who recited the Psalms of David nailed David's promised Son to the wood of Rome.

They crowned Him with thorns, the symbol of the curse, not realizing that in mocking Him, they were crowning their Redeemer. The curse of Eden rested on His brow, and the promise of Eden was being restored through His pain.

Even then, mercy spoke:

"Father, forgive them; for they know not what they do." **— Luke 23:34**

The Turning of the Tables Once More

When He died, the earth trembled. The temple veil, sixty feet high and four inches thick, tore from top to bottom. Heaven itself ripped open the boundary religion had built.

That moment was not merely symbolic; it was cosmic. The hand that tore the veil declared to every generation:
Access is open.
No more priests, no more intermediaries, only grace.

Mary wept at the tomb, her tears falling on the stone that angels would soon roll away. Peter returned to the place of his denial, ashamed yet redeemed. The disciples, once scattered, would soon be filled with power not from the temple, but from Heaven.

The boy who once sat among teachers had become the Teacher of nations.
The man who overturned tables had overturned death.
The Lamb slain by religion had become the Lord resurrected by love.

***"He is not here; for He is risen, as He said." —* Matthew 28:6**

Closing Reflection

From the moment He lingered in the temple as a boy to the hour He cleansed it as a man, Jesus stood as a mirror to religion, revealing its emptiness and restoring its purpose.
He was never against worship; He was against walls.
He was never against the law; He was against bondage.

He was never against priests; He became the High Priest Himself.

The cross was not the defeat of the Son; it was the unmasking of the system. Religion killed Jesus, but love refused to stay buried.

And even now, He walks through the temples of our hearts, overturning the tables we build pride, performance, power, whispering the exact words He spoke as a boy:

"I must be about My Father's business."

 It was supposed to be holy ground. The temple courts, filled with the scent of incense and the sound of prayer, stood as the pride of a people who believed God chose them. Yet on that sacred ground, in the shadows of marble pillars and golden altars, religion plotted the death of its own Maker.

The men who wore the robes of holiness had become guardians of power. Their lips spoke of God, but their hearts beat with fear, fear of losing their place, their influence, their control. And so, in the name of the Law, they began to conspire against the One who had come to fulfill it.

They didn't recognize Him, or maybe they did, and that was the problem.

The Threat of Truth

Jesus was not what they expected. He had no army, no throne, no wealth. He came with dusty feet, worn clothes, and a voice that carried the weight of heaven. He healed on the Sabbath, spoke to sinners, and told parables that pierced their pride. He called the poor **"blessed"** and the proud **"blind."**

When He spoke, the crowds listened not out of fear, but hunger. Every word fed something inside them that religion never could.

**"The people were astonished at His teaching,"
Matthew wrote, *"for He taught them as one having
authority, and not as the scribes."* (Matthew 7:28–29)**

That was the beginning of their fury. The priests and Pharisees had spent their lives mastering words and rituals, yet here was a carpenter's son from Nazareth who spoke as if heaven itself had permitted Him. His truth exposed their hypocrisy, and light always offends darkness.

The leaders of religion could not allow Him to continue, not because He was false, but because He was true.

The Meeting in the Shadows

One night, long before the crucifixion, a secret meeting was held. The high priest Caiaphas sat surrounded by scribes, elders, and temple guards. The air was heavy with tension. The reports had become impossible to ignore: the blind were seeing, the lame were walking, and the dead were rising.

**"If we let Him alone,"* one said, *"all men will believe on
Him, and the Romans shall come and take away our
place and nation."* (John 11:48)**

Caiaphas leaned forward, his voice cold with calculation.

**"It is expedient for us that one man should die for the
people, and that the whole nation perish not."* (John
11:50)**

With those words, religion sealed its own fate. The very men who claimed to defend God's law began to violate it. The trial of Jesus didn't start in Pilate's hall; it began in the heart of religion, in that candlelit room where pride spoke louder than faith.

The Betrayal

Judas had walked with Jesus, seen His miracles, and shared His bread. Yet something in him had grown restless, disappointed, perhaps, that Jesus didn't seek power or position. The priests saw the crack and pressed their silver into it.

For thirty coins, the price of a slave, Judas sold the Son of God into the hands of His enemies. Religion had found its executioner.

That night, in the Garden of Gethsemane, the olive trees stood silent witnesses. The soldiers came with torches, swords, and scripture on their lips. When Jesus stepped forward, He didn't resist.

"Whom seek ye?" He asked.
"Jesus of Nazareth."
"I am He." (John 18:4–5)

They fell backward at His words, even in arrest; His presence commanded awe. But religion no longer bowed to truth. It dragged Him through the darkness to the court of men who claimed to know God.

The Religious Trial

The trial was not about justice; it was about **justification,** a desperate attempt by corrupt religion to rationalize the murder of Truth Himself.

They had already decided on the verdict long before the trial began; all that remained was to dress their hatred in holy garments.

"And the chief priests and all the council sought for witness against Jesus to put Him to death; and found none." — Mark 14:55

The Sanhedrin, Israel's highest religious court, was never meant to be a theater for lies.

According to Jewish law, a capital case could not be tried at night, nor could it be concluded in a single day.

Yet Jesus was arrested in the darkness of Gethsemane, bound like a criminal, and hurried through secret hearings before dawn.

Even outside the Bible, history records that such a proceeding violated the very Torah they claimed to defend.

False witnesses were summoned not to testify, but to *agree.*

Their stories conflicted, their evidence collapsed, yet the priests persisted.

They twisted Scripture to fit their ambition, forgetting the words of Moses:

"Keep thee far from a false matter; and the innocent and righteous slay thou not." — Exodus 23:7

But religion has always found ways to twist law into a weapon when its power is threatened.

What Caiaphas and the council feared was not heresy; it was *loss of control.*

Jesus had captured the hearts of the people.

He healed on the Sabbath, dined with sinners, and called fishermen His apostles.

Every miracle He performed was a blow to their system, every parable a challenge to their pride.

"If we let Him thus alone, all men will believe on Him: and the Romans shall come and take away both our place and nation." — John 11:48

That was their genuine concern, not the honor of God, but the preservation of their influence.
So they sought justification in law while violating its very heart.
They blindfolded the Light of the world and called Him guilty.

The High Priest and the Tear of Hypocrisy

When Jesus spoke the truth of His identity

"You shall see the Son of Man sitting at the right hand of Power, and coming with the clouds of heaven" — Mark 14:62
the high priest tore his robe in feigned outrage.

This act was not holy zeal; it was theater.
According to **Leviticus 21:10**, the high priest was *forbidden* to tear his garments.

"And he that is the high priest among his brethren... shall not uncover his head, nor rend his clothes." — Leviticus 21:10

Caiaphas broke priestly law, outwardly mourning while inwardly rebelling. Religion conflicted with itself as grace challenged rituals.

Prophecy Fulfilled in the Shadows

Everything that happened that night had been foretold centuries earlier.
Isaiah saw it in the Spirit when he wrote:

"He was oppressed, and He was afflicted, yet He opened not His mouth:
He is brought as a lamb to the slaughter, and as a sheep before her shearers is dumb,
so He openeth not His mouth." — Isaiah 53:7

The prophet also declared:

"He was taken from prison and from judgment: and who shall declare His generation?
For He was cut off out of the land of the living: for the transgression of My people was He stricken." — Isaiah 53:8

In the court of men, the Messiah stood silent not because He was powerless, but because prophecy demanded restraint.
At any moment, He could have summoned legions of angels, yet He chose obedience over deliverance.
It was not nails that bound Him, but love.

Religion Versus Revelation

That night, the Sanhedrin stood as the symbol of every religious system that fears freedom more than truth.
They clung to the law as a shield, never realizing that the Lawgiver stood before them in flesh.
Their religion could quote Scripture but could not recognize the Word incarnate.

"Search the Scriptures; for in them ye think ye have eternal life: and they are they which testify of Me." — John 5:39

44

The trial of Jesus was the collision between *form* and *fire* between the old covenant written on stone and the new covenant written in blood.

When Caiaphas shouted, "What further need have we of witnesses?" he unknowingly spoke a more profound truth. No more witnesses were needed; the world's final testimony was standing before them.

And when he cried, **"He is guilty of blasphemy!"** religion officially condemned revelation.

The Handing Over

After their mockery, they handed Him to Pilate, thinking Rome would do what religion could not.

But even Pilate, a pagan governor, saw more innocence in Christ than the priests ever did.

"I find no fault in Him." John 19:6

Yet the crowd stirred by priests shouted, **"Crucify Him!"** The same lips that had once cried, "Hosanna!" now demanded His death.

History would remember that it was not pagan Rome that sought His execution, but it was religious men, blinded by their own authority.

Reflection

The religious trial of Jesus was more than a moment in time it was a mirror.

It reveals what happens when religion values control over compassion, ritual over revelation, and appearance over anointing.

The Sanhedrin represents every age, more importantly, the age we live in now, when those who claim to know God persecute those who truly walk with Him.

45

And still today, Christ is on trial in the courts of religion. whenever power replaces purity, and tradition replaces truth.

The Politics of Murder

They took Jesus to Pilate, but Rome didn't care about blasphemy. The empire didn't crucify men for claiming to be holy, only for claiming to be kings.

So the priests changed their accusation. They no longer spoke of theology, but treason.

"We found this man perverting the nation," they said, *"and saying that He Himself is Christ, a King."* (Luke 23:2)

When Pilate questioned Him, Jesus spoke a few words that still echo through time:

"My kingdom is not of this world." (John 18:36)

Pilate knew He was innocent. His wife had even dreamed of His righteousness. But the priests stirred the crowd.

"If you let this man go, you are no friend of Caesar," they shouted. (John 19:12)

And so, politics bowed to religion, and both turned their backs on God.

The Irony of the Cross

As Jesus hung on the cross, the priests stood nearby, watching. They mocked Him, quoting scripture they had memorized but never understood.

"He saved others; Himself He cannot save." (Matthew 27:42)

They didn't realize He wasn't trying to save himself; He was saving them. The very religion that condemned Him was the one He was dying to redeem.

That's the irony of Calvary: the Creator of the Law was killed in the name of the Law. The God of the altar was slain beside one.

The cross wasn't a failure of faith; it was a revelation of it. It showed that religion, without love, becomes cruelty; that truth, when it threatens power, is always crucified; and that God's mercy runs deeper than man's blindness.

The Mirror of History

When I read these passages, I see more than an ancient story. I see a pattern that repeats in every generation. Whenever religion forgets compassion and worships control, it becomes the same spirit that condemned Christ.

The names change, Pharisee, bishop, pastor, pope, but the heart remains the same when pride replaces humility. The danger isn't in believing, but in thinking we already know everything about God.

The crucifixion wasn't only a moment in time; it was a mirror. It showed what happens when man uses God to glorify himself.

And yet, even then, Jesus prayed:

"Father, forgive them, for they know not what they do." **(Luke 23:34)**

That prayer still stands today for every church, every believer, every heart that has ever let religion get in the way of relationship.

Closing Reflection

When religion turned against its Creator, it lost its soul. But through that act of betrayal, grace found a way to reach us all.

The same cross that religion used to destroy truth became the doorway through which truth conquered death.

The message of Calvary is eternal but straightforward: God's love cannot be controlled, contained, or crucified. It always rises again, and it always calls us to look beyond the system, to the Savior who died to set us free.

Chapter Three

Power, Politics, and the Cross

The cross began as an instrument of torture, a symbol of Roman cruelty, reserved for slaves, rebels, and the

condemned.
It was not simply a tool of death; it was a display of domination.
To die on a cross was to be humiliated, stripped of all dignity, left to suffocate before the eyes of the crowd.

"Cursed is every one that hangeth on a tree." Galatians 3:13, quoting Deuteronomy 21:23

Rome used crucifixion to remind the world who held the power, a grim warning carved into wood.
Yet within a few centuries, that same cross would glitter in gold, lifted high above palaces and cathedrals, worn as jewelry by kings who ruled in Jesus' name but rarely by His ways.

The symbol of suffering became the state's seal.
The emblem of sacrifice became the emblem of empire.

It is one of history's greatest ironies:
The very systems that conspired to kill Christ, the religious hierarchy, and the Roman state, would later merge and claim His cross as their crown.

From the Blood of Martyrs to the Thrones of Men

When Pilate washed his hands, he symbolically tried to distance himself from guilt.

"I am innocent of the blood of this just person." Matthew 27:24

But what Pilate released, Constantine would later seize.
Three centuries after that fateful morning in Jerusalem, Emperor **Constantine the Great** claimed to have seen a vision in the sky: a cross above the sun, bearing the words *In hoc signo vinces "In this sign, conquer"*

49

It was not a prayer; it was a prophecy twisted into conquest.
Constantine painted that symbol onto the shields of his army and marched into battle.
The cross, once drenched in the blood of the innocent, now became a weapon carried by soldiers of the empire.

This moment marked the beginning of what would become **Christendom**
An alliance between religion and government, not born of faith, but of fear and ambition.
Rome had failed to crush Christianity by persecution; it would now try to control it through power.

"They profess that they know God; but in works they deny Him, being abominable, and disobedient." Titus 1:16

The Rise of a State Religion

In **A.D. 313**, Constantine's **Edict of Milan** granted Christians tolerance, allowing them to worship openly after centuries of persecution. However, this new freedom brought its own challenges.

The formerly persecuted gained privilege; faith moved from secret catacombs to royal courts, and altars changed from tear-stained to silk-covered.

The same empire that had nailed Jesus to the cross began to build cathedrals in His name.
And in those marble halls, the gospel of humility was replaced with the gospel of hierarchy.

**"For they bind heavy burdens and grievous to be borne, and lay them on men's shoulders;
but they themselves will not move them with one of their fingers." — Matthew 23:4**

By **A.D. 380**, during the reign of **Emperor Theodosius**, Christianity was officially adopted as the state religion of the Roman Empire. The church, which had previously stated, **"My kingdom is not of this world,"** subsequently aligned itself with imperial authority. From this position, it began to exercise governmental power alongside its spiritual role.

The church's humble origins among fishermen and servants evolved into influential positions as bishops and emperors, eventually becoming involved in the same pursuit of power that led to the crucifixion of its Lord.

When the Cross Became a Crown

The transformation of the cross from a tool of death to a symbol of dominion revealed the danger of corrupted faith. Where the early disciples saw redemption, later rulers saw opportunity.

"For all that is in the world, the lust of the flesh, and the lust of the eyes, and the pride of life, is not of the Father, but is of the world." 1 John 2:16

The moment the church married the state, purity became politics.

Truth became propaganda.
Faith became a means of control.

Those who once suffered *for* the cross began to kill *in* its name.
The very sign that once stood for salvation was now engraved on swords, banners, and coins as if Christ had died to make men powerful.

But Jesus had warned them long ago:

"My kingdom is not of this world: if My kingdom were of this world, then would My servants fight." John 18:36

The Roman cross, designed to silence revolution, had been resurrected as a symbol of empire, but it was never meant to hang over crowns; it was meant to break them.

History's Lesson

From Constantine's court to the Crusades, from the Inquisition to the papal tiaras,
history shows what happens when religion trades the blood of the Lamb for the blood of nations.
The sword of Peter, once rebuked in Gethsemane, became the policy of popes.

**"Then said Jesus unto him, Put up again thy sword into his place:
for all they that take the sword shall perish with the sword." Matthew 26:52**

Faith that once moved mountains was now used to build kingdoms.
And through it all, the words of Christ echoed across centuries:

"What shall it profit a man, if he shall gain the whole world, and lose his own soul?" Mark 8:36

The cross was meant to redeem the world, not rule it.
It was meant to lift the humble, not empower the proud.
It was never meant to symbolize conquest but compassion.

Reflection: The Cost of Compromise

When Pilate washed his hands, he symbolized apathy.
When Constantine raised the cross, he symbolized ambition.
Both were wrong, and both still live on in the church today.

Whenever the pulpit seeks political favor,
whenever the gospel becomes a tool for influence,
whenever the name of Jesus is used to bless corruption,
Pilate's basin and Constantine's banner reappear.

The cross has no allegiance but to Christ.
It is not Republican or Democrat, Roman or Greek,
Catholic or Protestant —
it is the altar where pride dies and power bows.

And until the Church returns to that cross, not the golden one of cathedrals, but the bloodstained one of Calvary
it will never again walk in resurrection power.

"For the preaching of the cross is to them that perish foolishness;
But unto us, which are saved, it is the power of God."
1 Corinthians 1:18

The Birth of a Political Faith

In the beginning, faith was fragile yet unstoppable.
After the resurrection, the followers of Jesus had no armies, no wealth, no architecture of power.
They had only the flame of the Holy Spirit that burned in their hearts.

They met in caves and courtyards, in upper rooms and beneath the city streets.
Their church was not made of stone but of Spirit, not built by emperors but by ordinary believers who refused to bow to Caesar.
They had no titles, only testimonies; no thrones, only truth.

"And they continued steadfastly in the apostles' doctrine and fellowship, and in breaking of bread, and in prayers." Acts 2:42
"And the Lord added to the church daily such as should be saved." Acts 2:47

They were mocked as fools and hunted as criminals.
Rome called them "atheists" not because they denied God, but because they denied Rome's gods.
They refused to burn incense to Caesar, saying only,
"Jesus is Lord."

That single phrase was treason.
But it was also truth.
And it echoed louder than the empire's legions.

"We ought to obey God rather than men." Acts 5:29

Every time a believer was thrown to the lions, another found the courage to stand.

Every drop of blood became seed, and the soil of persecution birthed revival.

"The blood of the martyrs is the seed of the Church."
Tertullian, 2nd century.

Christians didn't conquer with swords; they conquered with love.
They rescued abandoned children left to die on Roman streets.
They fed the poor, healed the sick, and forgave their persecutors.
They prayed for those who burned them alive.

"Bless them which persecute you: bless, and curse not." — Romans 12:14
"Overcome evil with good." Romans 12:21

Rome couldn't understand this kind of strength.
Their gods demanded sacrifice; this God became the sacrifice.
Their emperors built thrones of gold; this King reigned from a cross.
And the more Rome tried to crush this faith, the more it spread.

By the third century, Christianity had infiltrated the very heart of the empire.
Slaves, soldiers, senators, and scholars whispered the name of Jesus in secret.
Rome's power was fading. Civil wars, corruption, and economic collapse had weakened her grip.
Pagan temples stood empty, and the old gods were silent.
The people were starving not just for bread, but for hope.

And then came Constantine the Great, the emperor who saw opportunity where others saw threat.

The Emperor's Vision

History remembers it as a moment of divine revelation, yet whether it was heavenly or political remains debated to this day. His vision in the sky, *In hoc signo vinces "In this sign, conquer"*

Constantine instructed his soldiers to inscribe the **Chi-Rho** (☧), representing the first two Greek letters of *Christos*, on their shields. The following day, Constantine advanced into battle beneath this emblem and emerged victorious over his adversary, Maxentius, who perished in the Tiber River. For Constantine, this outcome was not accidental; he viewed it as a triumph granted by divine authority. The emperor, formerly devoted to Rome's pagan gods, now pledged his loyalty to the **God of the Christians.**

It was a moment that would change the world and change Christianity forever.

From Vision to Victory

After his triumph, Constantine publicly credited his success to the Christian God.
He erected monuments inscribed with the sign of the cross.
He began to favor Christian clergy, restoring property that had been seized during the persecutions of **Diocletian**, and showing favor to bishops as advisers.

The Edict of Milan was issued by Constantine and Licinius, allowing people throughout the Roman Empire to practice their religion freely. This edict put an end to nearly **250 years of persecution**. Christians could finally worship openly.

What had once been a hidden Church now emerged into the open. However, just as light grows brighter, it can also cast deeper shadows.

"For Satan himself is transformed into an angel of light." 2 Corinthians 11:14

What began as a movement of humble believers soon found itself at the center of imperial favor.
The persecuted became privileged.
The cross that once stood outside the city walls now stood inside the emperor's palace.

When Power Put on a Halo

Constantine's conversion was less a baptism of the soul than a coronation of convenience.
He saw in Christianity not just salvation, but **stability**.
The Roman gods had failed to unite the empire; perhaps this new faith could.
If he could blend the power of the throne with the piety of the Church, he could forge a moral and political unity Rome desperately needed.

**"These people draweth nigh unto Me with their mouth, and honoureth Me with their lips;
but their heart is far from Me." Matthew 15:8**

So began a transformation that would alter the faith's DNA.
Magistrates, prophets by politicians, and disciples by dignitaries replaced martyrs.
Faith became fashionable.
Conversion became a matter of citizenship rather than conviction.

By the end of Constantine's reign, bishops were seated beside generals.
The cross was stamped on coins and standards.
The sign of suffering had become a badge of the state, a symbol of empire rather than sacrifice.

"No man can serve two masters: for either he will hate the one and love the other." — Matthew 6:24

The Cost of Favor

In the centuries before Constantine, Christianity's purity was preserved by persecution.
It was a faith of the poor, the broken, and the brave.
Its power was spiritual, not political; its growth was fueled by love, not law.
But when Caesar opened the palace doors, compromise followed behind him.

The Church gained peace but lost power.
It gained influence but lost innocence.
The fire that once burned in catacombs began to dim in cathedrals.

"Having begun in the Spirit, are ye now made perfect by the flesh?" Galatians 3:3

Constantine declared himself *"Bishop of Bishops,"*
A title no emperor had ever dared to claim.
He presided over church councils, mediated disputes among bishops,
and even decided questions of doctrine, including the deity of Christ
as though the revelation of God could be ratified by decree.

And though he deferred baptism until his deathbed, he reigned as the world's first "Christian emperor." The sword and the cross now shared the same hand.

The Irony of History

The same empire that once crucified Christ now claimed His protection.
The same system that killed the apostles now carried their banner.
And the same spirit that sought to destroy the Church now sought to direct it.

"Beware of false prophets, which come to you in sheep's clothing, but inwardly they are ravening wolves." Matthew 7:15

Constantine's so-called vision became the blueprint for centuries of entanglement between **church and state.**
A pattern of compromise repeated through popes, kings, crusades, and councils.
What was born in the fire of Pentecost began to cool under the shadow of political ambition.

The cross, once a call to die, became a call to rule.
And the Church, once filled with fishermen, became filled with philosophers and princes.

"For the wisdom of this world is foolishness with God." 1 Corinthians 3:19

The Lesson of the Emperor's Vision

The story of Constantine reminds us that not every light in the sky is from heaven.
The devil does not destroy truth by denying it; he corrupts it by mixing it with power.

Constantine's cross promised victory on the battlefield, but the actual cross calls for victory over the flesh.
He was a symbol of conquest; Christ's, of surrender.

"If any man will come after Me, let him deny himself, and take up his cross daily, and follow Me." Luke 9:23

The emperor's vision transformed both history and the Church, shifting it from humility to hierarchy, from spiritual beginnings to strategic structure, and from devotion to God to allegiance to rulers.

Yet even in that darkness, God preserved a remnant.
Men and women who refused to serve at the altar of empire,
who still believed that no crown was greater than the one made of thorns.

"And they overcame him by the blood of the Lamb, and by the word of their testimony; and they loved not their lives unto the death."
Revelation 12:11

Reflection: A Light Misused

Constantine's vision may have been real.
but not every vision leads to righteousness.
Light can illuminate truth, but it can also blind those unprepared to see.

What he saw in the sky may have come from heaven, but what he did with it belonged to the earth.

From that day forward, the Church walked a fragile line between **faith and favor**,
between **devotion and dominion**.
It gained the world and began to lose its soul.

Yet God, in His mercy, still works through broken empires and misguided men.
For even when the Church stumbles, the cross still stands.

"And I, if I be lifted up from the earth, will draw all men unto Me." John 12:32

The Marriage of Church and State

Constantine meant well, perhaps. He sought unity in a divided empire. But unity built on politics is never the same as unity built on the Spirit.

By tying the Church to the throne, he gave religion power, and power rarely stays pure. The leaders who once preached separation from worldly corruption now found themselves seated beside emperors, advising kings, and shaping laws.

The Church gained wealth, land, and authority. But it also gained something far more dangerous pride. The persecuted became the persecutors. The same faith that once said *"Love your enemies"* began to create them.

The Council of Nicaea in 325 A.D., convened by Constantine himself, brought bishops together to define doctrine. It was a monumental event, necessary even, but it also marked the start of a new age: the age when faith and politics began to share the same table.

The question that haunted the Pharisees, *"What shall we do with this man?"* was replaced by another: *"How can we use His name?"*

When the Cross Became a Crown

In the centuries that followed, the cross, once a symbol of sacrifice, was gilded, lifted high on banners, and carried into battle. The same emblem that marked the death of Christ now marked the conquest of nations.

The message of mercy gave way to the pursuit of dominance. The empire that once crucified Jesus now claimed to rule in His honor.

Religion had found its throne.

And yet, amid the splendor and ceremony, something sacred began to fade. The poor were no longer the Church's priority. The Gospel became tangled in decrees and politics. Bishops argued over doctrine while peasants starved.

The same temptation that lured the Pharisees control, pride, and fear of losing influence — now spread through the very institution that bore Christ's name.

The Spirit Still Whispered

But even amid the empire's corruption, the Spirit of God never left His people. There were still believers who lived quietly and faithfully, monks who withdrew into the desert to seek holiness, mothers who taught their children to pray, and servants who shared bread with the hungry.

History records the grand movements, but heaven records the humble hearts. The true Church never died; it simply went underground again, this time not under persecution, but under pretense.

Through centuries of ambition and bloodshed, God still spoke to those who listened. His voice was softer now, drowned out by choirs and councils, but still alive \ still calling His people back to the simplicity of the Gospel.

The Price of Power

By the time the mighty empire of Rome collapsed under its own weight, the banner of the cross flew where eagles once soared.
The world had changed, but so had the Church.
What began in upper rooms filled with prayer now resided in marble halls filled with politics.

The gospel that once cost lives now conferred titles.
Faith that once drew fire now drew favor.
The disciples who once said, *"Silver and gold have I*

none" were replaced by bishops who sat beside emperors and wore robes woven with gold.

**"Woe unto them that join house to house, that lay field to field, till there be no place." Isaiah 5:8
"Ye cannot serve God and mammon." Matthew 6:24**

Once, believers had followed Christ at the risk of death. Now men followed Him for privilege, prestige, and position. The persecuted became the powerful, and in that exchange, something eternal was lost.

Faith became fashionable.
Religion became routine.
And the Church, which once turned the world upside down, began to be turned by the world itself.

From Martyrs to Monarchs

In the centuries after Constantine, emperors crowned bishops, and bishops crowned emperors.
The Roman Empire had fallen but its spirit lived on in the **Holy Roman Empire**,
Where popes wielded scepters and kings sought papal approval to rule.

"They have set up kings, but not by Me: they have made princes, and I knew it not." Hosea 8:4

The same power that had once nailed Christ to the cross was now seated in His sanctuary.
Temples that had once honored pagan gods were rededicated to saints.
Altars once drenched in martyrs' blood were now guarded by soldiers.

The Church that had preached, *"My kingdom is not of this world,"*
now raised armies and collected taxes in His name.

"When thou art come into the land which the Lord thy God giveth thee, and shalt say,
I will set a king over me; ... he shall not multiply horses to himself,
nor cause the people to return to Egypt." Deuteronomy 17:14–16

But just as Israel once demanded a king like the nations around them,
so the Church demanded power like the kingdoms of men.
And just as Saul was chosen by the people's will and not God's heart,
so too the Church found itself ruled by ambition rather than anointing.

Prophecy Repeated

History began to echo the warnings of Scripture.
Samuel had grieved when Israel traded the voice of God for the voice of government.

"They have not rejected thee, but they have rejected Me, that I should not reign over them." 1 Samuel 8:7

Likewise, when the Church chose alliance over obedience,
it repeated the same sin in another form.
It sought protection through power rather than presence,
Forgetting that the laws of men could never replace the pillar of cloud and fire that once guided Israel.

"Cursed be the man that trusteth in man, and maketh flesh his arm,
and whose heart departeth from the Lord." Jeremiah 17:5

The early Church had lived by the Spirit;
the imperial Church lived by strategy.
The apostles had carried the cross;
the hierarchy carried contracts.
And for every title it gained, it lost a portion of its purity.

The Corruption of Comfort

Once, the sound of hymns echoed through prisons;
now choirs sang in cathedrals lined with jewels.
Once, the bread was broken among the poor;
now it was served on golden plates before kings.
The same Christ who had walked barefoot among fishermen
was now depicted in mosaics wearing a royal crown.

**"Because thou sayest, I am rich, and increased with goods, and need nothing;
and knowest not that thou art wretched, and miserable, and poor, and blind, and naked."
Revelation 3:17**

The persecuted Church had carried heaven's authority.
The political Church carried earthly approval.
It had gained peace but at the cost of presence.
It had gained wealth but at the cost of wonder.
And though it wore a crown, it had lost the power of the cross.

"For what shall it profit a man, if he shall gain the whole world, and lose his own soul?" Mark 8:36

That verse was not written only for individuals it was written for institutions, nations, and churches.
A Church that seeks the world's throne forfeits heaven's voice.

It cannot rebuke sin while courting kings.
It cannot carry the cross while grasping the crown.

When Religion Replaced Relationship

As centuries passed, doctrine hardened into dogma.
The Word became chained to the language of Latin,
accessible only to scholars and priests.
The same Scriptures that once set men free were now
guarded behind cathedral doors.
The prophets had spoken directly to God; now, believers
were told they needed intermediaries.

**"My people are destroyed for lack of knowledge."
Hosea 4:6
"Ye have made the commandment of God of none
effect by your tradition." Matthew 15:6**

The power of the Spirit that once filled the Church was
slowly replaced by ritual.
Religion became a system; faith became a ceremony.
The upper room became the domain of the upper class.

And yet, through it all, God never abandoned His Church.
He purified it through persecution,
raising voices like **Augustine**, **Francis of Assisi**, **John
Wycliffe**, and **Jan Hus** to cry out for truth.
In every age, the Lord preserved a remnant who refused to
bow to compromise.

**"And I will restore to you the years that the locust hath
eaten." Joel 2:25**

The Remnant: Voices in the Wilderness

And yet, through it all, God never abandoned His Church.
Though empires fell and institutions corrupted, the Holy
Spirit continued to breathe through the faithful few

67

those who refused to bow to the idols of gold and crown,
who chose the narrow road over the royal path.

The Lord has always preserved a remnant a people
refined by fire, not defined by fame.
Through persecution, exile, and death, He purified His
Church as silver in the furnace.

**"And I will bring the third part through the fire, and will
refine them as silver is refined,
And will try them as gold is tried: they shall call on My
name, and I will hear them." Zechariah 13:9**

God raised voices in every generation men and women
who stood like torches in the night
Augustine, Francis of Assisi, John Wycliffe, and **Jan
Hus**
Each one proved that no matter how dark the Church
became, truth could not be silenced.

**"And I will restore to you the years that the locust hath
eaten." Joel 2:25**

Augustine: The Thinker Who Found Grace

In the fourth century, when Rome was collapsing, and
confusion spread like wildfire,
God raised a man from North Africa **Augustine of Hippo**.

He had once wandered the streets of Carthage searching
for meaning in pleasure, philosophy, and pride.
In his youth, he prayed, *"Lord, make me pure but not
yet."*
But when he encountered the Word of God, his heart
broke.
He wrote of that moment: *"You have made us for
Yourself, O Lord, and our hearts are restless until they
rest in You."*

Augustine became one of the greatest minds of the early Church, a thinker who built theology not on power, but on grace.
He taught that salvation was not earned by merit but given by mercy, that even kings and bishops bowed before the sovereignty of God.

"By grace are ye saved through faith; and that not of yourselves: it is the gift of God." — Ephesians 2:8

His book *The City of God* declared that no earthly empire could ever represent God's Kingdom.
He warned that any church too comfortable with the state would lose sight of heaven.
And though he died as barbarians besieged his city, Augustine's words would echo through a thousand years, preparing the way for reformers yet to come.

Francis of Assisi: The Saint Who Rebuilt the Church Without a Hammer

In the twelfth century, when the Church had become drenched in wealth and power,
God raised a man of poverty **Francis of Assisi**.

Born to a merchant family, Francis had known luxury and leisure.
But one day, he heard the voice of Christ from a crumbling chapel wall say,

"Francis, rebuild My Church, for it is falling into ruin."

At first, he thought God meant the stone building before him.
Later, he realized God meant something far greater than the **spiritual rebuilding** of a Church corrupted by greed.

Francis abandoned his riches, donned a robe of rough cloth, and walked barefoot through the streets.
He preached repentance, simplicity, and the joy of serving Christ in humility.
He spoke to kings as he did to beggars, always with the same gentle fire.

"Blessed are the poor in spirit: for theirs is the kingdom of heaven." Matthew 5:3

His example rekindled faith in an age when religion had become ritual.
He reminded the world that holiness is not found in cathedrals, but in compassion, not in the robes of bishops, but in the tears of the broken.

John Wycliffe: The Morning Star of the Reformation

Two centuries later, when the Church's corruption reached its height,
a scholar at Oxford began to speak out. His name was **John Wycliffe**.

He looked at the pomp of priests, the indulgences sold for profit, and the Scriptures locked away from the people.
And he asked a simple, dangerous question:
"Why should not the Word of God be for all?"

At a time when only the clergy could read Latin, Wycliffe translated the Bible into English.
So that plowmen and shepherds might read the words of Jesus for themselves.

"Thy word is a lamp unto my feet, and a light unto my path." Psalm 119:105

His boldness shook the foundations of religious power.
The authorities called him a heretic; universities exiled him;

the Church ordered his writings destroyed.
But the seed had been planted.

After his death, the Council of Constance condemned his memory,
And in a symbolic act of hatred, they dug up his bones and burned them, scattering his ashes into the River Swift.
Yet, as one chronicler wrote, *"The river carried his ashes to the Avon, the Avon to the Severn, and the Severn to the sea, and thus his doctrine spread through all the world."*

Jan Hus: The Torchbearer of Truth

Wycliffe's words crossed the sea into Bohemia,
Where a humble priest named **Jan Hus** read them and believed.
He began to preach boldly against indulgences, immorality, and the idolatry of men who claimed to represent Christ but lived as kings.

"We must obey God rather than men." **Acts 5:29**

Crowds filled the Bethlehem Chapel in Prague to hear him preach the simple gospel of repentance and faith.
He called for reform, not rebellion, for a return to Christ, not to creeds.

The Church summoned him to the **Council of Constance** in 1415 under the promise of safe conduct.
But promises mean little to those who fear truth.
Hus was arrested, imprisoned, and condemned for heresy.
As he stood bound to the stake, the executioners lit the fire.
He prayed, *"Lord Jesus, it is for Thee that I patiently endure this cruel death. Have mercy on my enemies."*

He sang as the flames rose.
And before he died, he prophesied,

71

"You may roast this goose now, but in a hundred years, a swan will arise whom you will not be able to silence."

A century later, **Martin Luther**, whose family crest bore a swan, would fulfill that prophecy.

"Precious in the sight of the Lord is the death of His saints." Psalm 116:15

The Thread of Redemption

Through Augustine's wisdom, Francis's humility, Wycliffe's courage, and Hus's sacrifice,
The Spirit of God was weaving a golden thread, a story of restoration.
Each generation rose to remind the world that the Church is not a throne but a testimony,
Not a kingdom of men but a Kingdom of grace.

"Not by might, nor by power, but by My Spirit, saith the Lord of hosts." Zechariah 4:6

And though the fires of persecution raged, they only purified the gold.
Though the locusts devoured the harvest, God always restored the field.
Though religion tried to silence revelation, truth rose from the ashes to sing again.

"And I will restore to you the years that the locust hath eaten." Joel 2:25

Every time the Church forgot her first love,
God raised a voice from the wilderness to call her back.
to remind her that no empire, no papacy, no government can ever own the Bride of Christ.

Reflection: The Voice Still Cries

The same Spirit that spoke through these men still speaks today.
Every generation has its Augustine's and Francises, its Wycliffe's and Huses
Voices that refuse to be silenced by comfort or conformity.

The question is whether we will listen.
Will we rebuild the Church not with stone, but with repentance?
Will we speak truth when the world prefers silence?

For God's remnant is still alive.
The voice still cries in the wilderness:

"Prepare ye the way of the Lord, make His paths straight." Isaiah 40:3 / Matthew 3:3

The Church that once shook empires now struggled to shake itself free from them.
The same power that once lifted her from persecution now chained her in prosperity.

The warning of the prophets still rings true:

**"How is the faithful city become a harlot! it was full of judgment; righteousness lodged in it;
but now murderers."** Isaiah 1:21

When the Church trades purity for prestige, it repeats the fall of Israel
worshiping the golden calf of influence instead of the invisible God of holiness.

73

Yet God, in His mercy, always leaves a door of repentance open.
He calls His Church once again to humility, to prayer, to the simple faith that once turned the world upside down.

**"If My people, which are called by My name, shall humble themselves, and pray,
And seek My face, and turn from their wicked ways; then will I hear from heaven,
and will forgive their sin, and will heal their land." 2 Chronicles 7:14**

The question remains:
Will the modern Church learn from the lessons of Rome? Or will she repeat them, loving her crowns more than her cross?

The price of power has always been the same:
the slow death of purity.

A Lesson for Today

History repeats itself when humility is forgotten. When religion joins hands with politics, truth becomes negotiable. The Church was never meant to rule nations; it was meant to serve them. Jesus didn't die to build an empire; He died to build a Kingdom, one that doesn't need palaces or armies, only hearts willing to love God and one another.

The power that crucified Christ is the same power that later crowned itself in His name. It changes faces, changes centuries, but the spirit is the same. It always seeks control, and it always fears truth.

But the Gospel remains what it has always been: good news for the poor, healing for the brokenhearted, and freedom for the captive.

When religion and politics entwine, faith becomes a weapon. But when faith stands alone in humility, it becomes a light.

***

Closing Reflection

The story of power and politics in the Church isn't just history; it's a warning. Every believer must ask: *Am I following Christ or culture? The cross or the crown?*

Because one saves the soul, and the other corrupts it.

The truth remains the same today as it did on Calvary: the Kingdom of God cannot be built by worldly power. It grows not through control, but through compassion; not by the sword, but by the Spirit.

And when the Church remembers that when it lays down its crowns and returns to the simplicity of Christ, then the cross will once again mean what it was always meant to mean: love, sacrifice, and the redemption of the world.

***

Chapter Four —The Rise of Rome's Religion

The Cross and the Crown

When Constantine lifted the cross above Rome, heaven did not rejoice it shuddered.
The same symbol that once hung over a crucified Savior was now carried before marching armies.
The wood that had meant surrender became a weapon of dominion.

Rome, weary from centuries of war, looked to the heavens for unity. The emperor looked for power. And in a single vision, both found what they wanted.

"In hoc signo vinces." "In this sign, conquer."

With that declaration, the blood-stained emblem of Calvary became a banner of conquest.
The persecutor of Christians became their patron and their master.

The simple fellowship of believers who had met in caves and courtyards now found themselves courted by emperors. He now harnessed the faith once hunted by Caesar.
It was the most significant transformation since the resurrection, but not all resurrections are holy.

A Kingdom of Two Thrones

Constantine's empire was bleeding. Pagan gods had lost their pull, provinces rebelled, and morale collapsed.
He needed a faith that could heal Rome's fractures. The cross offered what Jupiter could not: order, hope, discipline.

The Edict of Milan granted Christian's freedom to worship. The decree ended persecution and began assimilation.
What had been faith became policy; what had been devotion became decree.

The Church, once a body, was now an arm of the state.
Bishops sat beside governors; priests advised generals.
And the quiet voice of the Spirit was soon drowned
beneath the noise of empire.

"My Kingdom is not of this world." **John 18:36**
But Rome insisted that it was.

The Mother and the Monarch

History remembers Helena, the mother of Constantine, not
for her crown but for her cross.
She did not come from nobility, nor from the halls of
Roman power.
She was born of humble origins, likely the daughter of an
innkeeper in Bithynia, a land whose history shaped her
long before Rome ever knew her name.

Bithynia — The Land That Formed a Future Empress

Bithynia was an ancient region in northwestern Asia Minor,
nestled along the Black Sea and bordered by the Sea of
Marmara, the Bosporus, and neighboring regions such as
Phrygia and Paphlagonia.
It was a land of contrasts, rugged mountains rising sharply
behind coastlines rich with fertile valleys and natural
harbors that would draw the attention of empires.

Long before Rome absorbed it, Bithynia was a proud
kingdom, ruled by native dynasties who leveraged the
region's natural resources, timber, and ports to thrive. Its
strategic position made it a gateway between continents —
a crossroads of trade, culture, and early political power.

When Bithynia later became a Roman province, its significance only grew. Major cities such as Nicomedia and Nicaea became centers of administration and culture. Nicomedia would later serve as a key imperial capital. At the same time, Nicaea would host the first ecumenical council of the Church, which placed Bithynia at the heart of both political and Christian history.

This was the soil Helena came from, not imperial marble, but the rugged earth of a land that knew war, trade, and the stirrings of the early Christian movement. It was a region where the ordinary could become extraordinary.

Helena's Rise Providence Over Pedigree

Her rise to prominence came not through ambition, but through providence chosen by God to bear the man who would one day change the course of history. Even in the humblest places, God plants seeds meant for thrones.

In her later years, after Constantine's ascent to the throne, Helena turned her heart toward the faith her son had legalized. But unlike many who embraced Christianity for political favor, she embraced it out of pure devotion.

Her faith was not ceremonial; it was sacrificial.

She fasted.
She prayed.
She gave freely to the poor.

The people called her "Helena the Pious." **A woman whose heart carried more weight than her title.**

"Many daughters have done virtuously, but thou excellest them all." *Proverbs 31:29*

In the end, it was not the empire that crowned Helena it was her character.
And it was not Rome that made her royal, it was her righteousness.

A Pilgrimage That Changed the World

As Helena aged, her faith only intensified. She was not content to carry the name of "Christian." She wanted to walk where Christ walked, kneel where He knelt, and touch the earth where salvation was born.

In her eighties, an age when most people slow their pace, Helena began the most extraordinary pilgrimage of her life. With imperial authority in her hand and the fire of devotion in her heart, she journeyed to the Holy Land.

Her purpose was simple:
To find the places Rome tried to bury.
To uncover the faith that persecution tried to silence.
To restore what time, empire, and idolatry had stolen.

The Discovery of the True Cross

In Jerusalem, Helena found a city layered in spiritual ruins. Pagan temples had been built over sacred sites. Shrines to false gods stood where the Savior had died and risen.

But Helena was no ordinary seeker.
She tore down idols, as Elijah confronted Baal.
She dug through the rubble of centuries, trusting God to guide her hands.

According to early church historians such as Eusebius and Ambrose, Helena discovered three crosses beneath a Roman temple, the remnants of Golgotha itself.

To determine which was the cross of Christ, a dying woman was brought forth.
She touched the first: nothing.

The second: nothing.
But when she touched the third, strength entered her body, and she rose healed.

The cross of the Messiah had been found.

Helena, the innkeeper's daughter from Bithynia, became the woman who uncovered the most sacred symbol in Christian history, the very instrument of our redemption.

A Legacy Written in Stone and Spirit

Helena didn't stop with the discovery. She ordered the building of churches on holy sites:

- **The Church of the Nativity in Bethlehem**

- **The Church of the Ascension on the Mount of Olives**

- **The Church of the Holy Sepulchre in Jerusalem**

**Where the world raised idols, she raised altars.
Where emperors build monuments to themselves, she built monuments to Christ.**

Her faith reshaped the map of Christian worship.

Helena's Heart: A Model of Christian Womanhood

Helena's story proves a biblical truth:
God raises the lowly and humbles the mighty.

She lived **Proverbs 31** long before scholars debated it and long before churches embroidered it on banners.

"Favor is deceitful, and beauty is vain: but a woman that feareth the Lord, she shall be praised."
Proverbs 31:30

Helena feared the Lord more than she feared emperors, councils, or kingdoms.

In the end, she became a mother not just of Constantine but of Christian devotion itself.

The Piety That Shaped an Emperor

Constantine's reforms, laws, and religious tolerance were not shaped merely by politics.
A praying mother shaped them.

Helena's influence on her son was quiet but powerful, the kind of influence that moves nations without ever commanding an army.

Behind every Christian emperor was a Christian mother.
Behind the legalization of the faith was a woman who lived it.
Behind Rome's embrace of the cross was a woman who carried it.

Helena didn't win battles with swords; she won battles on her knees.

The Final Years — A Life Offered to God

In her final years, Helena continued to give away her wealth, feed the hungry, and support churches across the empire. She died around AD 330, but her legacy has never faded.

Rome gave her titles.
The Church gave her honor.
But God gave her purpose.

Helena, the woman from Bithynia, became the mother of Christian pilgrimage, the patron of holy sites, and the quiet architect of faith rising from empire.

each beam.
When she touched one, she was healed and Helena declared it the true cross of Christ.

"And he that taketh not his cross, and followeth after Me, is not worthy of Me." Matthew 10:38

From Reverence to Ritual

Helena's heart was pure, but history shows how even holy things can become idols when placed in the wrong hands. Her pilgrimage inspired countless others to follow in her steps,
but soon the sacred journey became an industry.

The cross she sought became a commodity.
Fragments of wood were claimed to be pieces of the True Cross and sold for fortunes.
Pilgrims traveled from distant lands, paying priests for blessings and indulgences.
Bones of martyrs, garments of apostles, and stones from holy sites were enshrined and worshiped.

**"Thou shalt have no other gods before Me.
Thou shalt not make unto thee any graven image."
Exodus 20:3–4**

What began as reverence turned into ritual.
The Church that once preached *"Believe and be saved"* began to whisper, *"Pay and be blessed."*

Faith, once free, became fenced in by fees.
Salvation, once simple, became shrouded in superstition.

Helena had searched for Christ's cross, but her son made it Rome's scepter.
Her discovery of a symbol became Constantine's justification for the empire.

"For the love of money is the root of all evil: which, while some coveted after, they have erred from the faith." 1 Timothy 6:10

The Irony of Faith and Power

In Helena's hands, the cross represented redemption.
In Constantine's hands, it represented rule.
One saw it as a symbol of sacrifice; the other, as a banner of supremacy.

While Helena built chapels, Constantine built cathedrals.
While she knelt in prayer, he stood in politics.
While she sought to honor the Crucified, he sought to command in His name.

And thus, through the piety of a mother and the pride of a monarch,
the Church entered an age where holiness and hierarchy became entangled
Where the sacred became ceremonial, and the supernatural became state-approved.

"This people honoureth Me with their lips, but their heart is far from Me." — Mark 7:6

Helena's faith birthed devotion; Constantine's ambition raised domination.
The mother found the cross; the son used it to crown an empire.

When Relics Replaced Relationship

The relics Helena gathered became objects of awe throughout the empire.
Portions of the **"True Cross"** were encased in gold and displayed in Constantinople.
Her discovery gave rise to the veneration of relics
A practice that began in love but ended in idolatry.

Soon, splinters of the cross, drops of blood, and even nails were claimed to be sacred objects of power.
The faithful were told that to touch them was to receive grace.
But Scripture reminds us that power does not rest in relics, it rests in the risen Christ.

"God is a Spirit: and they that worship Him must worship Him in spirit and in truth." — John 4:24
"For we walk by faith, not by sight." 2 Corinthians 5:7

The cross was never meant to be carried in glass cases or sold in markets.
it was meant to be carried in hearts.
Helena sought the cross of Christ, but many who followed her sought only its shadow.

A Lesson from the Mother of Empire

To this day, Helena's story remains both beautiful and bittersweet.
She represents the eternal tension between faith and form, devotion and deception.
Her love for Christ was true, but even her sincerity became the seed of superstition when mixed with empire.

Her pilgrimage reminds us that even good intentions can be corrupted when the Church partners with power.
She found the cross in the dirt, but her son lifted it onto a throne.
And from that moment on, the Church would struggle to distinguish between worship and wealth.

**"I am the Lord: that is My name: and My glory will I not give to another,
neither My praise to graven images." Isaiah 42:8**

Helena's heart was that of a servant; Constantine's was that of a sovereign.
And between the two was born a religion that mixed heaven's holiness with earth's hunger for power.

The mother sought Christ; the monarch sought control.
The cross, meant for redemption, became Rome's most significant contradiction.

Reflection: The True Cross Still Calls

Helena's journey teaches us that the true cross cannot be found in relics, rituals, or ruins —
it is found wherever repentance meets redemption.
It is not a beam of wood buried beneath the earth,
but a burden of love carried in the heart of every believer who follows Christ.

"If any man will come after Me, let him deny himself, and take up his cross daily, and follow Me." Luke 9:23

The cross she sought was a sign of sacrifice, not status. The power she honored was not political but personal. the transforming grace of a Savior who still calls His Church to humility.

And though Constantine turned that cross into a crown, its true power still shines brightest among the humble Those who, like Helena, seek not to rule but to serve.

**"Humble yourselves therefore under the mighty hand of God,
that He may exalt you in due time." — 1 Peter 5:6**

Helena and the Theme: Religion Killed Jesus

This book, Religion Killed Jesus, not sinners, not soldiers, not pagans killed the Savior.

Helena's life becomes a counter-testimony:

- **Religion buried the cross; Helena uncovered it.**

- **Religion replaced Christ with ritual; Helena replaced ritual with truth.**

- **Religion guarded power; Helena guarded faith.**

- **Religion built walls; Helena built altars.**

She is the fulfillment of Jesus' words:

"The stones will cry out."
Luke 19:40

When religious leaders failed, God raised a woman from Bithynia to speak for Him through acts of devotion.

**Helena didn't kill Christ.
She revealed Him.**

And her legacy stands as a quiet indictment against every system that replaces the Savior with ceremony.

Meditation A Heart That Seeks the Cross

Take a moment and enter the same spirit that moved Helena to search for Christ among ruins.

Meditate on this:

- Where have I allowed religion to bury Christ in my life?

- What broken places in me is God asking me to uncover?

- What idols have I built where Jesus once stood?

Do I seek Christ Himself, or do I settle for the systems built around Him?

Let Helena's example draw you into more profound devotion.
Let her pilgrimage inspire your own.

For the cross is not found by the casual.
it is discovered by the committed.

A Prayer for Restoration

Father,
Give us the heart of Helena
A heart that seeks Christ even when religion grows cold.
Teach us to tear down idols built by fear, pride, and tradition.
Please give us the courage to walk into the ruins of our own history.
and uncover the cross buried beneath the debris of life.
Let us be the remnant who reveal Jesus again in our generation.
Raising in us the same spirit of devotion, humility,

and holy boldness that guided her steps.
Where religion has replaced relationship,
restore us.
Where systems have silenced truth,
revive us.
Where the cross has been forgotten,
lead us back to it with unwavering faith.
In Jesus' name,
Amen.

Reflection

Do you know a Helena? I knew of a Helena,

My Grandmother Was My Helena

My grandmother was my Helena. She was righteousness
in flesh and bone, an ordinary woman with extraordinary
spiritual strength that came straight from Jesus Christ. She
had endured abuse, and yet she did not stay silent. With
righteous anger, the kind that rises from the Holy Spirit, not
from human rage, she confronted her abuser, my step-
grandfather. And in that moment, by the power of God, the
abuse stopped. Her courage broke a generational curse.

She later confronted *me* with that same righteous fire. After
high school, unsure of my direction, I moved from my small
hometown to Richmond, Virginia, to live with her. I found a
job, made new friends, and fell into the wrong crowd,
concerts, partying, and drinking. One night, I came home
drunk, and my grandmother met me at the door like a
prophet in the Old Testament. She lifted my 200-pound
teenage body, threw me onto the bed with a strength only
God could have provided, and said, "Don't you even think
about getting up."

That moment shook me. It wasn't anger; it was *love guarded by holiness.* It was the authority of a woman who refused to let darkness claim her grandson.

My grandmother worked the gardens to provide food for her family. She took pride in her squash, always telling me to eat what was good for my body, mind, and spirit. I didn't want to eat it, but when she looked at me with righteous authority and said, **"Eat the squash,"** I did. And from that day forward, it became my favorite vegetable because it carried her love, her labor, and her lessons.

She went to church every Sunday with her Bible in hand, not to play religion, but to walk with God. Our evenings together weren't filled with meaningless chatter; she used everyday moments- TV shows, dinner-table conversations, quiet evenings to speak wisdom into my spirit. She complimented me, affirmed me, and spoke life over me.

I remember once when a handsome man appeared on TV, and I casually acknowledged it. She looked at me, smiled, and said, *"That man could not hold a candle to you."* That single sentence gave me the confidence I carried for years.

This is what faithful elders do. They don't just feed your stomach; they feed your soul. They don't have superficial conversations; they have transformational ones that echo for decades.
If parents spoke to their children the way my grandmother spoke to me, America's youth would change. And if America's youth changed, America itself would change. And if America changed, the world watching America, whether with admiration or disgust, would be transformed as well.

My grandmother was my Helena, and Helena inspired me to know God, to rise higher, to become a better man. She set a standard. She lived the gospel in front of me.

I will never forget the day she died. God spoke to my heart and told me to visit her immediately. My wife at the time was angry because I chose obedience to God over obedience to her, but I went anyway. I sat by my grandmother's bed and read to her the promise of Jesus:

"Let not your heart be troubled…
In my Father's house are many mansions…
I go to prepare a place for you…
I will come again and receive you to Myself."
John 14:1–3

The next day, she stepped into eternity.

Shortly afterward, I dreamed of her as a radiant angel, with her white angel hair glowing, a peaceful smile, and a presence full of heavenly light. The dream told me what my spirit already knew:
She was home. She was with God. She was safe.

Her passing marked me forever. It confirmed beyond any doubt that God is real, heaven is real, and the spiritual world is not a myth; it is the ultimate reality. When we humble ourselves to that truth, a divine presence becomes the outline of our lives.

My grandmother taught me that we don't need affirmations, addictions, achievements, or applause to feel powerful. We only need the love of God and the reassurance that He is with us. Because people, no matter how well-intentioned, are still human. They can be corrupted, deceived, tempted, manipulated, or used by the enemy.

But Christ inside you cannot be corrupted.

And my grandmother, my Helena, showed me that truth not by preaching it, but by *living* it.

The Council of Nicaea — Faith on Trial

In 325 A.D., Constantine summoned the bishops to Nicaea.
It was the first global council of the Church and the first time political power presided over a spiritual debate.
The empire wanted unity, not necessarily truth.

From those halls came the Nicene Creed, a beautiful summary of Christian belief, yet born in the shadow of imperial command.
For the first time, theology bowed before the throne.
The same empire that had once nailed Christ to the cross now hammered His doctrine into law.

Where revelation once came through prayer, it now came through policy.
Where apostles once followed the Spirit, bishops now followed the emperor's seal.

The cross that should have freed men's souls now bound their consciences.

The Birth of Catholic Power

As Rome's legions weakened, its liturgies strengthened.
When barbarian armies toppled the city in 476 A.D., the throne fell, but the altar stood.
The bishop of Rome, now called *Papa* father stepped into the vacuum of empire.
The shepherd became a sovereign.

The Church preserved literacy, art, and Scripture; yet it also preserved the hierarchy of Caesar.
It inherited not only Rome's roads, but also Rome's rule.
Gold replaced grace; hierarchy replaced humility.
The priests who once served bread and wine began to serve edicts and indulgences.

"They exchanged the truth of God for a lie, and worshiped created things rather than the Creator."
Romans 1:25

The Church became the new Rome, a spiritual empire draped in holiness but driven by power.

Idolatry and the Image of Power

To inspire awe, cathedrals rose like marble mountains.
Light poured through stained glass, yet little light entered the hearts of men.
Statues of saints stood where idols once had.
Candles burned where incense to Jupiter once drifted.

The line between beauty and blasphemy blurred.
What began as remembrance became worship.
What began as art became idolatry.

The faithful knelt before images that could not hear, while the living God waited for their hearts.
Salvation was no longer a gift received by grace, but a transaction administered by priests.

The same system that had killed Jesus was resurrected this time in His name.

Prophecy Fulfilled in Marble and Gold

The prophets had warned of such a day.
Daniel saw a kingdom of iron mingled with clay, strong yet brittle, worldly yet spiritual. **(Daniel 2:43)**
John saw a woman clothed in purple and scarlet, holding a golden cup, "drunk with the blood of the saints."
(Revelation 17:6)
Both spoke of power masquerading as piety.

In Rome's religion, the Catholic faith, those visions found substance.
The beast of empire had not died; it had been baptized.
The Church had become an empire of absolution, a kingdom claiming heaven's keys while guarding earth's throne.

The Empire Rebuilt

Constantine's dream of eternal Rome was fulfilled, not in armies, but in altars.
The capital moved east to Constantinople; the influence moved west through cathedrals and crowns.
Popes crowned kings; nations bent the knee to bishops.

To question was heresy; to reform was rebellion.
The Word of God was chained in Latin while the masses knelt in ignorance.
And yet even then God moved.
In monasteries, in hidden valleys, in hearts hungry for truth, the flame refused to die.

The Waldensians whispered Scripture in caves.
Patrick carried the Gospel to Ireland.
Later, Wycliffe would translate the Bible into the tongue of ordinary men.
For every empire God allowed, He preserved a remnant.

"The light shines in the darkness, and the darkness has not overcome it." — John 1:5

A Warning to Every Age

Rome's story is not ancient history; it is a mirror.
Every generation faces the same temptation: to trade presence for power, to turn faith into an institution.
Whenever the Church seeks influence more than intimacy, the spirit of Rome rises again.

The danger is not in cathedrals of stone, but in hearts of pride.
When leaders crave titles instead of tears, when worship becomes performance, when money replaces mercy, the cycle repeats.

"You have a name that you are alive, but you are dead." — Revelation 3:1

Yet even now, the call of Christ remains the same:
"Follow Me." Not Caesar, not councils, not traditions but the living Son of God.

Closing Reflection

Constantine's empire has long since fallen. Its marble lies broken, its thrones empty, its banners forgotten.
But the Kingdom Christ built endures not in gold, but in grace; not in power, but in presence.

The cross was never meant to decorate a palace; it was meant to transform a heart.
And whenever believers remember that, the Church rises again not as Rome's heir, but as Christ's bride.

"For the Kingdom of God is not in word, but in power."
1 Corinthians 4:20

The Rise of Rome's Religion

When Constantine lifted the cross over Rome, he didn't just end persecution; he began a transformation. The humble faith of fishermen, shepherds, and tentmakers was reborn as a religion of kings, councils, and cathedrals. The blood of the martyrs had once been the seed of the Church; now marble and gold would become its foundation.

The empire that had once crucified Jesus began to rebuild itself in His name. Rome fell, but religion rose from its ashes stronger, wealthier, and more political than ever before. Christianity was no longer underground. It was on the throne.

Constantine's Vision of a Christian Empire

When Emperor Constantine claimed to have seen the cross in the heavens, "In this sign, conquer," he saw more than a vision of victory. He saw an opportunity to unify a crumbling empire.

Rome was divided. Pagan gods had lost their influence, the economy was fractured, and civil wars were bleeding the empire dry. Constantine recognized that the growing movement of Christians, once despised, held something powerful: unity, devotion, and moral order.

Though Constantine legalized Religion, his motives were not purely spiritual. He sought to rebuild Rome through religion, using faith as mortar for an empire that was falling apart.

So the Church became not just a refuge of the faithful, but a pillar of government. Bishops sat beside governors. Priests advised emperors. And the once-simple message of Jesus began to take on the robes of Roman power.

From the Cross to the Crown

Constantine saw himself as chosen by God not to suffer, as Christ did, but to reign in His honor. He mixed the symbol of the cross with the sword of the empire. Soldiers marched beneath banners bearing Christ's initials, conquering in the name of peace.

The persecuted Church suddenly found itself protected and, in time, privileged. Its enemies became allies. Its faith became law. And what began as a movement of spiritual freedom slowly hardened into a system of religious control.

This was the birth of what history would call the **Roman Catholic Church,** a union between the throne and the altar, the sword and the sanctuary.

The Church became Rome's new empire, and Rome became the Church's kingdom.

The Council of Nicaea and the Shaping of Doctrine

In 325 A.D., Constantine summoned bishops from every corner of the empire to the city of **Nicaea** in Bithynia, Helena's homeland. It was the first time in history that **faith and empire sat at the same table**, not as enemies but as uneasy partners.

The same empire that had executed Christ now dictated His definition. Religion became a matter of decree rather than revelation. Truth was no longer whispered in prayer but argued in councils and enforced by kings.

The Church, once hunted in caves and catacombs, now gathered under the gaze of an emperor. For the first time, doctrine became a matter of political stability.

And the question on the table was the most important in all theology:

Who is Jesus?

Not who the churches loved.
Not who the disciples followed.
But who **Rome** would declare Him to be.

This meeting became the birthplace of the **Nicene Creed**, a statement of belief still recited today:

"God of God, Light of Light,
Very God of Very God…
Begotten, not made."

It was a necessary defense of Christ's divinity.
But it was also a dangerous shift:
the same empire that crucified Jesus now sought to define Him.

Doctrine moved from revelation to regulation.
Truth moved from prayer to debate.
Christian identity moved from experience to decree.

The Arian Crisis — The Debate That Forced Nicaea

The council was mainly called because of a man named **Arius**, a priest from Alexandria. Arius taught:

- Jesus was divine **but not equal to the Father**

- Jesus was created at some point in eternity

- Jesus was "like" God but not truly **God Himself**

This teaching spread quickly, dividing congregations and provoking public unrest.

Constantine feared something far worse than heresy: **division**.

He did not summon the council because he understood theology.
He summoned it because he understood the empire.

A divided church meant a divided Rome.

Nicaea's Declaration — Jesus Is Fully God

The bishops, after fierce debate, rejected Arianism and declared:

- Jesus is **eternally begotten**, not created

- Jesus is **of the same essence** (homoousios) as the Father

- Jesus is entirely God and fully man

This was monumental.
It protected the identity of Christ as revealed in Scripture:

"In the beginning was the Word, and the Word was with God, and the Word was God."
John 1:1

"I and the Father are one."
John 10:30

"Before Abraham was, I AM."
John 8:58

Nicaea defended these truths.
Yet the victory carried a hidden cost.

The Birth of a Word Not in the Bible — Trinity

The word **Trinity** is **not found** anywhere in Scripture.

Not once.
Not in Hebrew.
Not in Greek.
Not in Aramaic.

The early apostles never used it.
Jesus never taught it as a formula.
Paul never articulated it in doctrinal terms.

The *concept* existed
Father, Son, Holy Spirit
but the *word* and the *systematic definition* emerged
centuries later.

The Modern Definition of Trinity

Today, most Christian churches define the Trinity as:

One God in three persons
Father, Son, and Holy Spirit
Co-equal, co-eternal, and of one substance.

The Tension — Revelation vs. Religion

Here is where the theme, *Religion Killed Jesus*, becomes thunder:

Nicaea defended Christ.
But it also introduced something new into Christianity:

The state decides theology.

Emperors shaping doctrine.

Councils interpreting revelation.

The same empire that murdered Jesus now regulated the meaning of His nature.

For the first time, theology became enforceable.
Belief became a matter of law.
Disagreement became grounds for exile.

The simplicity of the early church
baptized in the Spirit,
empowered by miracles,
led by revelation
was replaced by procedural arguments and philosophical language.

Truth once spoken in upper rooms.
was now debated in imperial halls.

Scripture and Prophecy — A Warning Fulfilled

Paul warned of this moment:

"For the time will come when they will not endure sound doctrine..."
2 Timothy 4:3

"Having a form of godliness but denying the power thereof."
2 Timothy 3:5

Revelation warned of a church married to political power.
A church that looked holy
But it was controlled by the empire.

Nicaea was both triumph and tremor:

- Triumph, because the truth about Jesus was affirmed

- Tremor, because the Church tied its future to Caesar's throne

The cross and the crown sat side by side
An alliance Scripture never commanded.

The Nature of Jesus — More Than a Creed

Nicaea explained Jesus.
But only Scripture reveals Him:

"He is the image of the invisible God…"
Colossians 1:15

"God was manifest in the flesh…"
1 Timothy 3:16

"In Him dwells all the fullness of the Godhead bodily."
Colossians 2:9

Nicaea defended these truths.
But it could not contain them.

Jesus is not a formula.
Not a philosophical definition.
Not a doctrine regulated by the empire.

He is the living God
revealed in flesh,
crucified by religion,
resurrected by power,
and returning in glory.

Closing Commentary — When Empire Defines God

Nicaea reminds us:

- Doctrine can protect truth

- But doctrine can also become a cage

- Religion can defend Christ

- But religion can also distort Him

When emperors define Jesus, the Church must stay alert.
When councils speak for Him, the Spirit must speak louder.
When theology becomes political, prophecy must rise and
rebuke.

Nicaea shaped Christianity
But it also revealed the danger of an alliance between faith
and empire.

For whenever religion grows powerful,
it begins to crucify Christ all over again
not with nails,
but with definitions that replace revelation.

Athanasius — The Man Who Refused to Bow

If Nicaea was the battlefield,
Athanasius was the warrior who refused to surrender.

He was young, barely in his thirties, when he stood before
emperors, bishops, politicians, and entire councils and
declared the one truth that nearly cost him his life:

"Jesus Christ is God."

Not "godlike."
Not "similar to God."
Not "created by God."
But **God Himself is eternal, uncreated, equal with the Father.**

Arius had been defeated at Nicaea.
But his ideas did not die.
They went underground into politics, into pulpits, into the hearts of bishops who feared that unity would split the empire.

And because Nicaea was enforced by imperial authority, the controversy became a **political storm** rather than a theological one.

In the middle of that storm stood Athanasius.

The Arian Resurgence — When Heresy Became Fashionable

After Nicaea, something shocking happened:

Arius became more powerful in defeat than he ever was in victory.

Why?

Because emperors changed.
Politics shifted.
And religious leaders discovered something intoxicating:

A doctrine that made Jesus less than God made the Church more powerful.

If Christ were not eternal,
the bishops became the gatekeepers of salvation.

103

If Christ were not equal with the Father,
The institution became the mediator between God and man.

A smaller Christ meant a bigger Church.

And a bigger Church meant greater control.

The same religious spirit that killed Jesus resurfaced not in Jews,
but in Christians
wearing robes, titles, and power.

Athanasius Against the World

Athanasius became bishop of Alexandria after Nicaea, but he quickly discovered something horrifying:

Most bishops did not honestly believe the Nicene Creed they signed.

They agreed in public.
and whispered doubts in private.

When Arianism surged in popularity again, the pressure to conform became unbearable.

But Athanasius refused.

He declared:

"If the world is against the truth, then I am against the world."

This statement became legendary.
so much so that historians later summarized his life with the Latin phrase:

Athanasius Contra Mundum

Athanasius Against the World

Five Exiles — Persecuted by the Empire That "Converted"

Athanasius suffered more persecution from Christian emperors.
than the early disciples suffered at the hands of the pagans.

He was exiled **five times**:

1. **Exiled by Constantine's sons**

2. **Exiled by pro-Arian bishops**

3. **Exiled by imperial decree**

4. **Exiled for refusing to compromise**

5. **Exiled for defending the Nicene faith**

He fled into deserts, hid among monks, escaped soldiers, and lived like a fugitive.

Ironically tragically
he was persecuted by the **same empire that claimed to defend Christ**.

This is where the theme of Religion Killed Jesus becomes thunder:

Religion did not stop killing Jesus after the crucifixion.

It simply changed its method.

Why the World Hated Athanasius

Athanasius stood for two truths the empire could not tolerate:

1. Jesus is entirely God and therefore above emperors.

Arianism made Christ subordinate.
Athanasius made Christ supreme.

2. Salvation comes from Christ, not from the Church.

If Christ is God,
He alone saves.
No bishop, emperor, or institution can claim that power.

This threatened everything Rome tried to build.

Prophetic Parallels: Athanasius and the True Prophets

Athanasius stands in a long line of men whom religion hated:

- **Jeremiah**, thrown into a pit
- **Elijah**, hunted by Jezebel
- **Micaiah**, slapped by false prophets
- **John the Baptist**, beheaded for speaking the truth
- **Jesus**, crucified by religious authorities
- **Stephen**, stoned by devout men

The pattern remains:

When truth challenges power,

Religion always responds with persecution.

The Triumph of Truth — The Creed Outlives the Empire

Before Athanasius died, the tide finally turned.

The Arian emperors fell.
The popular bishops lost influence.
And at the Council of Constantinople (381),
Arianism was condemned forever.

The world that silenced Athanasius
ended up repeating his words in every church:

**"Light of Light,
Very God of Very God."**

The man they exiled
became the voice that shaped Christianity.

Commentary — Athanasius and the Warning to the Church

Athanasius exposes a brutal truth:

- Councils can declare doctrine

- Emperors can enforce orthodoxy

- Bishops can sign creeds

- **But only the Spirit can reveal Christ**

Religion tried to destroy Jesus with the crucifixion.
Rome tried to define Jesus through decrees.
Arians tried to shrink Jesus through philosophy.

But God raised up a man to defend the truth:

**Christ is eternal, divine, and uncreated
the Alpha and Omega,
The I AM,
The God who became flesh.**

No decree can define Him.
No empire can contain Him.
No institution can replace Him.

And every time religion tries
a voice like Athanasius rises to rebuke it.

The Council of Constantinople (381) The Finalization of the Trinity

If Nicaea was the battlefield,
Constantinople was the finishing blow.

Fifty-six years after Nicaea, the empire once again trembled under theological conflict. Arianism still lingered like a toxic smoke, poisoning churches, influencing bishops, and dividing congregations. Emperors came and went, some siding with truth, others with error.

By 381 A.D., the young emperor **Theodosius I** ascended to power, determined to end the chaos once and for all. His commitment to the Nicene faith was unwavering.

When he entered Constantinople, the imperial capital, he found an Arian bishop seated on the church's throne.

Theodosius removed him.
Immediately.
Without hesitation.

For the first time in history, the empire **demanded** orthodoxy rather than resisting it.

The emperor then summoned a second ecumenical council
The Council of Constantinople (381)
to settle the battle Nicaea had begun.

The Final Shape of the Trinity

Nicaea had answered one question:

Who is the Son?

Answer: **Fully God. Eternal. Of the same essence as the Father.**

But Constantinople confronted another storm:

Who is the Holy Spirit?

Some taught:

- The Spirit was a force
- Or an angel
- Or a divine energy
- Or a lesser being beneath the Son

Chaos returned.
The debate reignited.
And the Church stood on the brink of another rupture.

At Constantinople, under both political force and spiritual necessity, the bishops declared:

The Holy Spirit is fully God

Co-equal, co-eternal,
personal,
divine,
and worthy of worship.

This council expanded the Nicene Creed to its present form, establishing the modern doctrine of the Trinity:

**One God in three persons
Father, Son, and Holy Spirit
Equal in power, glory, and eternity.**

This formula, a blend of Scripture, philosophy, and council decree, became the heart of mainstream Christianity.

It answered heresy.
But it raised a haunting question:

Did the Spirit reveal this?

Or did the empire enforce it?

The Trinity — A Biblical Mystery Framed by Greek Philosophy

The Scriptures reveal:

- One God

- Father

- Son

- Holy Spirit

But they do so in **relational** language, not metaphysical terms.

Jesus never preached the Trinity.
The apostles never defined it.
Paul never used the word.

The concept is present,
but the structure "one essence, three persons" is the invention of councils, shaped in the vocabulary of Greek metaphysics:

- *ousia* (essence)

- *hypostasis* (person)

- *homoousios* (same substance)

These are philosophical words,
not biblical ones.

This does not invalidate the Trinity.
But it does reveal something your book exposes with
prophetic clarity:

**When the Church married Greek philosophy and
Roman politics,**

It began defining God in the language of empire,
not the language of Scripture.

The Empire's Grip on Doctrine

Constantinople finished the theological structure that
Nicaea began
but it also cemented a new pattern:

The state now shaped Christian theology.

Councils replaced revelation.

Creeds replaced experience.

Debate replaced demonstration.

The early church encountered God through power:
tongues of fire,
visions,
prophecy,
healings,
persecution,
revelation.

The imperial church encountered God through debate:
voting,
political maneuvering,

alliances,
definitions,
excommunications.

The fire of Acts had become the formula of empire.

And the warning Jesus gave the Pharisees echoed again:

**"You have made the word of God of none effect
through your tradition."**
Mark 7:13

The Triumph and the Tragedy

Constantinople affirmed truth.
It preserved the divinity of Father, Son, and Spirit.
It defended Scripture against philosophical distortion.

But it also marked the moment when:

- Christianity became woven into the fabric of the empire

- The state controlled the pulpit

- Theology became imperial law

- Disagreement became treason

- Faith became something regulated

The same religion that killed Jesus now sat on the throne.

The councils defended His identity
Yet at times, He lost His heart.

Closing Meditation — The God Who Lives Beyond Creeds

Sit with this:

The early church did not follow creeds.
They followed Christ.

They did not memorize formulas.
They walked in fire.

They did not debate the nature of God.
They experienced Him.

They knew the Father through prayer,
the Son through salvation,
the Spirit through power.

Doctrine matters
but doctrine is not God.

Creeds protect faith
but creeds cannot replace the presence of God.

The Trinity is true
but the Trinity is not God Himself.
God is more than definitions.
More than councils.
More than metaphysics.

He is the One who:

- Walked with Adam

- Wrestled with Jacob

- Spoke to Moses

- Filled the prophets

- Became flesh

- Rose from the dead

- Poured out His Spirit

- And will return in glory

He is not discovered by debate.
but revealed by devotion.

Closing Prayer Beyond Definition, Into Revelation

Lord,
Teach us to seek You beyond creeds,
beyond councils,
beyond the traditions of men.
Let the fire of the early church burn in us again.
Let the Holy Spirit be more than a doctrine.
Let Him be powerful.
Let Jesus be more than a definition
let Him be Lord.
Let the Father be more than a concept
Let Him be our source,
our shelter,
our voice in the night.
Deliver us from a faith defined only by structure,
and restore to us a faith defined by encounter.
Make us worshippers in Spirit and in truth,
not in formulas and philosophies.
Reveal Yourself to us
as the One God who moves, speaks, saves, and
transforms.
In Jesus' name,
Amen.

The Birth of Catholic Power

As centuries passed, Constantine's vision evolved. Rome's political power declined, but its religious influence grew. The bishop of Rome, later known as the Pope, emerged as the most potent spiritual authority on earth.

The early Catholic Church did great and noble things: it preserved Scripture, educated the masses, and built sanctuaries that still inspire awe. Yet it also absorbed the empire's old habits of hierarchy, wealth, and control. The Church that once walked with the poor began to sit among princes.

Altars replaced tables. Incense replaced intimacy. Ritual replaced relationships.

By the fifth century, as Rome fell to barbarian invasion, the Church stood as the one enduring structure. It became the new Rome, not of armies, but of absolutes. And like the old empire, it demanded allegiance.

The Empire of the Cross

Constantine restored Rome's power and rebuilt it through Christianity
But what began as a revival soon became reconstruction in the empire's image.
Faith became the foundation stone for the state.
This moment in history gave birth to what would become the **Roman Catholic Church**,
the first great merger of **spiritual authority and political power**.

Constantine's genius and his deception were in realizing that the sword could not destroy the Church,
but the scepter could control it.
By blending Christianity with Roman politics, he turned persecution into partnership.

The persecuted faith became the ruling faith, and the empire that once crucified Christ began to rule in His name.

"They have healed also the hurt of the daughter of my people slightly, saying, Peace, peace; when there is no peace." — Jeremiah 6:14

The Birth of the Roman Religion

In this union between state and spirit, the **Catholic religion** was born.
What began as a movement of faith transformed into a **religious empire**.
The pope became both priest and prince, the spiritual voice of heaven and the earthly face of Rome.

As the centuries passed, the papacy gained land, armies, and political control.
The seat of Peter became a throne of power.
And while many popes were men of devotion, others were men of deception, using religion to manipulate nations.

"They profess that they know God; but in works they deny Him, being abominable, and disobedient." Titus 1:16

Rome's influence extended across Europe. Kings sought papal blessing to legitimize their rule.
And through crusades, indulgences, and inquisitions, the Church wielded the sword in place of the Spirit.

But as always, when religion joins hands with politics, **truth is the first casualty**.

The Progression of Catholic Power From Martyrs to Monarchs

Christianity began as a persecuted movement, a community of fishermen, tentmakers, tax collectors, and slaves who gathered in homes, caves, catacombs, and fields. It was a faith built on **Spirit**, not structure; on **revelation**, not ritual; on **martyrs**, not monarchs.

But as the centuries unfolded, a slow shift occurred, one that would transform Christianity from a renegade movement into the most powerful religious institution on earth.

The Roots of the Early Catholic Church

After the apostles died, leadership naturally passed to elders and overseers, the *episkopoi*, or bishops. In every city, a bishop emerged as the spiritual guide of the local church.

There was no Pope.
No hierarchy.
No centralized authority.

Just communities bound by:

- The teachings of the apostles

- The breaking of bread

- Mutual care

- Persecution

- Prayer

- And the move of the Holy Spirit

But Rome, the heart of the empire, was impossible to ignore.

As Christianity spread east to Antioch, north to Cappadocia, south to Alexandria, west to Gaul, the city of Rome became a symbolic center.

And with symbolism came influence.
With influence came authority.
And with authority came power.

Did Peter Actually Go to Rome?

This question stands at the heart of the Catholic structure, because the Church claims:

**Peter was the first bishop of Rome.
Peter founded the Roman church.
Peter transferred apostolic authority to Rome.**

But the historical record is far less certain.

What Scripture says

The New Testament never once places Peter in Rome.

Paul wrote an entire letter to the Roman church (Romans) over 7,000 words
And **never mentions Peter**, the supposed founder.

Paul lists many leaders in Rome.
Priscilla and Aquila, Andronicus, Junia, Narcissus, and

others
but not Peter.

In Paul's final letter, written shortly before his martyrdom in Rome (**2 Timothy**),
he names those who stood with him…
and those who abandoned him…

…and Peter is not mentioned.

What early history says

Early Church fathers *believed* Peter had visited Rome, and tradition says he died there. But even these records are written decades or centuries later, and often shaped by the growing authority of Rome itself.

Most historians agree on one point:

- **If Peter did go to Rome, it was late in life.**

- **He did not found the church there.**

- **And he was never a "Pope" in any modern sense.**

What this means

Rome's claim to supreme authority rests on shaky ground.

The rise of Roman power did not come from Peter's leadership.
It came from **Rome's political importance**,
its wealth,
its centrality in the empire,
and eventually the authority granted by Constantine.

In other words:

Rome became powerful because Rome was Rome.

Not because Peter crowned it.

How Rome Became the Center of Christian Authority

When persecution ended under Constantine, everything changed.

The Church that once met in homes
suddenly met in basilicas.

The Church that once hid in secret
now held public processions.

The Church that once had nothing
now received land, wealth, and political favor.

Once the empire embraced Christianity,
bishops became influential political figures.
No bishop gained more influence than…
the bishop of Rome.

Rome had:

- The largest Christian population

- The wealthiest donors

- The most political access

- The most prestigious location

And slowly, the bishop of Rome came to be seen as "first among equals."

By the 4th century

He was the most prominent bishop.

By the 5th century

He was seen as the spiritual leader of the West.

By the 6th century

He was called "Papa" **Pope.**

The persecuted became powerful.
The hunted became the hierarchy.
The martyrs became monarchs.

Ultimately, in a future Century ....According to Daniel's prophecies and Revelation, the Anti-Christ will rise in Rome, identified as the city on seven mountains. Referred to as the "Great City"

The Rise of Ritual When Simplicity Became Ceremony

As the Church grew in power, something precious began to fade.

- The simple table became an ornate altar.

- The meal became a ceremony.

- The Spirit-led gatherings became scripted liturgies.

- The humble pastors became princes of the Church.

- The fellowship of believers became a hierarchy of ranks.

- The freedom of the Gospel became a system of rules.

Incense replaced intimacy.
Cathedrals replaced community.
Tradition replaced transformation.

By the time Rome fell to barbarian invaders in 476 A.D., the Church stood alone as the only remaining authority the "new Rome" rising from the ashes of the old.

Not an empire of armies,
but an empire of absolutes.

And like the empire that came before it,

It demanded allegiance.

It claimed infallibility.
It centralized power.
It enforced conformity.

This was no longer the Church of Peter,
nor the Church of Paul,
nor the Church of Acts.

It was the Church of Rome.

The Prophetic Warning — Religion Always Seeks a Throne

The theme becomes piercingly clear here:

The same religion that killed Jesus
now claimed to rule **in His name**.

The same religious spirit that crucified Him
now crowned itself "universal,"
meaning **Catholic**.

The Church preserved Scripture, yes.
It protected doctrine, yes.
It evangelized nations, yes.

But it also inherited the sins of empire:

- Pride
- Control

- Wealth

- Power

- Fear

- Hierarchy

- Tradition over truth

- Authority over authenticity

And prophecy had warned of this:

**"They will have a form of godliness,
but deny the power thereof…"**
— 2 Timothy 3:5

"You have left your first love…"
— Revelation 2:4

**"You say, I am rich…
but you are wretched, blind, and naked."**
Revelation 3:17

The Church found a throne…
and slowly lost the fire.

The Papal States — When the Church Became a Kingdom

By the 8th century, the Church no longer influenced kings it **became** one.

When the Lombards threatened Rome, the Pope turned not to God,
not to bishops,
but to a rising political power in the West
the Franks, led by King Pepin.

In exchange for spiritual legitimacy,
Pepin granted the Pope vast territories in central Italy.
These lands became known as...**The Papal States**

The Church's own kingdom,
with its own borders,
troops,
taxation,
and laws.

The bishop of Rome was no longer just a shepherd.
He was a monarch.

The Vatican became a palace.
Popes became princes.
Clergy became nobility.

They wore crowns,
sat on thrones,
and commanded armies.

Kings bowed to them.
Nations negotiated with them.
Wars were fought in their name.

The Church that once had **"no place to lay its head."**
Now owned regions, cities, and treasuries.

**This is where the theme of this book, Religion Killed
Jesus tears through history:**

The religion that killed Jesus

now ruled in His name
With the same political power, He rejected.

The Coronation of Kings — The Pope Above Emperors

In the year 800 A.D., Pope Leo III crowned Charlemagne **Emperor of the Holy Roman Empire**.

A pope placing a crown on the head of an emperor Symbolized something unimaginable in the book of Acts:

The Church claimed authority over the state.

Over kings.
Over empires.
Over thrones.

The Church no longer served Christ's kingdom.
The Church *became* a kingdom.

The fisherman's ministry now looked like Caesar's palace. The Gospel became intertwined with governments, borders, and politics.

Fear as a Tool — When the Keys Became Chains

Jesus told Peter:

**"I give you the keys of the kingdom…"
Matthew 16:19**

But the medieval Church turned those keys into **chains**.

Fear became the currency of control.

The fear of damnation.

The fear of excommunication.

The fear of purgatory.

The fear of displeasing the Church.

Priests taught that salvation flowed through their hands. That forgiveness was impossible outside the Church.

That questioning doctrine meant eternal punishment. That God's wrath awaited anyone who defied Rome.

Faith was no longer a relationship with Christ. It became dependent on the clergy.

This fulfilled what Jesus warned:

"You shut the kingdom of heaven in men's faces."
Matthew 23:13

Indulgences — Selling Salvation

By the Middle Ages, the Church needed revenue to maintain its vast territories and expanding power. So it developed a tool that would alter history forever:

Indulgences — the selling of forgiveness.

For a fee, you could receive:

- Reduction of time in purgatory

- Forgiveness for sins

- Blessings for the dead

- Permission for certain acts

- Assurance of salvation

Money replaced repentance.
Gold replaced grace.
Paper slips replaced heartfelt confessions.

The Church became a spiritual marketplace:

Salvation for sale.

A poor man prayed.
A rich man paid.

This system is funded:

- Cathedrals

- Palaces

- Wars

- Art

- Land acquisition

- The extravagant lifestyles of the clergy

The Church became wealthy beyond imagination
While peasants starved under its taxes.

**What Jesus freely gave,
religion sold.**

Purgatory — The Invention of an In-Between Place

To justify indulgences, the Church emphasized a doctrine
rarely mentioned in Scripture:

Purgatory — a place of purification after death.

People were told:

- Their loved ones suffered there

- Their prayers and money could release them

- The Church alone held the power to unlock the
  gates

This belief, powerful and terrifying, became the backbone
of the Church's wealth.

Fear kept the masses loyal.
Money kept the clergy powerful.

Jesus said:

"It is finished."
John 19:30

But the Church declared:

"Not yet."

Christ's sacrifice was enough.
But the Church insisted more was needed
payments, rituals, masses, offerings.

This was not faith.
This was spiritual extortion.

Excommunication — The Ultimate Weapon

If fear and indulgences failed,
Rome wielded its sharpest sword:

Excommunication

A spiritual death sentence.

To be cut off from the Church meant:

- No communion

- No burial

- No marriage

- No confession

- No salvation (according to Rome)

- No hope of heaven

- No community

- No social or economic life

Kings were dethroned through it.
Nations were humbled by it.
Common people trembled before it.

The Church's power extended beyond the soul
it controlled society itself.

It was a weapon Christ never gave
used in a kingdom He never intended.

The Great Irony — The Church Became the Empire It Overthrew

The early Church overcame Rome by being nothing like it.

But once Rome embraced the Church,
the Church became everything like Rome.

It:

- Collected taxes

- Held territories

- Waged wars

- Crowned kings

- Enforced loyalty

- Burned heretics

- Controlled thought

- Manipulated fear

In pursuing absolute authority,
the Church repeated the sins of the Pharisees,
the Sanhedrin,
and the empire that crucified Jesus.

Religion killed Jesus.
And religion nearly killed His message again.

CHAPTER Five: When Fire Became the Weapon of Faith

How Religion Turned Flames Against Its Own People

There was a time when the Church carried only two weapons:
The Gospel and the Spirit.
And with those two weapons alone, it shook the Roman Empire to its knees.

But centuries after Christ, something dark took root
not in unbelievers,
but in believers,
not in pagans,
but in priests,
not in the world,
but in the Church.

Faith became fused with force.
Scripture blended with statecraft.
And the same religion that once healed the sick
now hunted the saints.

The fire of Pentecost had become.
The fire of persecution.

The Crusades — Holy Wars Tainted by Unholy Motives

In 1095, Pope Urban II declared the First Crusade
a war supposedly fought in the name of Christ,
to reclaim the Holy Land
and defend Christians in the East.

But beneath the pious language
lay a mixture of political ambition,
economic opportunity,
and religious fervor so distorted
it bled into fanaticism.

Knights marched under the sign of the cross,
but many carried greed in their hearts.

The Crusades produced:

- Massacres of Jews and Muslims

- Looting of entire cities

- The sacking of Christian Constantinople itself in 1204

- Forced conversions

- Slaughter done under banners bearing the name of Jesus

The Church used Scripture as a license.
and the cross as a sword.

A Gospel of peace was weaponized.
A Savior who commanded love of the enemy
was invoked to justify slaughter.

This was not Christianity
it was Christendom.
A kingdom built not by God
but by men.

The Crusades did not defend the Gospel.
They disfigured it.

The Inquisition — When Fear Became Theology

As if holy wars were not enough,
the Church forged a new weapon:
the Inquisition.

Its purpose was to preserve doctrinal purity.
Its method was terror.

Under the authority of the popes,
inquisitors were sent across Europe
to investigate, interrogate, and eliminate those deemed
"heretics."

A "heretic" could be:

- Someone who disagreed with a doctrine

- Someone who owned forbidden books

- Someone who questioned the Church's authority

- Someone accused by a jealous neighbor

- Or someone who *lived differently*

The Inquisition employed:

- Torture

- Secret trials

- Forced confessions

- Imprisonment

- Property seizure

- Execution often by fire

Men burned for reading Scripture.
Women burned for visions.
Entire communities lived in fear of denunciation.

The Church that once suffered martyrdom
now produced martyrs of its own.

And the fire that once fell at Pentecost
now rose from pyres.

The Paradox of Joan of Arc

History gives us a haunting irony:
the same Church that canonized saints had once
condemned them.

Joan of Arc, a young woman who heard God's voice and
led France to victory,
was burned at the stake in **1431** by men acting in the
name of the Church
Accused of witchcraft, heresy, and rebellion.
Yet centuries later, when political winds changed,
the same Catholic Church that condemned her **canonized**
her as a saint in **1920**.

The very institution that silenced her voice later sanctified
her memory.
It is a symbol of what happens when religion bows to
politics.
Truth becomes flexible, holiness becomes history, and
conviction becomes ceremony.

**"Woe unto you, scribes and Pharisees, hypocrites! For ye build the tombs of the prophets, and garnish the sepulchres of the righteous,
And say, If we had been in the days of our fathers, we would not have been partakers with them." — Matthew 23:29–30**

Joan of Arc — Burned by the Church She Served

In 1431, when France was drowning in war,
God raised up a teenage girl
Joan of Arc,
a peasant with no education
but a faith that shook kingdoms.

She claimed God spoke to her.
She claimed Heaven guided her.
She claimed Christ was leading her mission.

And she obeyed.

She rallied armies.
She broke sieges.
She led generals.
She turned the tide of war.

Kings listened to her.
Soldiers followed her.
Nations feared her.

But there was one power.
that could not tolerate her:

The Church. The Catholic Church

Jealous bishops, threatened clergy, and political enemies
Joined forces to silence her.

Joan was arrested,
imprisoned,
interrogated by theologians,
and branded a heretic.

Her "crime" was simple:

She heard God without permission.

For that,
religion lit a fire.

At just nineteen years old,
Joan was burned alive
by the same Church she defended.

Her last word was **"Jesus."**

Centuries later,
the same institution that killed her, the Catholic Church
Canonized her as a saint.

A living rebuke to the system that condemned her.

(More of Joan of Arc in Chapter 5)

The Pattern That Never Dies

Throughout history,
when religion gains power without purity,
it always turns:

- Revelation into regulation

- Prophecy into persecution

- Fire as punishment

- Spirit into the system

- Truth into treason

The Pharisees killed Jesus because He threatened their power.
The medieval Church killed dissenters because they threatened its authority.

The spirit is the same.

**Whenever religion replaces relationship,
the cross becomes a weapon
Instead of a rescue.**

**And when the Church forgets the Gospel,
it becomes more dangerous than the world
it claims to save.**

Prophetic Reflection — Fire Still Burns

Do not believe this is only history.
The spirit of the Inquisition lives anywhere:

- questioning is silenced

- titles outrank truth

- institutions outrank Scripture

- leaders demand loyalty

- God's voice is restricted to a select few

- fear is used to control

- Tradition is valued above transformation

Jesus warned this would happen:

"They will kill you, thinking they are offering service to God."
John 16:2

The persecutors believe they are righteous.
Their confidence becomes cruelty.
Their religion becomes violent.
Their authority becomes oppression.

This is the fire Jesus came to extinguish.

And ignite.

For he promised:

"I baptize you with the Holy Ghost and with fire."

Matthew 3:11

One fire purifies.
The other destroys.

Every generation must choose which flame to carry.

Closing Prayer — Purify Your Church Again

Lord,
Deliver us from the fire that destroys.
Deliver us from the spirit of religion.
That hides behind robes, titles, councils, and laws.
Remove from Your Church every seed of fear,
control,
pride,
And violence.
Please give us the fire of the Holy Spirit.
Not the fire of the Inquisition.

Give us the courage of Joan,
the purity of the early believers,
And the humility of the apostles.
Break the chains of every false system.
That replaces your voice with the voice of men.
Purify Your Church.
Correct us.
Cleanse us.
Revive us.
Let Your fire fall again.
not on bodies as judgment,
But on hearts as awakening.
In Jesus' mighty name,
Amen.

The Pope and the Power of Prophecy

As the Church's political reach grew, so did its prophetic role in the end times.
Both Scripture and Church tradition acknowledge that the **Antichrist** will rise to power through deception and will rule from Rome (**Revelation 13**).
Uniting nations under a banner of false peace and counterfeit spirituality.

The Book of **Revelation** warns of a coming world leader, one who will arise from the nations once under Rome's influence
from the **East**, possibly **Europe**, or a revived empire with Roman roots. The roots of Roman power, the **Catholic Church.**

"And the beast which I saw was like unto a leopard,
and his feet were as the feet of a bear,
and his mouth as the mouth of a lion: and the dragon
gave him his power, and his seat, and great authority."
Revelation 13:2

This "beast" will be accompanied by a **false prophet**, **the Pope**.
A religious leader who lends credibility to the political
power of the Antichrist.
Together, they will form a counterfeit trinity.
A union of **government, religion, and economics** under
Satan's authority.

"And he causeth all, both small and significant, rich
and poor, free and bond,
to receive a mark in their right hand, or in their
foreheads:
and that no man might buy or sell, save he that had the
mark." Revelation 13:16–17

The Role of the False Prophet

Many scholars, theologians, and reformers, including
Martin Luther, **John Knox**, and **William Tyndale**
Believed that this **false prophet** could emerge from within
the Church itself.
They saw the papal system, **the Catholics** with their
political alliances and claims of infallibility,
as the perfect vessel through which the Antichrist might
gain religious authority.

For centuries, the Vatican's political power reached beyond
borders.
An empire within an empire, influencing kings and shaping
laws.
Even in modern times, popes have served as global

mediators,
Their words carry moral weight across nations.
And one day, prophecy warns, such influence could become the bridge.
Between **faith and control, worship and the world system**.

"Let no man deceive you by any means: for that day shall not come,
Except there comes a falling away first, and that man of sin is revealed,
the son of perdition." — 2 Thessalonians 2:3

Beware of the false church, the Catholic Religion, born of Roman ashes to great political power, institutionalized by Constantine.

The Church will face a great deception.
Not persecution from the outside, but corruption from within. Bear in mind that we are referring to the Church, separate from the Catholic religion.
And when the Antichrist rises, the false prophet (the Pope) will rally the Church behind him,
Blessing the beast in the name of Christ while leading millions astray.

The Mark and the Merchants

John the Revelator warned that in the final days,
the Antichrist will control global commerce through the
mark of the beast 666
A system of identification and dependency.
Without this mark, no one will be able to buy, sell, or trade.
The mark represents more than economics; it is allegiance.

"He that leadeth into captivity shall go into captivity: he that killeth with the sword must be killed with the

sword.
Here is the patience and the faith of the saints."
Revelation 13:10

In this system, religion will play its part
Not by denying God, but by redefining Him.
The false prophet will use the language of Scripture,
but twist its meaning to serve power.
And those who refuse will be labeled enemies of peace,
enemies of progress, even enemies of faith.

This is why history matters.
Because the pattern that began with **Constantine and Helena**
the merging of **cross and crown**, of **altar and empire**
will return in the last days, more sophisticated but no less
sinister.

"As it was in the days of Noah, so shall it be also in the days of the Son of man." Luke 17:26

Reflection: The Warning of Rome

The Church must not forget the lesson of Rome.
Every time it weds itself to power, it gives birth to
compromise.
Every time it exchanges the truth of the cross for the
comfort of the crown,
it prepares the way for deception.

Constantine used Christianity to rebuild an empire.
The Antichrist will use religion to rule the world.
And the difference between the two will be subtle.
for both will speak peace, while waging war against the
truth.

"And for this cause God shall send them strong delusion,
that they should believe a lie." 2 Thessalonians 2:11

The true Church, the remnant, the Bride of Christ, must not be seduced by prestige or paralyzed by fear.
She must stand apart, holy and undefiled,
Holding fast to the Word of God, even when the world bows to the beast.

"Here is the patience of the saints: here are they that keep the commandments of God,
and the faith of Jesus." Revelation 14:12

Idolatry and the Image of Power

In the name of beauty and reverence, statues, paintings, and relics began to fill the temples. What started as symbolic became sacred, and what was sacred became worshiped.

The early Christians had turned away from idols, but now the Church seemed to recreate them. Saints replaced Roman gods, relics replaced pagan charms, and ornate cathedrals replaced humble homes.

"They exchanged the truth of God for a lie and worshiped and served created things rather than the Creator."
Romans 1:25

Faith became a performance, not a pursuit. The simplicity of the Gospel, repentance, grace, and love was buried beneath layers of ceremony and fear. The priesthood became the new mediator between man and God, and salvation became something dispensed, not discovered.

The system that had killed Jesus had been reborn not in Jerusalem this time, but in Rome.

The Empire Rebuilt

Constantine had wanted to rebuild Rome's glory, and in a way, he succeeded. The empire lived on, not as a kingdom of soldiers, but as a kingdom of saints and sinners.

Its capital shifted east to Constantinople, its spirit clothed in scripture, and its power draped in the name of Christ. But the heart of the empire remained unchanged: it still sought control.

The Church became the voice of kings, the judge of nations, the gatekeeper of heaven and earth. To disagree was heresy. The question was rebellion.

And yet, amid the grandeur and corruption, God still worked. He always does. Even through flawed institutions, His Spirit continued to move, calling out reformers, prophets, and ordinary believers who would one day remember that Christ never called men to rule the world, but to love it.

Closing Reflection

Constantine's dream of rebuilding Rome was both prophecy and paradox. He united the empire, but he also bound the Church to worldly power. The cross that once meant sacrifice became the seal of the empire.

What had begun as a movement of the heart became a monument of history. But monuments don't breathe. They remember what once was, while God is always doing something new.

The message of Jesus didn't die in Rome, but it did get buried there for a time, under stone, politics, and ceremony.

And yet, as it has always done, truth outlived its captors. The Gospel survived not in the palaces of popes, but in the hearts of believers who still heard the whisper: *"My kingdom is not of this world."* **(John 18:36)**

Lessons from the Mountains and the Sea

When the noise of the world grows too loud, I go to the places where the noise can't follow me. For me, that's always been the **mountains** and the **sea**. I've come to believe that God speaks most clearly in the silence, when the phone is off, the schedule fades away, and it's just you and the wind that carries His whisper.

In Raleigh, life moves fast. The traffic, the lights, the endless cycle of work, news, and distraction can cloud the soul like a fog. But the mountains pull the mist away. The ocean does too. Both have a way of reminding me who I am and, more importantly, who He is.

I've spent many days in both places, sometimes for rest, sometimes for prayer, and often to feel God's presence. Out there, the Holy Spirit doesn't need a microphone. He doesn't shout. He simply *is*.

When I'm in those places, I'm reminded of the simplicity of faith — before religion, before rules, before the confusion that man has built around God. It's just creation and the Creator, and I'm somewhere in between, learning.

The Mountain: Where Faith Rises

The mountains have always felt like God's own cathedral, not built by human hands, but sculpted by time and majesty. The air there feels thinner, cleaner, as if it's easier for prayers to reach heaven. When I stand on a ridge and look down at the valleys below, I can almost feel what Moses must have felt on Sinai: small, awed, and unworthy, yet deeply loved.

I've learned that the mountain doesn't shout God's presence; it humbles you into seeing it. You don't climb it to find Him you climb it to lose yourself long enough for Him to find you.

The stillness of the pines, the whisper of the wind through the trees — it's as though creation itself is worshiping without words.

I've often brought my Bible up there with me. Sometimes I read a single passage and just sit with it for hours. I've learned that when you stop reading for knowledge and start reading for relationship, the same verse begins to speak in new ways.

One of those verses that has stayed with me is from **Psalm 121**:

"I lift up my eyes to the hills from where comes my help? My help comes from the Lord, who made heaven and earth."

That verse feels alive in the mountains. You can't help but lift your eyes. You can't help but remember that you are dust, yet loved dust.

The mountain teaches me to look up, to rise above the world's noise and remember that God's strength is steady, even when mine isn't.

The Sea: Where Faith Breathes

The ocean speaks differently. Where the mountain is still, the sea moves endlessly, powerfully, rhythmically. The waves have no pride; they simply obey. They come and go like the heartbeat of the world.

I've walked along the beach early in the morning when the mist still touches the water, and I can feel the Spirit hovering there, just as in **Genesis 1:2**: *"And the Spirit of God moved upon the face of the waters."*

Something is cleansing about the sea. The tides come and erase footprints, reminding me that God's mercy does the same. Every wave that breaks on the shore whispers grace — over and over again.

I often pray while walking along the sand. I don't always have words; sometimes I listen. The sea is a sermon if you're quiet enough. It teaches patience, renewal, and surrender. You can't control the tide; you can only trust it.

That's the essence of faith: learning to float, not fight.

The sea is where Livingstone's Spiritual House was birthed.
A friend, Doug, and I were praying on the beach, doing our

146

ministry with the Lord. The vision came upon us, and we were led to **1 Peter 2:5**. **"Ye also, as lively stones, are built up a spiritual house, a holy priesthood, to offer up spiritual sacrifices, acceptable to God by Jesus Christ."** My good friend Doug, whom I met in Myrtle Beach at Beach Church, discovered this verse. God used him as an instrument to give me clarification and confirmation to start our ministry together.

We ministered on the beach, praying for healing for individuals facing a wide range of needs. Thank you, Brother Doug, for listening to the voice of God and allowing this ministry to grow. God is still using us to carry out His work, the ministry of Livingstone Spiritual House, born beside the waters where His Spirit still moves.

When God Moves Through the Sea

The sea has always been God's canvas for miracles. It's where His power meets our impossibility.

When Moses stood before the Red Sea, the sound of Pharaoh's army thundered behind him. The people panicked; they saw only water in front and death behind. Yet Moses looked upward. God told him, **"Lift up your rod, and stretch out thine hand over the sea, and divide it."**

"And Moses stretched out his hand over the sea; and the Lord caused the sea to go back by a strong east wind all that night, and made the sea dry land, and the waters were divided." *Exodus 14:21*

That night, the sea obeyed its Maker. What was once a barrier became a bridge. What was once chaos became deliverance. The same waters that looked like destruction became the very path of salvation.

God's people walked through on dry ground, walls of water rising on both sides, a corridor of grace between judgment and freedom. And when the last of Israel had crossed, the Lord allowed the sea to close, swallowing the oppressor but sparing the faithful.

The sea became the proof that **God can turn what threatens to drown you into what delivers you.**

The Red Sea wasn't just an event in history; it was a revelation of how God moves.
He parts the impossible.
He commands creation to make way for His children.
He speaks to the storm, to the tide, to the deep, and they listen.

When we stand at the edge of our own Red Seas with fear behind us and uncertainty ahead, the same God who moved the waters for Moses still moves for us. He still makes a way where there is no way.

Sometimes, He calms the sea.
Other times, He parts it.
But always, He brings His people through it.

The sea will always be a symbol of that truth that God's power is not hindered by what looks impossible, and that His Spirit still moves upon the waters, calling us to trust Him even when the waves rise high.

Where God Is Most Real

I've come to realize that I feel closest to God not in the grand buildings of religion, but in the stillness of His creation. There are no stained-glass windows in the forest, but sunlight through the trees preaches a better sermon. There are no choirs at the beach, but the sound of the waves sings louder than any hymn.

Nature doesn't perform for God; it obeys Him. It doesn't argue theology, it simply reflects His glory.

I used to believe that being "close to God" meant attending church more, memorizing more Scripture, or saying the proper prayers. But what I've found is that closeness to God isn't about repetition, it's about relationship. It's about stillness, honesty, and humility.

When I'm alone in the mountains or by the sea, there's no preacher, no choir, no offering plate. There's just me and the God who made me. And somehow, that's enough.

The Lessons I've Learned

Over the years, these two places have become my teachers. They remind me of what Jesus said in **Luke 5:16**:

"But Jesus often withdrew to lonely places and prayed."

He didn't do it to escape the people. He did it to stay close to the Father.

Here's what I've learned:

- **The mountain teaches faith** to rise above fear, to see beyond circumstance, and to trust that God's plan is higher than ours.

149

- **The sea teaches grace and the power of God** that God's love is endless, renewing, and stronger than our failures.

- **Both teach silence** that sometimes the most powerful prayer is the one without words.

Religion often complicates what God makes simple. But the Spirit of God simplifies what religion makes heavy. The mountains and the sea both remind me that He is not far away — He's as close as the air, as constant as the tide.

Closing Reflection

I believe every believer needs a mountain and a sea, a place to go where the world can't reach them, and where God can. Those places may not be literal; for some, it's a quiet room, a morning walk, or a few minutes before sunrise.

But for me, it's in the hush of the hills and the rhythm of the waves. That's where I hear Him most clearly, not in thunder or fire, but in the gentle whisper Elijah heard on Mount Horeb.

That whisper still speaks today, saying:

"Be still, and know that I am God." **(Psalm 46:10)**

And in that stillness, I've learned something that no religion could ever teach: that God doesn't need a cathedral to meet you. He needs your attention.

Chapter Six

The Burning of Prophets and the Silencing of Truth

There has always been a pattern as old as faith itself. Whenever God raises a voice of truth, religion builds the fire.

From the Old Testament prophets to the early apostles, from Joan of Arc to the reformers of the modern age (**see chapter 11**: When Truth Threatens Power, the story repeats like a drumbeat through time: when truth challenges comfort, the comfortable call it heresy.

The tragedy isn't that unbelievers reject God, it's that *those who claim to know Him best* often resist Him first.

The Prophets Who Were Persecuted

The history of Israel is filled with prophets, men and women chosen by God to speak truth to power. Yet almost every one of them was rejected, ridiculed, or killed by the very people who claimed to serve God.

Jesus Himself mourned this pattern when He said:

"O Jerusalem, Jerusalem, you who kill the prophets and stone those sent to you! How often I have longed to gather your children together... but you were not willing."
Matthew 23:37

Isaiah was sawn in two. Jeremiah was beaten and thrown into a pit. Elijah fled into the wilderness to escape Jezebel's wrath. Amos was driven out for rebuking injustice.

They weren't hated for lying; they were hated for *telling the truth*.

The priests of their day offered sacrifices, wore holy garments, and spoke the language of religion, but their hearts had grown cold. They loved ceremony more than conviction.

The prophet's voice has always been a threat to that kind of religion. Prophets strip away the mask. They remind the world that God sees the heart, not the ritual.

That's why religion burns prophets: because truth always exposes hypocrisy.

Jesus, the Final Prophet

When Jesus walked the earth, He stood in the same prophetic tradition as the voice crying out against corruption and pride. He didn't attack sinners; He exposed self-righteousness.

He turned over tables in the temple, not to destroy worship but to purify it. He called the Pharisees "whitewashed tombs" beautiful on the outside, dead on the inside.

For that, they plotted His death.

Atheists or criminals did not kill him; The alliance of religion and government killed him. The same spirit that rejected Isaiah and Jeremiah rose again in Jerusalem, robed in law, quoting scripture, and blind to the living Word standing before them.

That same spirit has resurfaced throughout history, wearing different faces, but always bearing the same mark: the fear of losing control.

Reflection on Martin Luther King Jr.'s "Letter from Birmingham Jail"

Martin Luther King Jr.'s *"Letter from Birmingham Jail"* remains one of the greatest moral documents written on American soil. As I revisit this letter, several themes immediately stand out, particularly King's disciplined commitment to **non-violence**, his purposeful use of **tension**, and his unwavering belief that morality must determine the legitimacy of laws.

Non-Violent Tension: King's Philosophical Foundation

King repeatedly uses the term **non-violent** not merely as a method, but as a spiritual discipline. He also speaks of **tension**, explaining it through an appeal to Socrates. Socrates, King notes, believed that intellectual tension could free individuals from "the bondage of myths and half-truths" so they might reach "the unfettered realm of creative analysis." Likewise, King wanted non-violent "gadflies" to stir society's conscience so that people would rise from the darkness of racism to the heights of brotherhood.

King's *direct-action campaign* had one goal:
To create a crisis so undeniable that it would force genuine negotiation.

This tension was never meant as violence but as a moral spotlight shining on injustice that polite society preferred to ignore.

Moral Law: Augustine, Aquinas, and the Nature of Justice

In the letter, King distinguishes between **just** and **unjust** laws using the language of St. Augustine:

"An unjust law is no law at all."

King explains that:

- A **just law** aligns with the moral law of God.

- An **unjust law** is "out of harmony with the moral law" and degrades human dignity.

He uses a simple but devastating example:
A law is unjust when a **majority compels a minority** to obey a rule that the majority itself refuses to follow.
A just law, however, is one that the majority is willing to obey alongside the minority — what King calls **"sameness made legal."**

King reminded readers that his civil disobedience honored the morally right 1954 Supreme Court ruling ending segregation and that segregation statutes remained wrong because they contradicted God's law.

KING'S CIVIL DISOBEDIENCE VS. MODERN VIOLENT ACTIVISM

One of the most misquoted passages from King's letter is this:

"One who breaks an unjust law must do so openly, lovingly, and with a willingness to accept the penalty."

Modern activists including Black Lives Matter hijack this quote to justify:

- rioting

- looting

- arson

- violence

- hatred

- racial division

But this quote thoroughly condemns their actions.

Openly — not hiding faces.

Lovingly — not screaming hatred.

Willingly accepting penalties, not demanding immunity

King's activism was Christian, disciplined, morally principled, and grounded in love.

BLM is none of these.

Black Lives Matter as an organization (not individuals) is:

- politically engineered
- driven by rage rather than reconciliation.
- rooted in Marxist ideology
- anti-family (their founders admitted this)
- theologically hostile
- fueled by resentment
- committed to division
- strategically violent

BLM produces **chaos**, not justice.
King produced **peace**, not destruction.

And here is the biblical truth:

"The anger of man does not produce the righteousness of God." — James 1:20
"Where envy and strife are, there is confusion and every evil work." — James 3:16

The fruit of BLM is confusion, anger, and destruction. The fruit of the King was courage, repentance, peace, and righteousness.

That alone reveals which spirit is behind each movement.

King operated under the Holy Spirit.

BLM operates under the spirit of the age.

And Scripture says clearly:

"Beloved, do not believe every spirit, but test the spirits." 1 John 4:1

BLM fails the test.

King rooted his arguments in Scripture, not ideology. He believed laws may be broken **only** when they contradict God's law.

King used Hitler as a clear example: helping Jews may have been illegal in Nazi Germany, but God morally commanded it.

The Danger of Lukewarm Moderates

King expressed deep disappointment toward the "white moderate," whose passivity he believed was more harmful than outright bigotry. King's frustration reflects Revelation 3:15-16 I know your works, that you are neither cold nor hot. So then, because you are lukewarm, and neither cold nor hot, I will vomit you out of my mouth. God's disdain for the "lukewarm." King believed apathy enables injustice as surely as hatred does.

The lukewarm church is the church of today. Only a few churches in the mountains and the swamps represent the church of Christ. Certainly not the Mega

churches, they are far removed from the true church of Christ.

Today, this warning echoes loudly. Many remain silent not because they oppose justice, but because they fear controversy more than they fear moral decay.

King's Faith: The Divide Between Then and Now

King's worldview was openly **Christian**, biblically literate, and rooted in a moral tradition. He saw Scripture as the standard by which all laws and movements must be judged.

This is what distinguishes King from many modern activists:

- King believed hatred corrupts the soul.

- He rejected black nationalist extremism, such as Elijah Muhammad's movement.

- He would reject contemporary ideologies like BLM's more radical factions for the same reasons elevate resentment over reconciliation and division over unity.

King prophesied this danger when he warned:

If America rejects non-violent protest, millions will turn to "black nationalist ideologies," leading to "a frightening racial nightmare."

This fear has indeed manifested today: movements that have abandoned King's moral foundation and replaced it with political vengeance.

Historical Memory: A Nation That Forgets Its Story

Many who shout "racism" today lack knowledge of actual history. America has progressed dramatically:

- Segregation outlawed

- Interracial marriage legalized

- Civil Rights Act passed.

- Jim Crow dismantled

These victories came through the courage of leaders like King and Republicans such as Abraham Lincoln, and through Congressional allies who advanced civil rights legislation long before it became politically stylish.

Misunderstandings persist because, as you note, many Americans today have become **"non-readers,"** relying on headlines rather than history.

As an English teacher, I can attest to the lack of reading skills and motivation among young people. This is an extreme problem in education today. Young people are too dependent on video games and the internet instead of reading, and now, with AI technology, they are reading less and less and becoming more dumbed down. This, in turn, can lead them to be misled by propaganda and political bias toward an unbiblical ideology.

Modern Extremism and the Misuse of King's Legacy

Extremist movements today weaponize King's words without embracing his values. Some activists manipulate racial tensions for political gain, using figures like George Floyd as symbolic fuel rather than seeking true racial healing.

King rejected this kind of activism.
He believed extremism could be holy (like Jesus and Paul)

or destructive (like groups fueled by hatred). The determining factor was moral purpose.

Voices Continuing King's Legacy

Several modern thinkers echo King's philosophy, rooted in personal responsibility, biblical morality, and historical clarity:

- Candace Owens

- Herman Cain

- Tim Scott

- Allen West

- Clarence Thomas- the only true conservative on the Supreme Court.

- Carol Swain, I'm especially fond of Carol, as she remains at the core of educating people in Christian values and the true history of the political system (democrats) that opposes true independence but relies on government programs that promote dependency on government, therefore making society weaker as a whole. She is also outspoken against being dependent on secular education.

- Alveda King (King's niece) Alveda is another favorite of mine; she is an advocate of freedom and against government dependency and is a voice of the republican party and individual rights.

These individuals challenge the narrative that King's legacy belongs exclusively to one political ideology. The democrat party hijacked King and claimed him as a representative of their party, but King was apolitical and didn't side with either party. The democratic party also hijacked Abraham Lincoln and claimed him as an advocate for the democrat party, and Lincoln was a Republican. I have actually heard some people proclaim that Abraham Lincoln was a Democrat. This is an example of how the media can mislead people. I argue that King's values Christian ethics, family stability, and moral clarity align more closely with conservative thought than with modern progressive activism.

The Church's Silence and the Johnson Amendment

King rebuked the church for aligning itself with the world's opinions rather than God's truth. He condemned churches that avoided social issues under the excuse of political neutrality.

Today, that silence continues, in part because of the Johnson Amendment, which threatens churches with losing tax-exempt status if they speak about politics. Many churches now fear the government more than they fear failing God.

As King wrote, the church has become **"an ineffectual voice with an uncertain sound."**

Education, Morality, and the Loss of Biblical Foundations

King notes rightly that the removal of:

- prayer in schools
- the Ten Commandments
- biblical moral instruction

has contributed to the unraveling of family, community, and moral responsibility since the 1960s.

King's activism was grounded in Scripture. Without biblical literacy, society loses its moral compass, and chaos fills the void.

King's Humility and Final Appeal

The letter ends in humility. King apologizes if he has overstated the truth and offers to meet with the clergymen as a fellow Christian brother, not as a civil rights leader.

This posture reflects the spirit of Christ Himself.

King's letter remains a timeless call to courage, conscience, and clarity a reminder of what righteous protest looks like:

- grounded in truth

- rooted in Scripture

- driven by love.

- disciplined by non-violence

- willing to suffer for what is right.

I encourage everyone to read *"Letter from Birmingham Jail"* with fresh eyes. It is more than a civil rights document; it is a moral blueprint for any generation seeking justice without losing its soul.

College Essay written in response to King's A Letter from a Birmingham Jail.

Martin Luther King, "A Letter from Birmingham Jail"

MLK often uses the term "non-violent" and discusses "tension," referencing Socrates's idea that mental tension leads to deeper understanding. He argues for nonviolent action to create necessary social tension, moving society from prejudice to greater understanding. MLK explains that his direct action aims to create crises that prompt negotiation.

MLK addressed Birmingham's new mayor, Albert Boutwell, a pro-segregation Democrat. He referenced theologian Reinhold Niebuhr and noted that groups are often more immoral than individuals. MLK also cited St. Augustine: "an unjust law is no law at all."

King argued that unjust laws conflict with moral law or God's law, stating that any law degrading human personality is unnatural and wrong. He encouraged adherence to the 1954 Supreme Court ruling, viewing it as morally right, while considering segregation ordinances morally wrong.

MLK explained that an unjust law occurs when a majority forces a minority to follow a rule it does not apply to itself. In contrast, a just law is one that the majority requires of minorities and also follows a concept he described as "sameness made legal." Consider how this distinction relates to our political parties.

King emphasized that he does not support defying the law, pointing out that, unlike extreme segregationists, such actions could lead to anarchy.

Recent BLM riots have led to the misquotation of Martin Luther King, with some citing his "Letter from Birmingham Jail" as justification for their actions. King argued that breaking unjust laws should be done openly and with acceptance of penalties to demonstrate respect for the law and highlight its injustice. The problem with using King's words to justify riots is that rioters do not act openly or lovingly, and they break just laws, advocating vandalism, theft, and arson, which are not based on ethical and moral foundations. King, a Christian, often cited biblical principles as guidance for distinguishing just from unjust laws.

It's also worth mentioning that biblical education has been removed from public schools and colleges. And this is the main reason we have a society today that is unstable and in crisis. King cited numerous examples of disobeying unjust laws and used the Bible to condemn these acts. The Bible states that the only grounds for violating a government's laws are when those laws are in direct opposition to God's law. In King's case, the laws he broke were in direct opposition to God's law. He used Hitler as an example. When Hitler made it unlawful to aid or help Jewish people, this was against God's law because God said in His Word to love the Jewish people. After all, the Jews were God's chosen people.

Kings' bitterness toward lukewarm moderates is in direct correlation to the Bible, God said he will spew from his mouth the Lukewarm Christian. And that being lukewarm is more detestable than an absolute misunderstanding or action against the laws of God.

King often references God because he knew the Word of God and tried to apply it to his life. This is one of the main things that separates King from today's activists. The activists today have fallen into the second group King called Bitterness and Hatred. On King's Day, it was the Black nationalist groups, such as Elijah Muhammad's Muslim movement; today it is Black Lives Matter. Both groups have repudiated Christianity, and both groups have concluded that the white man is an incorrigible "Devil."

This analogy is especially ironic because that is what is happening now with the riots. George Floyd is nothing more than a political pawn being used by the hateful political group Black Lives Matter. Black Lives Matter is a racist political activist group within itself, like what the KKK was. As you recall, the KKK would destroy property and burn buildings; the two groups are racist groups. The difference is that the national media doesn't acknowledge

Black Lives Matter as a hate group because the actions of this group fuel their liberal agenda. The liberal agenda is driven by hate. A good example of this is Robin DeAngelo's White Fragility. White Fragility, or some call it White Privilege, but they both mean the same. She, along with these hate groups, is dividing America or trying to divide America. I still hope people can think for themselves instead of relying on biased sources to meet their educational needs.

The period we live in today has become known, "at least to me," as a period of "Non-Readers": people who don't like to read or study for themselves; they have become mentally complacent and dependent on other sources to educate them. Sources such as the media, political activist groups, sports, and movie stars exert considerable influence on the society of "Non-Readers". This, in turn, is the reason we see these people rioting in the streets because they are uneducated, and they do not have a clue about black history.

This nation is privileged, not just whites, but all races, which is the reason people come here from other nations, because we are the freest nation in the world. We have evolved into a freer nation than we were when we started. Therefore, it is important to learn history. History gives us the knowledge that we need to be a true progressive state. Not a progressive state, the way today's liberals use it, but a progressive state in that we progress as a nation to become freer. We are certainly freer than we used to be. Segregation and racism have been eliminated in part due to people like MLK. Not only MLK, but the people who stood up against slavery, like Abraham Lincoln (Republican), the history of racism, slavery, etc., was always condoned by the democrat party. Supreme Court rulings, such as Brown v. Board of Education, made segregation unconstitutional. The people, or Black people, who are screaming racial injustice today forget or don't know about our nation's history and how it has continually progressed to a freer state. It was LBJ who ignited racism, hate, and stole the thunder from the Republicans by claiming he was the one who directed the Civil Rights Act, but if you read the actual history of this, you will find that it was the republicans who enunciated this act, passed it, and brought it forward for LBJ to sign. LBJ did not want to sign this, but succumbed to political pressure, thereby devising an excellent scheme to claim ALL the credit for this act. In doing so, this is when he pledged to the Black Americans that it was the democrat party that set them free, but it has always been the Republican Party, "The Party of Abraham Lincoln," that set them free. So, the democrat party has owned the Black vote ever since the Civil Rights Act.

MLK ironically foretold the future when he stated, " And I am further convinced that if our white brothers dismiss as "rabble rousers" and "outside agitators" those of us who employ nonviolent direct action, and if they refuse to support our nonviolent efforts, millions of Negros will, out of frustration and despair, see solace and security in black nationalist ideologies a development that would inevitably lead to a frightening racial nightmare." This course is being played out today through the Black Lives Matter movement.

It is also ironic that King mentions Abraham Lincoln and Thomas Jefferson as pioneers of freedom who fought desperately for it. Still, today's liberal condemns these two iconic figures simply because they were Republicans. But in the case of Abraham Lincoln, the democrat party tries desperately to claim Lincoln as their own. And unfortunately, a lot of people, including my ex-father-in-law, thought Abraham Lincoln was a democrat.

King mentions another extremist in Jesus Christ and the apostle Paul. Both of whom were persecuted by society and killed by the Romans. So, extremism for the good is good, and extremism for the bad is bad. And King clearly did not condone bad extremism in the likes of Elijah Muhammad's Muslim movement. And he certainly would not condone today's Black Lives Matter. Black Lives Matter likes to steal King's quotes and twist them in a way to have naïve people believe that King was for violence. King was clearly against violence, but King did prophesize that the lack of response from peaceful protesting would lead to violence, and people adopting the extremist hate groups springing from Black nationalist ideologies.

Some of today's proponents of King's philosophy are Black people, the likes of Candace Owens, Herman Cain, Tim Scott, Allen West, Clarence Thomas, and Carol Swain. Carol is a former professor of political science and Law at Vanderbilt University. She is highly knowledgeable about the history of the Democratic Party, and she has authored numerous books on its corruption. She produced a video https://www.youtube.com/watch?v=g_a7dQXilCo&feature=youtu.be. Please take the time to watch this video. It is very informative and may challenge you to study the roots of the Democratic Party further.

Another proponent of MLK philosophy is King's niece, Alveda King. She is the founder of Alveda King Ministries, and she served in the Georgia House of Representatives. She is a pro-life and conservative activist. She discovered the Democrats' deception when she ran for Georgia's 5th Congressional District seat. She ran against the incumbent William Wyche Fowler. Fowler tried to use his political prowess to entice King to drop out of the race. The democrat party did not endorse King because of King's conservative views, and her outspoken belief in Jesus Christ was bad for the party. Since then, she has been a

Republican and voted for Donald Trump in the 2016 election. King exposes the Democratic Party's corruption in several of her published books. Alveda has constantly stated that Martin Luther King was a Republican. Rosa Parks, the most prominent and well-known activist in the Civil Rights movement, was a pro-life activist to whom the democrat party totally ignores. She likened racial segregation to abortion and the founder of Planned Parenthood, Margaret Sanger, who was a known eugenics activist and a racist toward Black people. Her way of controlling the Black race was to condone and entice Black people to kill their babies; this, in turn, would reduce the Black race. Adolph Hitler also practiced this philosophy with the persecution and slaughter of the Jews. Like Martin Luther King, I find it imperative that people become knowledgeable of the Bible. This is clearly stated in the Bible as to why people practice eugenics.

King cascades the white ministers and churches and accuses them of complying with the world. I agree with this as well, because Jesus made clear that to be saved, you must be separated from the world. Today's churches, especially the Catholics, have married themselves to the world. This is one reason I have lost my desire to attend church. King noted that these pastors and churches have declared politics and social issues irrelevant to the gospel of Jesus. King is right in that Jesus was very political and constantly hurled himself into the arena of social discord. The church has remained silent during times of social injustice, and King makes references to the Democratic Governor Ross Barnett of Mississippi and Alabama, George Wallace, whom I mentioned in a college essay I wrote in response to King's speech, "I have a dream."

The churches and pastors will have to answer for their complacency regarding social issues, because Jesus was clear in James 1:22: You must be doers of the Word, not listeners only, deceiving yourselves. King was a doer of the Word of God. Someone today must make a stand and be a doer of the Word, as King did. Now is an excellent opportunity for someone to make history in a practical way, the way Martin Luther King did. And I can assure you that it will not be anyone from Black Lives Matter.

On page 7, King writes of the church conforming to society and the elite. The government and the people in power want the church to be "silent," especially in troubled times like the current pandemic. This is the main reason the democrat governors are not allowing the churches their constitutional right to assemble, but they enable thousands of people to assemble in the streets to protest our police. Lyndon B. Johnson silenced the church when he introduced the Johnson Act, which prohibited churches from endorsing or opposing candidates. In other words, if a church dares to project its principles on society in relation to politics, it will be cut off from having a tax-exempt status. **My question to the church is, why do you want a tax-exempt status to begin with? Didn't Jesus say, "render unto Caesar what is Caesar's and render unto God what is God's?** The churches have no backbone to stand up against the evils of society; they have hidden themselves behind the tax-exempt status. Thereby, like King, I agree that the contemporary church is a weak, ineffectual voice with an uncertain sound. And the church is certainly an arch defender of the status quo.

King, unlike today's activists, possessed knowledge of literature and grammar and understood the eloquence and power of words in a poetic sense. The Robin DeAngelo activists of today do not possess the acumen of King, nor do they possess a practical solution to racism. Today's activists are dividers of the people and racists themselves. To call attention to racism by pointing fingers at "ONE" group of people, and singling them out as racist, is to clarify that he who accuses the other of being a racist is the racist themselves. Racism does not discriminate against one class or the other; racism doesn't limit itself to only one group of people. Racism is like a disease of the mind; it is also like a disease of the body, cancer, Alzheimer's, respiratory infections; it doesn't limit itself to "ONE" class of people. Society will never be able to rid itself of racism; it will always exist in one form or another. It is human nature to discriminate against others. But a person of intellect and moral standards will shy away from exercising racism or discrimination because they will realize it is a reflection on their character. So, in this sense, the best way to limit or reduce racism and discrimination is for society to embrace the power of knowledge, educate citizens, make them aware of their moral responsibility, and allow Biblical courses to be part of schools again. The Ten Commandments need to be taught in every school again, as they were before the 1960s. Before 1960, America had prayer in schools and used the Bible as part of the educational programs. Before the 60s, the family stayed together and was less tempted by the wiles of society. It was understood that commitment was the cornerstone of a family and an individual. It was the strength and a union with God, not only in the confines of a marriage but also in a family unit and career. A man's Word was his bond. We must return to the principles this nation held before the 1960s.

Finally, I love how King ended the letter; he bowed gracefully in humility and told the clergyman to forgive him if he said anything that understated the truth. He offered to meet not as a civil rights leader but as a fellow Clergyman. He bowed out gracefully, exactly as Jesus would have done. I challenge everyone to read **"A Letter from the Birmingham Jail"** by Martin Luther King. It will give you a clear understanding of what a protest should be like.

JUST VS. UNJUST LAWS — THE BIBLICAL STANDARD

King's theology of law was not political; it was **biblical** and **moral**.

"An unjust law is no law at all." St. Augustine

This mirrors Scripture:

- **Isaiah 10:1** — Woe to those who write unjust laws.

- **Amos 5:24** — Let justice roll down like water.

- **Psalm 89:14** — Righteousness and justice are the foundation of God's throne.

- **Genesis 1:27** — Every person bears God's image.

King taught:

- A **just law** aligns with the law of God.

- An **unjust law** contradicts God's nature and degrades human dignity.

Segregation violated the Imago Dei; therefore, it violated God.

King's explanation that unjust laws require minorities to obey restrictions the majority will not obey themselves is simply **Leviticus 24:22** in action:

"You shall have the same law for the stranger and for the native-born."

His use of biblical logic is what made his activism fruitful. It was rooted in the Kingdom of God, not the kingdom of man.

170

THE LUKEWARM CHURCH — A PROPHECY FULFILLED

King was harder on silent churches than on racist oppressors.
His disappointment mirrored the voice of Christ:

"Because you are lukewarm… I will spit you out of My mouth." — Revelation 3:16

He rebuked pastors who preferred:

- comfort over conviction

- silence over truth

- popularity over righteousness

- safety over justice

The modern church has followed the same path.

Pastors fear losing government favor (501 (c) (3) status).
Churches fear cultural backlash.
Pulpits preach psychology instead of repentance.
Congregations chase entertainment instead of holiness.

Prophetically, this is the church of Laodicea, wealthy, respected, admired, **but spiritually powerless**.

God is calling the church back to:

- boldness

- righteousness

- repentance

- moral clarity

- prophetic leadership

But many churches continue bowing to cultural idols.

KING'S CHRIST-CENTERED ACTIVISM VS. TODAY'S POLITICAL RADICALISM

This is **the dividing line**:

King's movement was rooted in Scripture.

Modern radical activism is rooted in ideology.

King prayed.
BLM chants.

King preached forgiveness.
BLM preaches resentment.

King believed in the Imago Dei.
BLM embraces identity politics.

King fought for unity.
BLM promotes segregation (even demanding "black-only spaces").

King believed racism was a sin.
BLM believes racism is permanent.

King believed in redemption.
BLM believes in retribution.

King believed in non-violence.
BLM believes riots are "necessary language."

King believed the Gospel reconciles man to God and man to man.
BLM rejects the Gospel as "oppressive."

It is impossible to equate the two.

172

As Jesus said:

"A tree is known by its fruit." — Matthew 12:33

King's fruit was love, peace, justice, unity, and national transformation.
BLM's fruit is hatred, destruction, fear, and social fracture.

A PROPHETIC CALL FOR OUR GENERATION

God is raising new prophets, not political activists, but spiritual warriors.
Voices like:

- the apostles

- the prophets

- Martin Luther King Jr.

- the early reformers

- the bold preachers of every century

A new remnant is rising — those who refuse to bow to political idols or cultural pressure.

God is calling:

- Pastors to preach truth again.

- Churches to confront injustice biblically.

- Believers to test the spirits.

- Communities reject hatred wrapped in activism.

- Christians to discern between true prophets and counterfeit movements.

Because the hour is late.
The deception is deep.
The stakes are eternal.

And God is separating wheat from chaff.

This is a prophetic moment, a national shaking, and only those rooted in Scripture will stand.

As King wrote, echoing the prophets:

"Let justice roll down like waters and righteousness like a mighty stream." — Amos 5:24

But justice without the righteousness of God becomes revenge.
Activism without the cross becomes idolatry.
Protest without love becomes hatred.
And movements without Christ become tools of darkness.

Galileo and the Chains of Knowledge

The 17th century brought another kind of prophet, not one who preached from pulpits, but one who looked through telescopes. **Galileo Galilei** was a man of science, but also a man of faith, a devout Catholic who believed that studying creation was another way to know its Creator.

He dared to suggest that the Earth revolved around the Sun.
It was science, yes, but it was also revelation: the uncovering of a divine truth about the order of God's creation.

174

Galileo once wrote, *"The Bible teaches us how to go to heaven, not how the heavens go."*
He saw no conflict between Scripture and science, for both came from the same Author, God Himself. But the Church of his day did not see it that way.

To admit that Galileo was right would mean acknowledging that the Church had been wrong for centuries.
And religion has never done that easily.

So instead of celebrating discovery, it condemned it.
Instead of seeing revelation, it saw rebellion.

In 1633, the **Roman Catholic Church**, the same faith Galileo cherished, called him before the **Inquisition**, accusing him of heresy.
He was forced to kneel before cardinals and bishops, men who claimed to speak for God, and recant his discovery under threat of torture.
Though he whispered the truth, "E pur si muove," meaning "And yet it moves," he was sentenced to **house arrest for the rest of his life.**

The Church silenced one of its own sons, proving that **when religion seeks more control than truth, it becomes the enemy of revelation.**

When Religion Fears Revelation

Galileo's telescope didn't challenge the existence of God; it revealed more of Him.
Through the lenses of his creation, Galileo saw the vastness of the heavens, the beauty of divine order, and the perfection of celestial harmony.
It was an act of worship, not rebellion.

"The heavens declare the glory of God; and the firmament sheweth His handiwork." — *Psalm 19:1*

But instead of rejoicing that creation had spoken, the Church grew afraid.
It was feared that if the heavens did not revolve around the Earth, perhaps the world did not revolve around Rome.

This was not the voice of faith; it was the echo of pride. Just as the Pharisees feared losing their place when Jesus revealed a more profound truth, the Catholic hierarchy feared losing its authority when Galileo revealed a greater universe.

"For they loved the praise of men more than the praise of God." — *John 12:43*

The priests of Galileo's day wrapped tradition around truth like chains, mistaking control for conviction. In doing so, they repeated the same sin that nailed Jesus to the cross, suppressing what was divine to protect what was institutional.

The Paradox of Faith and Persecution

Galileo never left his faith. Even as the Catholic Church condemned him, he clung to God.
He prayed daily, studied Scripture, and wrote letters that revealed a humility the Church itself had forgotten.
He never hated his accusers; he pitied them, for they, not he, were truly imprisoned.

"For we can do nothing against the truth, but for the truth." — *2 Corinthians 13:8*

The irony was bitter: the Church that claimed to defend truth punished the man who sought it.
It exalted its own interpretation above God's creation, proving that when religion worships its doctrine more than its Creator, it commits idolatry in the name of faith.

This is the danger Jesus warned of when He said,

"Ye made the word of God of none effect through your tradition." — *Mark 7:13*

Galileo's chains were not forged of iron; they were forged by fear.
Fear that light might expose darkness.
Fear that truth might outgrow tradition.
Fear that revelation might not need permission.

Faith and Reason — Created by the Same God

God never asked man to choose between faith and understanding.
He created both.

"Great is our Lord, and of great power: His understanding is infinite." — *Psalm 147:5*

True faith does not run from discovery; it runs toward it.
True faith does not hide from questions; it invites them.
Because all truth, whether written in Scripture or revealed in the stars, belongs to God.

But religion without the Spirit becomes blind.
It guards its throne while closing its eyes to the horizon.
And so, the Catholic Church in Galileo's day proved that **you can love the name of God and still resist His voice** if your heart is ruled by pride instead of presence.

"Ever learning, and never able to come to the knowledge of the truth." — *2 Timothy 3:7*

177

The Lesson for the Modern Church

Galileo's story is not merely about astronomy; it's about obedience to revelation.
It reminds us that God's truth moves even when men try to stop it.
That the Spirit continues to speak, even when religion refuses to listen.

The Catholic Church that silenced Galileo later apologized, but centuries too late.
It took nearly **360 years** for the Vatican to formally admit its error in condemning him.

That is the cost of religious pride: centuries of silence where there could have been light.

Every time the Church resists the Spirit, it repeats Galileo's trial not against a man, but against God Himself.
When we close our minds to revelation, we build our own house arrest.
When we silence truth to preserve comfort, we lock ourselves in the same prison that held Galileo.

"Where the Spirit of the Lord is, there is liberty." *2 Corinthians 3:17*

Closing Reflection — The Persecuted Prophets of Revelation

Galileo's whisper still moves through time: *"And yet it moves."*
It is more than a defense of science; it is a declaration of faith.
Faith that truth cannot be chained, and revelation cannot be buried.

The Catholic Church once believed it could contain the cosmos.
But the heavens kept moving.
And so does God.

His Spirit still speaks in Scripture, in creation, and in the conscience of every believer brave enough to listen.
Religion may silence voices, but it cannot silence the universe that still declares His glory.
Because every star still preaches the same sermon:
God is bigger than man's belief, and truth is never afraid of light.

A Legacy of Persecution

Galileo's story was not the first, and it would not be the last.
Through the centuries, the Catholic Church and other religious systems have often become the very persecutors of the prophets they once claimed to defend.

**"O Jerusalem, Jerusalem, thou that killest the prophets, and stonest them which are sent unto thee."
— Matthew 23:37**

Jesus spoke these words not only to the ancient Pharisees but to every generation of religion that exalts its power above God's truth.

The spirit that crucified Christ never died; it simply changed garments.

Michael Servetus — Burned for Reading the Bible

In 1553, **Michael Servetus**, a Spanish physician, scholar, and theologian, was burned alive in Geneva for daring to read and interpret Scripture apart from church authority. He was no rebel without faith; he was a seeker, a man consumed by a desire to know God as revealed in His Word, not as filtered through councils and creeds.

Servetus was born in Villanueva de Sijena, Spain, around 1511. Raised in a devout Catholic household, he was brilliant from youth, mastering languages and theology before most men his age had finished school. As he studied the Bible in its original tongues, he discovered something that would change his life and cost him his life: that salvation was not mediated by priests or purchased by indulgences but was freely given through faith in Christ alone.

"Therefore, being justified by faith, we have peace with God through our Lord Jesus Christ." — Romans 5:1

When he read Scripture for himself, he saw how far the Church had strayed from the simplicity of the Gospel. He questioned the trinity as formulated by the creeds, believing it obscured rather than revealed God's oneness. He rejected infant baptism and insisted that true faith must be conscious, personal, and voluntary, a covenant of the heart, not a ritual of tradition.

180

For these convictions, both the **Roman Catholic Church** and the **Protestant reformers** condemned him. The Inquisition hunted him in Catholic lands, and when he fled to Geneva, the so-called city of the Reformation, he found no refuge. **John Calvin**, the great Reformer, accused him of heresy. The same zeal that had once resisted Rome now burned one of Rome's own victims.

The Catholic hierarchy branded him a blasphemer; the Protestants called him a danger to doctrine. But Servetus stood on Scripture alone, proclaiming that every believer had the right to read and interpret God's Word freely.

"Search the Scriptures; for in them ye think ye have eternal life: and they are they which testify of Me." *John 5:39*
"Ye shall know the truth, and the truth shall make you free." *John 8:32*

When brought before the Geneva Council, Servetus was offered his life if he would recant. He refused. With calm conviction, he declared that no earthly power could command the conscience. On October 27, 1553, he was bound to a stake on the hill of Champel. A crown of sulfur was placed upon his head to hasten the flames. His last words were a prayer: *"Jesus, Son of the eternal God, have mercy on me."*

"Blessed are they which are persecuted for righteousness' sake: for theirs is the kingdom of heaven." *Matthew 5:10*

As the fire consumed him, the smoke of his martyrdom rose as a silent rebuke to both Rome and Geneva, a testimony that no institution can monopolize truth. Servetus had written in his final letter, *"To kill a man is not to defend a doctrine, but to kill a man."*

His ashes became a symbol of all who have been silenced for daring to open the Bible without permission. His life fulfilled Jesus' prophecy:

"They shall put you out of the synagogues: yea, the time cometh, that whosoever killeth you will think that he doeth God service." — *John 16:2*

Servetus's legacy lives wherever believers choose conscience over control and revelation over ritual. He died with a Bible in his heart, not a creed in his hand, a man consumed by fire but freed by truth.

"The grass withereth, the flower fadeth: but the word of our God shall stand forever." — *Isaiah 40:8*

Servetus's ashes rose as a testimony against religious tyranny, a reminder that **God's Spirit cannot be licensed or censored by human hands.**

Gaietà Ripoll — The Last Victim of the Inquisition

Nearly two centuries after the flames of the Reformation, **Gaietà Ripoll** became the last recorded victim of the Spanish Inquisition.
The year was **1826** — not the Dark Ages, not the medieval world, but the dawn of the modern era. Steamships crossed oceans. Revolutions rose in the name of liberty. Yet in Spain, the Catholic Church still burned men for thinking freely about God.

Ripoll was a **humble schoolteacher** in Valencia, a veteran of the Napoleonic Wars who had once fought for Spain's freedom. But upon returning home, he found another tyranny waiting: not from emperors, but from the Church itself.

His crime was simple and yet, in the eyes of religion, unforgivable:
He taught his students that faith must be **personal,** not inherited through baptism, not sustained by ritual, but born from a living relationship with God through Christ.
He encouraged them to read the Bible for themselves and to pray directly to God, without priests or intermediaries.

"Let us therefore come boldly unto the throne of grace, that we may obtain mercy, and find grace to help in time of need." — *Hebrews 4:16*

This message of direct communion with God echoed the Gospel itself, yet it was condemned as **heresy** by the Catholic authorities. To question the Church's authority, even gently, was to threaten its entire foundation.

In 1824, Ripoll was arrested and charged with **Deism,** believing in God but rejecting the dogmas and sacraments of the Catholic Church. His accusers called him a **"corrupter of youth,"** echoing the ancient accusation made against Socrates. But Ripoll's teachings were rooted in Scripture, not rebellion.

"God is a Spirit: and they that worship Him must worship Him in spirit and in truth." — *John 4:24*

For two years, he was imprisoned and interrogated by the Inquisition in Valencia. This institution should have died centuries earlier, but which clung to power like a ghost of Rome's former glory. The tribunal found him guilty of *obstinate heresy*. The sentence was death.

On **July 26, 1826**, in the public square of Valencia, Gaietà Ripoll was paraded before a crowd of townspeople. His head was encircled with a garland of thorns made from straw — a mockery of Christ's own suffering.
Before his execution, he was offered one final chance to recant. He refused.

He said, **"I die reconciled to God and to man,"** and commended his soul to the mercy of Christ.

"Be thou faithful unto death, and I will give thee a crown of life." — *Revelation 2:10*

Ripoll was **hanged** from wooden gallows. Afterward, the Catholic Church, still fearful that his death might inspire others, ordered his body placed in a barrel and burned publicly.
They called it *"an act of faith."*

"They shall put you out of the synagogues: yea, the time cometh, that whosoever killeth you will think that he doeth God service." — *John 16:2*

That day, the Inquisition ended outwardly, but not in spirit. The tribunal's fires went cold, but the mentality that fueled them, the idea that religion can police belief, that the Spirit must submit to structure, still lingers wherever men exalt tradition above truth.

The Spirit of Ripoll's Faith

Ripoll's faith was not rebellion; it was a return to the simplicity of the Gospel.
He believed what the apostle Paul declared:

"For by grace are ye saved through faith; and that not of yourselves: it is the gift of God." — *Ephesians 2:8*

He trusted in Christ's finished work, not in the mediation of priests or the repetition of rites. Like the reformers before him, he rediscovered that faith is not granted by the Church, but the Spirit awakens.

"Now the Lord is that Spirit: and where the Spirit of the Lord is, there is liberty." — *2 Corinthians 3:17*

Ripoll's quiet defiance revealed a truth the Church feared to admit: that the authority of heaven cannot be institutionalized.
The same power that parted the Red Sea, raised the dead, and filled the apostles at Pentecost cannot be confined to cathedral walls or priestly decrees.

The freedom Ripoll died for is the same freedom Christ purchased with His blood: the freedom to approach God directly, to know Him personally, to walk with Him without mediation.

"Stand fast therefore in the liberty wherewith Christ hath made us free and be not entangled again with the yoke of bondage." — *Galatians 5:1*

A Modern Parable

The execution of Gaietà Ripoll stands as one of history's great ironies: the Church that preached mercy killed a man for teaching grace.
He was not a soldier, not a revolutionary, not a criminal, but a teacher.
He died not for what he denied, but for what he believed that **salvation is a matter of the heart, not the hierarchy.**

His death marked the final chapter of the Inquisition, a system that had once burned thousands in the name of Christ, but which now ended with the death of a single, humble believer whose only weapon was truth.

Even in his final moments, Ripoll embodied the words of Christ:

"Father, forgive them; for they know not what they do." — *Luke 23:34*

And though his body was burned, his message could not be silenced. His life reminds the Church — and the world — that God's Word and Spirit cannot be chained by fear, forbidden by councils, or owned by any religion.

"The word of God is not bound." — *2 Timothy 2:9*

Eternal Testimony

Gaietà Ripoll's name may be little known, but his faith still speaks.
He was the last to die by the Inquisition's han.

His death was the Church's shame, but heaven's victory and the first of a new age of spiritual liberty, where faith began to rise again, unchained.
For even as the last flames of the Inquisition faded, the Spirit of truth, the same Spirit that moved upon the waters, that inspired the prophets, that comforted the martyrs, continued to move.

"The light shineth in darkness; and the darkness comprehended it not." — *John 1:5*

And that light still shines, calling every believer to reject the chains of religion and walk in the freedom of revelation.

"If the Son therefore shall make you free, ye shall be free indeed." — *John 8:36*

Joseph Smith — Silenced by the Sword of Religion

In 1844, **Joseph Smith**, founder of the **Latter-day Saint movement**, was assassinated by a mob driven by religious hatred, many of whom believed they were defending the purity of Christianity.
Smith's death was not the end of a cult; it was the echo of a pattern that has repeated since Cain and Abel: religion often destroys what it cannot dominate.

A Prophet in a Nation of Churches

Joseph Smith was born in **1805**, in the burned-over district of upstate New York, a region aflame with religious revivals and competing denominations. In that environment, every preacher claimed to speak for God, and every church claimed to possess the truth.

As a young man, confused by the divisions he saw among Christians, Smith turned to the only authority he could trust, the Bible.
He later wrote that he read **James 1:5** one night by candlelight:

"If any of you lack wisdom, let him ask of God, that giveth to all men liberally, and upbraideth not; and it shall be given him." — *James 1:5*

Taking that verse literally, he knelt in the woods and prayed for guidance. What followed would alter the course of American religion. Smith claimed that God the Father and Jesus Christ appeared to him, telling him that all churches had strayed from the fullness of truth and that he must help restore it.

Whether one accepts that vision or not, the reaction of organized religion was immediate and violent. Local ministers ridiculed him. Church leaders denounced him. Newspapers branded him a heretic and a blasphemer. Yet Smith continued preaching, teaching that God still spoke, that revelation had not ceased with the apostles.

"Surely the Lord God will do nothing, but He revealeth His secret unto His servants the prophets." — *Amos 3:7*

The Restoration and the Rebellion

In 1830, Joseph Smith organized the **Church of Christ**, later called **The Church of Jesus Christ of Latter-day Saints**. He claimed that an angel named Moroni had guided him to ancient plates buried in the earth, scriptures he translated as *The Book of Mormon*.

The movement grew rapidly. Converts flocked from across America and Europe, drawn by his message of direct revelation, spiritual gifts, and the gathering of a holy people. But growth provoked hostility. Traditional churches feared losing influence; politicians feared losing power. Smith and his followers were expelled from one state after another **Ohio**, **Missouri**, and finally **Illinois**.

In Missouri, mobs destroyed homes, burned farms, and drove families into the wilderness. In one infamous event, the **Haun's Mill Massacre (1838)**, seventeen Latter-day Saints were murdered, including children, by armed mobs acting in the name of God.

Smith himself was imprisoned multiple times. In one letter written from a jail cell, he reminded his followers:

"The things which we have written are nothing compared to the spirit of God which is poured out upon us."

His faith mirrored that of the apostles, who also preached under persecution:

"We are troubled on every side yet not distressed; we are perplexed, but not in despair; persecuted, but not forsaken; cast down, but not destroyed." — *2 Corinthians 4:8–9*

Martyrdom at Carthage Jail

In **June 1844**, Smith and his brother **Hyrum** were arrested on false treason charges and taken to the **Carthage Jail** in Illinois. Outside the jail, a mob of over 200 armed men gathered, many were professing Christians, some even ministers, swearing that Smith would never leave alive.

On the evening of **June 27**, the mob stormed the jail, firing through the door. Hyrum fell first. Joseph returned fire with a pistol in self-defense, then ran to the window, crying, *"O Lord, my God!"* as bullets struck him. He fell from the second-story window, landing dead in the courtyard below.

He was 38 years old.

"Precious in the sight of the Lord is the death of His saints." — *Psalm 116:15*

Some clergy celebrated his murder as the righteous judgment of God. Newspapers rejoiced that "the impostor was no more." But heaven's silence that day spoke louder than the mob's gunfire. **Once again, religion had silenced what it could not understand.**

"They have persecuted Me; they will also persecute you." — *John 15:20*

The Rise of a People

Smith's death did not end the movement. It scattered it like the early disciples after Stephen's stoning, and from that scattering came a new strength.
Under **Brigham Young**, thousands of Latter-day Saints journeyed westward, crossing the plains to settle in the Salt Lake Valley. They built communities in the desert, raised families, and preached the same message Smith had begun that revelation was still alive, that heaven had not closed its mouth.

Though many have questioned or opposed Mormon doctrine, the story of its survival bears witness to a divine pattern: that truth, or even the search for it, cannot be exterminated by persecution.

"The light shineth in darkness; and the darkness comprehended it not." — *John 1:5*

The Mormon migration became a modern Exodus, a people fleeing religious oppression to find freedom in the wilderness, echoing the Israelites led by Moses.

"And the Lord went before them by day in a pillar of a cloud, to lead them the way; and by night in a pillar of fire, to give them light." — *Exodus 13:21*

Religion Versus Revelation

Joseph Smith's story is not merely about one denomination; it is about what happens when revelation confronts religion.
Every revival, every reformation, every awakening begins the same way: with one voice hearing from God and many others calling it blasphemy.

Like Jesus before the Sanhedrin, Smith was condemned for claiming to hear the Father.
Like Stephen before the council, he was stoned not by pagans but by the religious.
Like Paul, he was hunted for preaching grace beyond the law.

"Ye stiffnecked and uncircumcised in heart and ears, ye do always resist the Holy Ghost: as your fathers did, so do ye." — *Acts 7:51*

Religion without revelation always fears what it cannot define and condemns what it cannot control.
The death of Joseph Smith was not the death of a heretic; it was the death of another man who believed that God still speaks.

"For the word of God is quick, and powerful, and sharper than any twoedged sword." — *Hebrews 4:12*

Legacy and Warning

Today, the Latter-day Saint church has millions of members worldwide. It stands as one of the few American-born faiths that survived violent persecution and endured. Yet Joseph Smith's story remains a warning to every generation of believers not to repeat the sins of the past.

The question is not whether all his revelations were perfect; the question is whether the Church has learned to listen to the God who still speaks.

Because every time religion kills what it cannot understand, it kills part of its own soul.

"For we can do nothing against the truth, but for the truth." *2 Corinthians 13:8*

And though bullets silenced Joseph Smith, his cry still echoes across the centuries, a cry that all who seek God must be free to hear Him for themselves.

Closing Reflection — Revelation Over Religion

The mob thought it had stopped a man; instead, it awakened a movement.
The same Spirit that whispered to prophets in the wilderness and apostles in prison still speaks to hearts unafraid of heaven's voice.
Religion builds temples; revelation builds testimonies.
One seeks control. The other seeks communion.
And in the end, only one will stand for the truth that cannot be buried, and revelation cannot be silenced.

"He that hath an ear, let him hear what the Spirit saith unto the churches." *— Revelation 2:7*

A Personal Journey of Seeking Truth

When I think of Joseph Smith and his quest for truth, I cannot help but reflect on my own.
Like Smith, I was a seeker. In my twenties and early thirties, I longed to understand God in a deeper, more personal way. I wasn't searching for a denomination; I was searching for truth.

I remember reading the same verse that changed Joseph's life:

"If any of you lack wisdom, let him ask of God, that giveth to all men liberally, and upbraideth not; and it shall be given him." — *James 1:5*

That scripture resonated in my spirit. I wasn't given a divine vision, but I was given a hunger, the same hunger that drives every believer who wants to know the real God beyond religion's noise.

My Encounter with the Latter-day Saints

It was during that time, in my twenties, when I first met elders Brock and Verig from the Church of Jesus Christ of Latter-day Saints. I remember their names like it happened yesterday.
They were kind, polite, and eager to share their faith. I respected their sincerity. They began by studying the Bible with me, and I welcomed that. But as time passed, they shifted more toward the Book of Mormon, and less toward the Holy Bible I loved.

I often asked them to stay grounded in Scripture, but their focus remained on their own book. Still, I kept listening to it. I wanted to understand what they believed and test everything through the Word, as Scripture instructs:

"Beloved, believe not every spirit, but try the spirits whether they are of God: because many false prophets are gone out into the world." *1 John 4:1*

Their persistence eventually led to an invitation to be baptized into the Mormon faith. I was hesitant but open, wanting to discern the truth. Yet, on the day of the proposed baptism, something happened that I will never forget.

The Voice That Spoke

As I sat beside the two elders in the church that morning, I heard a voice as clear as day say:

"Leave the church now."

I froze. The words were unmistakably gentle yet firm, filled with authority and peace. I didn't argue, I didn't analyze, I obeyed. I stood up and walked out, without saying a word.

Hours later, the two elders came to my home, asking where I had gone. I told them truthfully: *"I heard a voice tell me to leave."*
They told me the voice was of Satan. But in my spirit, I knew differently. I felt the same stillness that Elijah felt when he heard the *still small voice* on the mountain.

"And after the earthquake a fire; but the Lord was not in the fire: and after the fire a still small voice." — *1 Kings 19:12*

I closed the door quietly. I wasn't angry, I was certain. God had spoken, and I knew that was enough.

The Discernment Between Spirit and Religion

That moment taught me a truth I've carried all my life:
It is not our place to condemn what we do not fully understand.
If Joseph Smith's visions were truly from God, then those who condemned him committed blasphemy against the Spirit. If they were not, then God Himself would be the judge.

"Judge not, that ye be not judged." — *Matthew 7:1*

As believers, we must walk carefully when it comes to spiritual revelation. To deny something outright, without discernment, risks opposing God Himself just as the Pharisees did when they accused Jesus of casting out demons by Beelzebub. Christ warned them that blasphemy against the Holy Spirit is the one sin that will not be forgiven.

"Whosoever speaketh a word against the Son of man, it shall be forgiven him: but whosoever speaketh against the Holy Ghost, it shall not be forgiven him."
— *Matthew 12:32*

Religion, in its fear, too often becomes the voice that stones prophets rather than tests prophecy.

What I Learned

Looking back now, at sixty years old, I see that my encounter with the Mormon faith wasn't about conversion; it was about confirmation.
God used that moment to teach me discernment: how to listen for His voice above the noise of men.

I don't condemn the Latter-day Saints; there were good men among them, sincere hearts seeking truth. But I saw how easily religion can drift from revelation, how tradition can replace transformation.

That day I learned something Joseph Smith himself discovered:
Faith must be personal. Revelation must be tested. And obedience must belong to God alone.

"My sheep hear My voice, and I know them, and they follow Me." — *John 10:27*

The Spirit Still Speaks

Religion will always try to control what it cannot comprehend. But God still moves. He still speaks. He still calls His people out of systems and into intimacy.

Like Joseph Smith, like every prophet who dared to ask, "Lord, what is truth?" I learned that the true Church is not built of stone, but of surrender.

"Ye also, as lively stones, are built up a spiritual house, a holy priesthood." — *1 Peter 2:5*

The voice that told me to leave the church was the same Spirit that tells all believers to follow Him over everything else, over titles, temples, and traditions.

That day wasn't the end of my search. It was the beginning of understanding that revelation never contradicts the Word of God; it fulfills it.

Final Reflection

The mob that murdered Joseph Smith thought they killed a man, but they only proved the truth of Scripture:

"For we can do nothing against the truth, but for the truth." — *2 Corinthians 13:8*

And the same Spirit that spoke to Smith through *James 1:5* spoke to me thirty years ago, reminding me that God still guides, still reveals, and still warns.

Religion can build empires and doctrines, but it cannot own the voice of God.
For when God speaks, the wise listen, and the humble obey.

"Where the Spirit of the Lord is, there is liberty." — 2 Corinthians 3:17

The Bible's Warning Against Religious Blindness

From the Old Testament to Revelation, God warns His people about the danger of exalting religion over righteousness.
Israel built the golden calf while claiming to worship the Lord.
The priests in Jeremiah's day burned incense to Baal while standing in the temple.
And in Jesus' time, the Pharisees "compassed sea and land to make one proselyte" (*Matthew 23:15*) yet missed the very Messiah standing before them.

The Catholic Church, like ancient Israel, began with divine revelation but became entangled in worldly power. It clothed truth in tradition and replaced the living voice of the Spirit with stone rituals.

"Having a form of godliness but denying the power thereof." *2 Timothy 3:5*

Every era of religion carries this warning:
When men build walls around revelation, they also build prisons around themselves.

Truth Still Moves

Though Galileo was chained, Servetus burned, Ripoll hanged, and Smith slain, the truth of God has never stopped moving.
Revelation continues to unfold.
The Spirit still breathes.

And no system, no church, no government, and no pope can stop what God has spoken.

"For the word of God is not bound." — *2 Timothy 2:9*

The same sun that Galileo saw still shines as a constant reminder that God's truth does not revolve around man's authority.
The same Spirit that spoke through the prophets still whispers today to those willing to hear.

The question is not whether God is still speaking.
The question is whether religion is still listening.

Final Reflection

Galileo's whisper, "And yet it moves," was more than defiance.
It was a prophecy.

It spoke for every voice silenced by the Church, every seeker of truth condemned by fear, and every believer who dared to see God beyond the walls of religion.

The heavens still declare His glory.
The prophets still cry from the ashes.
And the Spirit still moves upon the waters, breaking chains, tearing veils, and calling His people back to the truth that no church can own and no empire can contain.

Because the truth was never Rome's.
It was never the pope's.
It was never the councils.

The truth was and forever is **Christ Himself.**

"I am the way, the truth, and the life: no man cometh unto the Father, but by Me." — *John 14:6*

The Spirit Still Speaks

Though the Church has often failed, God has never stopped raising voices. The Spirit of truth continues to move not just through preachers, but through poets, teachers, scientists, and ordinary people whose conscience won't let them stay silent.

History may silence the body, but it cannot silence the truth. The same fire that burned the prophets also forged the Gospel's endurance. The blood of the martyrs became the seed of faith.

Every time religion tried to contain God, He broke out. Every time it tried to silence Him, He spoke louder through someone else.

The Spirit doesn't live in cathedrals. He lives in hearts that are willing to listen, even when it costs everything.

A Warning and a Hope

When it punishes those who question, it repeats the sins of the Pharisees.

God doesn't need defenders; He needs followers. The truth never needed permission to speak, only courage to be heard.

The tragedy of history is that those who loved God most were often condemned by those who claimed to represent Him. But the hope of history is this: God always vindicates His prophets, even if the vindication comes long after the fire.

"You shall know the truth, and the truth shall make you free."
— John 8:32

And freedom, not control, was always God's plan.

The lesson is clear and timeless: when religion replaces **revelation** with **ritual**, it loses its soul. When it trades the living Spirit for lifeless ceremony, it becomes the very thing Christ came to confront. The lesson is clear: when religion replaces revelation with ritual, it loses its soul. When it punishes those who question, it repeats the sins of the Pharisees.

God doesn't need defenders; He needs followers. The truth never needed permission to speak, only courage to be heard.

The Pharisees once stood at the gates of the temple, convinced they were protecting holiness, yet they were the ones who crucified it. Their descendants now wear different robes, but their spirit remains the same. Whenever control takes precedence over compassion, and authority silences authenticity, the Cross is raised again not as salvation, but as indictment.

"Having eyes, they see not; and having ears, they hear not." — **Mark 8:18**

Ritual without revelation is religion without relationship.
Doctrine without discernment is law without love.
And faith without humility becomes idolatry in holy clothing.

God doesn't need defenders, He needs followers.
He never asked for protectors of His throne; He asked for people who would carry His heart.

The truth never needed permission to speak, only courage to be heard.

Throughout history, those who dared to speak that truth paid the highest price.
Prophets were stoned. Apostles were imprisoned.
Reformers were burned. And yet, through every age of persecution, the Word of God refused to stay buried beneath the ashes of fear.

That is the tragedy of history: that those who loved God most were often condemned by those who claimed to represent Him.
But the hope of history is greater still: **God always vindicates His prophets**, even if vindication comes centuries later.

When the Church crucified Christ, the resurrection proved its error.
When the inquisitors burned Joan of Arc, history revealed her as Heaven's warrior.

When institutions fall silent, God still finds a voice in deserts, prisons, and quiet hearts that refuse to bow.

"For there is nothing hidden which shall not be revealed, neither secret that shall not be made manifest." — Mark 4:22

Truth cannot be chained. It may be silenced for a season, but it cannot be destroyed. It waits in tombs, only to rise again when the stone of fear is rolled away.

The warning is to those who build walls where God is trying to open doors.
The hope is for those who still listen when His Spirit whispers in the wilderness.

"You shall know the truth, and the truth shall make you free." — John 8:32

And freedom, not control, was always God's plan.
Freedom of the heart, not permission from hierarchy.
Freedom to love without limits, to serve without recognition, to speak without fear.

So let the warning echo through history but let the hope echo louder:
God will always raise new voices when the old ones grow silent.
And even when religion builds its fires, revelation will always find its way through the smoke.

Closing Reflection

If you listen closely, the voices of the prophets still echo through time in Scripture, in history, and sometimes, in our own hearts.
Their voices are not silent; they only sound different now.

They speak in the cries of the broken, in the courage of the faithful, and in the whispers of those who still dare to believe that truth matters.

They remind us that truth is not popular, and faith is not safe.
For truth does not serve culture; it confronts it.
And faith does not follow the world; it calls the world to repentance.

The prophets of old lived in days not unlike our own, marked by confusion, moral decay, and political corruption.
Isaiah warned of a nation that honored God with its lips while its heart was far from Him.
Jeremiah wept for a people who shouted, *"The temple of the Lord!"* while living in rebellion.
Amos thundered against the wealthy who trampled the poor and called their luxury "a blessing."
And **Ezekiel**, standing among exiles, saw dry bones and dared to believe they could live again.

Their message was simple and eternal: **repent, return, remember.**

Pagans did not kill them, but the priests did.
Not rejected by atheists, but by those who claimed to know God best.
Their message threatened power, not faith, and power always crucifies what it cannot control.

"O Jerusalem, Jerusalem, thou that killest the prophets, and stonest them which are sent unto thee..." **— Matthew 23:37**

From the Scroll to the Screen

Today, the setting has changed, but the spirit is the same.
The platforms have multiplied, but the prophets are still

mocked.
Truth has become a headline debated, diluted, and dismissed.

We live in a world that tweets its convictions but trembles to live them.
A culture that trades discernment for distraction, and reverence for entertainment.
We have knowledge without wisdom, connection without communion, and noise without revelation.

Just as Israel once bowed before golden calves, modern man bows before glowing screens.
The idols are no longer carved from stone; they are coded in pixels.
And yet the same voice still calls:

"Little children, keep yourselves from idols." — 1 John 5:21

We are the generation of **Laodicea** rich, self-assured, and blind to our spiritual poverty.
The Church of today stands at the same crossroads as Israel once did:
to choose between popularity and purity, between performance and presence, between religion and relationship.

The Prophets Still Speak

Listen carefully, and you can still hear them.
Moses speaks when leaders must choose between obedience and the approval of Pharaoh.
Elijah speaks when truth stands alone on Mount Carmel, outnumbered but unshaken.
John the Baptist speaks when voices cry out in the wilderness of corruption and pride.

204

Joan of Arc speaks when courage refuses to bow to fear or hierarchy.
And **Jesus Christ** the Prophet, Priest, and King still speaks above them all, calling His Church back to Himself.

The fire that burned them did not destroy their message, it refined it.
Their ashes became seeds.
Their silence became song.
And their deaths became doorways through which truth would march into the next generation.

The Mirror of Our Time

We are witnessing, once again, the collision of truth and power.
Prophets are not being burned at the stake, but they are being canceled, silenced, and ridiculed in digital flames.
False teachers build empires, while true shepherds are branded extremists.
The world applauds compromise but crucifies conviction.

Yet, amid this darkness, a remnant remains the same remnant that has always stood when the world bowed.
The same Spirit that filled Daniel in Babylon and Esther in Persia still fills men and women today who will not be silent in the face of evil.

God has not changed.
He still raises voices from unexpected places: the young, the broken, the outcast, the obedient.
The question is not whether God still speaks; it is whether His people still listen.

"He that hath an ear, let him hear what the Spirit saith unto the churches." — **Revelation 3:22**

The Unburned Truth

The Church may lose its buildings, its influence, or its reputation, but it must not lose its voice.
For the gospel was never meant to be managed; it was meant to be proclaimed.
And even if the world builds its fires again, truth will not burn.

Because truth is not an idea; it is a Person.
It is Christ the Word made flesh, crucified by religion, resurrected by God, and enthroned forever as the unshakable revelation of divine love.

Religion ignites, but truth endures.
And through every age of deception, division, and decay, the Spirit of God still moves.
calling the Church to rise, to repent, and to remember who she was meant to be **a light on a hill, not a system in the dark.**

So let the prophets speak again, not from pulpits alone but from every life set on fire by the living God.
And may this generation be the one that chooses revelation over ritual, courage over comfort, and faith over fear.

For the world is still watching.
And the same God who spoke in the burning bush still speaks in the burning heart.

"Is not My word like fire," saith the Lord, "and like a hammer that breaketh the rock in pieces?" — **Jeremiah 23:29**

And so it is:
The fire burns,

the truth endures,
and the Word lives on.

Chapter Seven

Idolatry in the Name of God

When most people hear the word *idolatry*, they think of
stone statues, golden calves, or pagan temples. But idols
have evolved. They no longer stand in the open air — they
sit in pews, hang on walls, and sometimes preach from
pulpits.

Idolatry is not just about what we worship; it's about what
replaces God in our hearts.
And through the centuries, **religion itself** has become the
most subtle form of idolatry of all.

The Ancient Warning

When God delivered Israel from Egypt, His first
commandment was not about murder, theft, or adultery; it
was about worship.

**"Thou shalt have no other gods before Me." — Exodus
20:3**

He knew the human heart would always be tempted to
create visible substitutes for the invisible God.
From the golden calf at Sinai to the bronze serpent that
King Hezekiah later destroyed because people began to

worship it **(2 Kings 18:4),** Scripture shows us how easily sacred symbols become sacred traps.

Man always seeks to turn revelation into ritual to make what was once living into something manageable.

From Pagan Shrines to Christian Statues

When the early Church spread through the Roman Empire, it confronted a world saturated with idol gods of stone, marble, and gold.
Yet, over time, as the Church gained influence, it absorbed the culture it was called to transform.

The Roman Catholic Church, once persecuted by Rome, became Rome.
Temples were renamed churches, and pagan statues were given Christian names.
Jupiter became Peter; Venus became Mary; pagan feasts were rededicated as saints' days.
The images once condemned by the prophets were merely repainted in holy colors.

What began as an effort to redeem culture became a compromise that corrupted the gospel.

"They feared the Lord, and served their own gods." — 2 Kings 17:33

Even now, the faithful kneel before carved images, pray to saints as mediators, and venerate relics believed to contain divine power, all practices the early apostles would have rebuked.
The danger is not in honoring saints or remembering holy people, it is in replacing the living Christ with created things, giving glory to the symbols instead of the Savior.

The False Comfort of Visible Faith

The human soul longs for something it can see, touch, and control.
Invisible faith demands trust; idols offer convenience.
We trade the presence of the Spirit for the security of ceremony.

That is why Jesus confronted the Pharisees, not because they prayed, but because they had turned prayer into performance.
He overturned the tables in the temple because worship had become commerce.
He rebuked the scribes who loved the greetings of men more than the approval of God.

And today, the same spirit lives on when the Church worships its traditions, defends its image, and measures holiness by outward devotion rather than inward transformation.

The truth is simple: idolatry does not begin in the temple; it starts in the heart.

Throughout history, one of the clearest examples of this has been seen within the **Catholic Church.** What began as a movement of faith centered on the living Christ slowly transformed into a system centered on hierarchy, ritual, and icons. The cross that once represented sacrifice became gilded in gold; the name of Jesus, once whispered in prayer, became guarded behind Latin liturgy and priestly mediation.

The early church fathers warned of this drift. They knew how easily devotion could turn into dependence, how quickly reverence could become replacement. Over time, faith was replaced by form, and a relationship with God was replaced by reverence for men who claimed to stand in His stead.

Statues of saints, relics, and images meant to remind believers of holiness became objects of prayer and adoration. Instead of coming boldly before the throne of grace, people were taught to approach God through a priest, a pope, or an image. What began as symbolism became substitution.

Yet the Scripture speaks plainly:

"Thou shalt have no other gods before Me. Thou shalt not make unto thee any graven image, or any likeness of any thing that is in heaven above, or that is in the earth beneath, or that is in the water under the earth." *Exodus 20:3–4*

True worship has never been about statues or ceremonies — it has always been about the heart. Jesus said,

"God is a Spirit: and they that worship Him must worship Him in spirit and in truth." *John 4:24*

But over centuries, idolatry disguised itself as reverence. Images were called "holy." Rituals were declared "sacred." Men were given titles reserved for God alone. The Church that once carried the truth began to carry the traditions of men.

This is not to condemn every Catholic believer, for many within that system have sought Christ sincerely, and God sees the heart. But it is to expose the danger of any religion that replaces the living presence of God with man-made intermediaries.

When the church bows to statues instead of the Spirit, when people confess to priests instead of to Christ, when rituals overshadow repentance, **idolatry wears a robe and carries a rosary.**

The tragedy of idolatry in the name of God is that it blinds us with beauty while robbing us of power. Gold, incense, and ceremony may stir emotion, but only the Holy Spirit transforms the soul.

God never asked for images to remind us of Him. He gave us His Spirit to dwell within us.
He never asked for marble cathedrals He asked for living temples made of hearts.
He never asked for repetition. He asked for a relationship.

When religion begins to glorify its structure more than its Savior, it becomes an idol in itself.
And perhaps the greatest idolatry of all is when man builds a system so ornate that the simplicity of the Gospel *Christ alone* can no longer be seen.

Mary, Saints, and the Subtle Deception

The Catholic Church teaches the veneration of Mary, calling her "Queen of Heaven," "Co-Redemptrix," and "Mediatrix of All Graces."
But Scripture gives that role to Christ alone.

"For there is one God, and one mediator between God and men, the man Christ Jesus." — 1 Timothy 2:5

Honoring Mary for her obedience is biblical. Worshipping her, praying to her, or attributing to her powers of intercession is not.
It is the same ancient deception in a new disguise, exalting creation over the Creator.

Likewise, the use of relics, rosaries, and icons has blurred the line between remembrance and reliance.
These objects may have begun as symbols of faith, but for millions, they have become substitutes for it.
A cross worn around the neck means nothing if the heart beneath it is unrepentant.

"This people draweth nigh unto Me with their mouth, and honoureth Me with their lips; but their heart is far from Me." Matthew 15:8

Modern Idols in Sacred Clothing

The Church no longer bows before carved stone, but it bows before something far more dangerous: power, pride, and politics.
Some worship their denomination. Others worship their doctrine. Still others worship their leaders.

A cathedral can become an idol just as easily as a golden calf.
A pulpit can become a throne, and a preacher can become a substitute for the Savior.
Whenever we exalt the visible over the invisible, the system over the Spirit, we are no different from Israel bowing to Baal.

"Little children, keep yourselves from idols." 1 John 5:21

The irony is that the greatest idol of all is not carved from marble; it is made from ego.
We do not need to build altars to worship ourselves; we already carry them in our hearts.

The Call to Return

True worship is not about images, incense, or institutions.
It is about spirit and truth.

"The hour cometh, and now is, when the true worshipers shall worship the Father in spirit and in truth." John 4:23

Christ does not dwell in cathedrals of stone; He dwells in temples of flesh in the hearts of those who love Him.
And until the Church lays down its idols, its pride, its politics, its hierarchy, it will never know the power that once turned the world upside down.

The Church does not need another monument; it needs another Pentecost.
It does not need more rituals; it needs more revelation.
It does not need more priests; it needs more prophets.

Only when religion releases its grip on control will the Spirit once again fill the sanctuary

The Forgotten Body

In the book of Acts, believers broke bread house to house.
They prayed together, prophesied, laid hands on the sick, and shared what they had.
There was no hierarchy, only harmony.
No celebrity, only community.

But as the centuries passed, the clergy replaced the community, and hierarchy replaced humility.

The church that was born in an upper room now hides in boardrooms.
The Spirit who once empowered fishermen now waits outside church walls, while polished programs fill the schedule but not the soul.

"Now ye are the body of Christ, and members in particular." 1 Corinthians 12:27

We were never meant to be spectators of one man's calling but participants in one divine mission.
The call to ministry belongs not to a class of clergy but to the entire body of believers.

When every believer preaches, the Church multiplies. When only one man preaches, the Church fossilizes.

The early Church was never built on performance, but participation. They gathered not to be entertained, but to encounter God. Their worship wasn't confined to temples, their power wasn't tied to titles, and their faith wasn't measured by attendance but by obedience.

Somewhere along the way, the Church forgot her identity. She traded her simplicity for structure, her anointing for approval, her movement for maintenance.
She built walls instead of wells, pulpits instead of partnerships, and pews instead of pathways.

We call it progress. Heaven calls it paralysis.

Because the Church is not an audience, it is an army.
The Body of Christ was never designed to be divided between clergy and laity. Every believer is both priest and prophet, called to carry the fire of God beyond the sanctuary into the streets, schools, and cities.
Christ never anointed spectators. He anointed servants.

The forgotten truth of the Body is that revival is not found in the pulpit alone; it's found in the participation of the people.

The Spirit was poured out not upon one preacher, but upon one hundred and twenty believers, men and women, young and old, rich and poor, all filled, all sent, all aflame.

The miracle of Pentecost was not the tongues of fire on a few, but the fire on all.
The Church was never meant to be an institution but an incarnation — Christ multiplied in every believer.
The Body is not built by committees or clergy but by connection: one Spirit, one heart, one mission.

It is time to return to the upper room, not the conference room.
It is time to remember that the head of the Church is Christ, not the pastor, not the bishop, not the brand.
It is time for the Body to rise, for the saints to step out of the pews, for faith to become flesh again.

The forgotten Body must awaken, for the world will never see Christ until the Church becomes His hands and feet again.
Not a divided institution, but a united incarnation.
Not a religious machine, but a living movement.
Not a place we go, but a people we are.

A Call Back to the Body

The Church must return to the pattern of the New Testament, a living body where Christ is the Head and every member ministers.
Pastors were never meant to stand above the flock, but among it.
Their authority is not to dominate, but to disciple.
Their calling is not to perform, but to prepare.

When the pulpit becomes a stage, and the pastor becomes the star, the gospel becomes entertainment.
But when the Church becomes a body again, the world becomes our mission field, not our marketplace.

Religion may light candles before its images, but only the Holy Spirit lights fire within the soul.
And when that fire burns again, not in one man, but in the whole congregation, idols will fall, and revival will rise.

In the first century, there were no cathedrals, no titles, no stained glass.
There were homes filled with prayer, upper rooms filled with power, and believers filled with the Holy Spirit.

The apostles understood that leadership was service, not status.
They followed the words of Jesus, who said,

"He that is greatest among you shall be your servant."
Matthew 23:11

Paul wrote not as a ruler but as a father in the faith. To the Ephesians, he said,

"He gave some, apostles; and some, prophets; and some, evangelists; and some, pastors and teachers; For the perfecting of the saints, for the work of the ministry, for the edifying of the body of Christ." —
Ephesians 4:11–12

Notice the purpose of these roles was not to create a class of professionals, but to equip the saints.
Every believer was a minister. Every home is a sanctuary. Every heart is a temple.

The early Church thrived because the Spirit was its structure and love was its law.
They met daily, broke bread, prayed, and shared all things in common **(Acts 2:44–47)**.

216

They had no seminaries, yet they had power.
No boards or budgets, yet they turned the world upside down. **(Acts 17:6)**

But history changed the Church's rhythm.
By the third and fourth centuries, as Christianity gained imperial favor under Constantine, the living organism of the body began to fossilize into an organization.
Faith moved from homes to halls, from Spirit to ceremony.
Bishops replaced brotherhood.
The altar replaced the table.
The priest replaced the people.

The flame of participation dimmed under the weight of position.
The very structure that was meant to serve began to rule.
The Church forgot that Jesus never called men to build thrones He called them to carry crosses.

"Ye know that the princes of the Gentiles exercise dominion over them, but it shall not be so among you." Matthew 20:25–26

When the Church began to mirror the empire instead of the kingdom, power replaced presence, and the Body became divided.
The reformation, centuries later, began to break those chains, restoring the authority of Scripture and the priesthood of all believers.
But even today, the temptation remains to build platforms instead of altars, brands instead of brothers, programs instead of prayer.

The New Testament pattern still stands like a lighthouse in the fog of modern religion:
Christ is the Head.
The Spirit is the guide.
Every believer is a minister.

"For as the body is one, and hath many members, and all the members of that one body, being many, are one body: so also is Christ." — 1 Corinthians 12:12

When every joint is supplied, the Body grows.
When every believer prays, the Church breathes.
When every heart burns, the world sees Christ again.

It is time for the Church to remember that the kingdom of God does not operate through hierarchy, but through harmony, not through control, but through communion.
The greatest revivals in history did not begin in cathedrals, but in living rooms, barns, and hidden prayer meetings where ordinary believers believed an extraordinary God.

The Church must rediscover that same fire.
Not a borrowed flame from one preacher's charisma, but a shared blaze of Spirit and truth.
When that happens, when Christ is truly the Head, and His people truly the Body, the world will not find religion; it will find resurrection.

True worship is not about images, incense, or institutions.
It is about spirit and truth.

"The hour cometh, and now is, when the true worshipers shall worship the Father in spirit and in truth." **John 4:23**

Christ does not dwell in cathedrals of stone; He dwells in temples of flesh in the hearts of those who love Him.
And until the Church lays down its idols, its pride, its politics, its hierarchy, it will never know the power that once turned the world upside down.

The Church does not need another monument; it needs another Pentecost.
It does not need more rituals; it needs more revelation.
It does not need more priests; it needs more prophets.

Only when religion releases its grip on control will the Spirit once again fill the sanctuary.

"How True Understanding Comes: Study, Revelation, and the Death of Religious Dependence"

Many people claim, *"I could never read the Bible all the way through; it's boring, confusing, and impossible to finish."*
But anyone who says this misses the entire point of Scripture. You do not learn the Word of God by forcing yourself through Genesis to Revelation like a textbook. You learn through **Spirit-led revelation**, not religious duty.

I have never read the Bible straight through from beginning to end. Instead, I began in the New Testament, where the covenant of Christ speaks directly to the world we live in today. From there, I used cross-references in the Bible and let it lead me into the Old Testament whenever the Holy Spirit connected the dots. I studied the Scriptures the way the apostles taught:
letting the Spirit illuminate truth instead of following a man-made reading plan.

My study Bible is called The MacArthur Study Bible New King James Version.

Reading the Bible is not the same as **studying** the Bible.
Reading gives information.
Studying brings revelation.
And revelation comes only from the Holy Spirit.

Jesus promised this Himself:

"The Holy Spirit will teach you all things." John 14:26

This is how Scripture becomes alive. When you let the Holy Spirit guide you, passages open doors to other passages, and the entire Word ties together in a way no human teacher could ever reveal.

And this is why I wrote this book to show you that **you do not need religious gatekeepers to know God.**

"You Do Not Need a Mediator- Christ Alone Is Enough"

The modern church teaches believers to depend on pastors for understanding, as if spiritual knowledge requires a middleman. But the Bible calls this **idolatry,** replacing the Holy Spirit with human authority.

Paul commanded:

"Study to show yourself approved unto God." — 2 Timothy 2:15

That command was not given just to pastors.
It was given to **every believer.**

Salvation is not earned.
It is a gift.
And after receiving that gift, every believer is called to grow in knowledge directly from God, **not through a mediator, not through a religious hierarchy, and not through a professional priesthood.**

We are *all* called to minister.
We are *all* called to be pastors.
And we are *all* called to walk in the authority Christ gave us.

The early church understood this. Religious institutions today do not.

"Stop Going to Church — YOU Are the Church"

Scripture never commands Christians to gather inside a building, raise money, maintain programs, or listen to one man speak every week. The Church is not a building, it's a people. Jesus said:

"Where two or three are gathered in My name, there am I." Matthew 18:20

Two or three believers fellowshipping in truth is more "church" than a thousand people sitting in a million-dollar sanctuary listening to a polished performance.

Hebrews 10:25 commands us to assemble.
but it does not say where, how, or under a religious structure.

The early Church met in homes, courtyards, and marketplaces, not temples.
The idea of a "church building" came centuries later when Rome institutionalized Christianity, turning it into a political system. That system became the foundation for Catholic power, religious wealth, and ultimately the same spirit that crucified Jesus:
a man-made structure pretending to represent God.

And yes, Rome hijacked Christianity for political control. Yes, the story of Peter founding the church in Rome is historically fabricated.
Religion built an empire; Jesus built disciples. If you must go to church, don't waste time sitting in the pews listening to a pastor; instead, teach or attend Bible study and allow God to minister to all of you in class or during Bible study. Or serve in another capacity. Join the ministry program and minister to others instead of sitting in the pews doing nothing. Living Stones Spiritual House is a living ministry; we never sit for any length of time except to lead others in prayer and to fulfill our duty to minister to others.

"Grace Flows Through Forgiveness — Not Religion"

You did the will of God by forgiving. Forgiveness is the greatest act of spiritual authority available to a believer. It is the key that unlocks grace. Most people cannot forgive because their hearts are controlled by pride and pain.

But you forgave, and in doing so, you stepped into the rare air of true spiritual maturity. You became a vessel God can use. When you choose forgiveness, heaven responds. The Holy Spirit flows freely. Ministry is born.

This is why Jesus said:

"Blessed are the merciful, for they shall obtain mercy."
Matthew 5:7

Forgiveness separates you from the world.
Forgiveness reveals Christ within you.
Forgiveness proves you belong to God.

"A Ministry Without Walls: The Way of Jesus"

You do not need a building, a stage, or a pulpit.
You need **two or three people**, the Word of God, and the Holy Spirit.

That is how the real Church grows.
That is how Jesus started His ministry.
That is how the apostles discipled the world.

This is the heartbeat of Christianity, not religion, not rituals, not institutions.

Just believers filled with the Spirit, gathering wherever God places them.

This is the movement that Religion tried to kill.
This is the Church Jesus actually built.
This is the Church rising again.

Ministry Begins With Relationship — Not Religion, Not Texting, and Not Spiritual Performance

The most effective way to minister to others is simple: **see the person before you see the sin.**
Too many people jump into "pastor mode" before they've taken the time to understand the human heart in front of them. Every person is different. Every heart carries its own wounds, hopes, fears, and history. To minister like Christ, you must **first know their heart**.

And you cannot know someone's heart through **texting**.

Texting is impersonal. It is unclear. It is easily misunderstood. It creates confusion, distance, and assumptions. You cannot win a soul to Christ through text messages. At best, texting is a tool to set an appointment:

"Can we talk at 8 o'clock?"
"Can we meet tomorrow?"

That is where texting should end.

If a person lives nearby, the ministry must be **face-to-face**.
If they live far away, the ministry must be **voice-to-voice**.
Human connection brings understanding, tone, empathy, and sincerity, none of which exist in texting.

Dependency on texting destroys relationships.
It complicates business.
It confuses friendships.
It ruins dating and marriage.

A relationship built on texting is no relationship at all. It lacks the very ingredients God designed for human connection: presence, voice, emotion, discernment, and shared experience.

Relationship Builds Trust — Trust Opens the Heart to Christ

Before you ever mention Jesus, **let Christ shine through you.**
People must first feel:

- Safe

- Heard

- Understood

- Respected

- Equal

If someone enjoys a beer or wine, don't elevate yourself above them. Jesus turned water into real fermented wine to continue the celebration of a Jewish wedding festival that historically lasted for days or even weeks **(John 2:1 10).** He did not condemn celebration. He condemned **hypocrisy.**

Wine is not sinful.
Alcohol is not sinful.
Dependency is sinful.
Abuse is sinful.
Running to alcohol instead of God is sinful.
The heart determines whether something becomes sin, not the substance itself.

Scripture even acknowledges:

"Give strong drink to the one who is perishing, and wine to those in bitter distress."
 Proverbs 31:6

It is not wine that destroys a person;
It is the emptiness and brokenness in their soul.

The Holy Spirit Moves Through Humility, Not Superiority

The Holy Spirit does not live in perfect people; there are none.
The Holy Spirit lives in those with:

- A contrite heart

- Humility

- Sincerity

- Weakness that leans on God

- A desire to serve Christ truthfully

The Spirit works through a heart that knows its need for God.

When ministering to someone, if they enjoy a drink, and you are comfortable, have a drink with them. Sit at their table. Be their friend. Jesus did not place Himself on a pedestal. He did not pretend to be "better." He walked among the hurting, the broken, the confused, and the lost.

You cannot win anyone to Christ by acting superior.
You cannot help someone who feels beneath you.
This is why Jesus said:

"Let him who is without sin cast the first stone." John 8:7

The heart of ministry is not judgment.
The heart of ministry is relationship.

This Is Why Religion Fails at Winning Souls

Religion tries to "save" people without **knowing** them.
Religion preaches before it listens.
Religion condemns before it connects.
Religion draws lines rather than builds bridges.

But Jesus built relationships first.
He earned trust.
He sat at tables.
He asked questions.
He shared meals.
He understood hearts.
Then He ministered.

This is the model every believer must follow.

The True Church

The true Church is not built on personality, but presence.
It is not sustained by charisma, but by communion.
It does not gather to watch; it gathers to work to serve, to love, to lift.

When every believer becomes a minister, every city becomes a sanctuary.
When every heart becomes an altar, every day becomes holy ground.

That is the Church Jesus died to build, not a cathedral of stone, but a kingdom of servants.
Not a pastor at the top, but a Savior at the center.

"But speaking the truth in love, may grow up into Him in all things, which is the head, even Christ." — **Ephesians 4:15**

So let the modern Church repent of its idolatry of leadership and return to the simplicity of love.
Let pastors lead, but let the people live their calling.
Let pulpits equip, but let the streets preach.

For when the body moves again as one, Christ will be seen again as Head.

"Little children, keep yourselves from idols." **1 John 5:21**

Religion ignites, but truth endures.
And when the Spirit reclaims His Church, no idol, no title, and no tradition will stand.

The true Church was born not in marble halls but in an upper room in the sound of a rushing mighty wind, in tongues of fire, in hearts made new.
There were no robes, no ranks, no divisions, only disciples.
The apostles did not compete for titles; they contended for truth.
Peter stood and preached, but the Spirit fell on all men and women, servants and free. (*Acts 2:1–4***)**

That was the Church as Christ intended:

- **One Lord. One faith. One baptism. (***Ephesians 4:5***)**

- **One body, and one Spirit, even as ye are called in one hope of your calling. (***Ephesians 4:4***)**

As history unfolded, this unity was tested.
By the second century, structure began to replace Spirit.
Bishops rose to power; councils replaced the community.
By the fourth century, when Constantine crowned

Christianity as the empire's religion, the Church traded her sandals for scepters.
What began as a movement became a monument.
Faith that once walked the streets of Jerusalem now sat on the thrones of Rome.

The Church of Acts turned the world upside down; the Church of Empire turned the gospel inside out.
And yet the true Church never died.
Through persecution and corruption, through reformations and renewals, there has always been a remnant of those who kept their eyes not on men but on the Master.

"Nevertheless, the foundation of God standeth sure, having this seal, The Lord knoweth them that are His." *— 2 Timothy 2:19*

Throughout history, the Spirit has called the Church back to her roots:
Back to prayer instead of politics.
Back to presence instead of programs.
Back to power instead of popularity.

From the deserts of the early monastics to the fires of the Reformation, from Wesley's revival tents to Azusa Street's humble gatherings — God has never needed a palace to pour out His power.
Every time man tried to institutionalize what was born of the Spirit, God raised up men and women outside the system to remind the world that *the Church is alive because Christ is alive.*

"Know ye not that ye are the temple of God, and that the Spirit of God dwelleth in you?" *— 1 Corinthians 3:16*

The true Church is not a denomination or a dwelling.
It cannot be confined to a brand or a building, for it was

born in blood and built on grace.
It is not the creation of men but the continuation of Christ.

"Upon this rock I will build My Church; and the gates of hell shall not prevail against it." — *Matthew 16:18*

The Church Jesus builds is not a stage for personalities but a sanctuary for presence.
Not a crowd gathered around a celebrity, but a people centered around a cross.
It is where the poor are fed, the broken are healed, and the lost are found.

Let the true Church rise again not to reclaim power, but to release love.
Not to boast in its name, but to bear His.
Not to entertain, but to embody.

When the Church stops chasing platforms and starts carrying crosses, the world will see Jesus again.
When the Church stops defending religion and starts demonstrating resurrection, revival will return.

For the true Church is not a movement of man, it is the manifestation of Christ on earth.
And until He is once again the Head, the Body will never be whole.

The Old Idol in a New Temple

The first commandment was clear:

"You shall have no other gods before Me." (Exodus 20:3)

The second made it even clearer:

"You shall not make for yourself a carved image, or any likeness of anything in heaven above or on the earth beneath... You shall not bow down to them nor serve them." (Exodus 20:4–5)

Yet from the very beginning, mankind has struggled with that simple truth. When Moses came down from Sinai, he found the Israelites worshiping a golden calf, created by their own hands, celebrated in God's name. They didn't think they were abandoning God; they thought they were *honoring* Him.

That's the deception of idolatry: it disguises itself as devotion.

And that same spirit still lives on today, not in deserts or shrines, but in sanctuaries and steeples. We may no longer melt gold, but we still shape God into images that make us comfortable.

We build our idols from habit, culture, pride, and power.

We worship the symbol of the cross more than the sacrifice it represents.
We venerate the building more than the Body of Christ.
We quote the preacher more than the Word of God.

And sometimes, we defend religion more fiercely than we obey the truth.

How Idolatry Changed Its Face

In the centuries after Christ, the Catholic Church began to absorb the customs of the world it sought to convert.

When Emperor Constantine declared Christianity the religion of the Roman Empire, pagan temples were renamed as churches.
Pagan festivals became "holy days."
Pagan idols were repurposed, their faces reshaped into saints and apostles.
The gods of Olympus were replaced with the saints of Rome.

It was not always rebellion; sometimes it was compromise.
But compromise is the slow poison of truth.
In an effort to make the gospel more acceptable, the Catholic Church became more imperial and less inspired.
The altar of repentance became an altar of relics.
And over time, the Church began to confuse reverence with ritual, and faith with formality.

"Having a form of godliness, but denying the power thereof: from such turn away." — 2 Timothy 3:5

By the Middle Ages, cathedrals across Europe were filled with statues, incense, and relics.
Pilgrims traveled not to encounter the living Christ, but to touch the bones of dead saints.
Prayers were offered not to God directly, but through intermediaries, priests, popes, and Mary herself.
The Scriptures, once given freely to the people, were locked behind Latin walls, accessible only to the educated elite.

The very faith that began with fishermen and tents became a religion of thrones and gold.
And the commandment that forbade images became the very law religion learned to bend.

What the Word Declares

The prophets cried against such things:

"They have mouths, but they speak not; eyes have they, but they see not." — *Psalm 115:5*
"They that make them are like unto them; so is every one that trusteth in them." — *Psalm 115:8*

Isaiah thundered the same warning:

"They lavish gold out of the bag, and weigh silver in the balance, and hire a goldsmith; and he maketh it a god: they fall down, yea, they worship." — *Isaiah 46:6*

And even the Apostle John, in his vision of Revelation, saw a religion that would one day blend truth and blasphemy, a "woman clothed in purple and scarlet, decked with gold and precious stones," holding a golden cup of abominations (*Revelation 17:4*).

History bears witness that the Church began to mirror the empire it once resisted.
It was no longer the persecuted bride of Christ, but the crowned queen of men.
Her incense rose higher than her prayers.
Her processions grew longer than her compassion.

The Spirit's Call Back to Purity

Yet even amid corruption, God always preserves a remnant.

From the desert fathers who fled the cities to pray, to the reformers who dared to read the forbidden Word, to every believer today who refuses to bow to ritual, the Spirit still whispers:

"Come out of her, My people, that ye be not partakers of her sins." — *Revelation 18:4*

True worship is not found in statues or in ceremony, but in spirit and in truth.
Jesus told the Samaritan woman:

"The hour cometh, and now is, when the true worshipers shall worship the Father in spirit and in truth: for the Father seeketh such to worship Him." — *John 4:23*

The cross is not a charm to wear, but a call to die.
The saints are not mediators, but models of faith who point to Christ alone.
Mary was blessed because she believed, not because she was divine (***Luke 1:45***).
And no pope, priest, or preacher can replace the direct relationship between the believer and the Savior.

"For there is one God, and one mediator between God and men, the man Christ Jesus." — *1 Timothy 2:5*

Idols of the Heart

The idols of today no longer stand in temples of stone; they stand in the hearts of men.
An idol is anything that takes the place of Christ, even if it carries His name.
It can be a denomination, a tradition, a political cause, or even a ministry.
The heart is the new temple, and what we enthrone there determines whom we truly worship.

233

"Son of man, these men have set up their idols in their hearts." *Ezekiel 14:3*

The Church must tear down its golden calves, both ancient and modern.
Whether carved from stone or built from pride, they all stand in the way of revival.
When we return to the simplicity of the gospel to the Word, the Spirit, and the blood, the idols will fall, and the presence will return.

"Do not turn to idols or cast images of gods for yourselves. I am the LORD your God". Leviticus 19:4:

The Church's Image of God

When Constantine rebuilt Rome under the banner of Christianity, faith became art. Churches were filled with marble saints, painted angels, and gold-leaf ceilings. What began as an expression soon became an obsession.

The beauty was meant to glorify God, but the people began to praise the beauty. They bowed before images, prayed to relics, and kissed the feet of statues.

Religion taught them that these things connected them to heaven, but in truth, they distracted them from the living God who said plainly, *"I am Spirit, and those who worship Me must worship in Spirit and in truth."* **(John 4:24)**

Worship turned from the inward to the outward, from the heart to the hand, from faith to form.

And once again, man began to control what should only belong to God.

When Art Became an Idol

In the beginning, the Church had no art, only awe.
Early believers met in caves and homes, their symbols simple: a fish, a cross, a loaf of bread.
Their faith was plain but powerful. They carried Christ in their hearts, not in their hands.

But as Rome embraced Christianity, something shifted.
The Church began to reflect the empire more than the upper room.
Art became theology, and theology became theater.
The very commandment that forbade carved images was reinterpreted to accommodate the empire's new religion.

By the sixth century, mosaics of Christ began to fill the domes of cathedrals.
By the eighth century, the *Iconoclastic Controversy* divided the Church, with one side defending the veneration of icons and the other declaring them idolatry.
Even emperors took sides: Constantine V destroyed icons, while others restored them.

Through centuries of debate, the truth became buried under tradition.
The argument was not over whether God should be worshiped, but *how*.
And as men debated, the Spirit grieved.

"To whom then will you liken God? Or what likeness will you compare to Him?" — *Isaiah 40:18*
"They exchanged the glory of the incorruptible God for an image made like corruptible man." — *Romans 1:23*

When the Image Replaced the Invisible

God forbade images not because He feared art, but because He is infinite.

No statue, painting, or relic can contain His glory. To reduce Him to form is to deny His fullness.

Yet throughout the Middle Ages, the Catholic Church multiplied images of saints, relics, crucifixes, icons, and shrines.
Worshipers were told that the images were "windows to heaven."
But over time, the window became the wall.
Faith was filtered through form, and people began to pray to what they could see rather than to the God who cannot be seen.

"We walk by faith, not by sight." — 2 Corinthians 5:7

The danger of image-based worship is not in art itself, but in attachment when the symbol becomes sacred, and the holy becomes replaced.
The same spirit that built the golden calf in the wilderness built cathedrals filled with gilded saints.
The Israelites said, "This is the god who brought us out of Egypt." (*Exodus 32:4*)
And centuries later, believers were told, "This image will bring you to God."

Both were lies born of impatience and fear, the desire to see what should only be believed.

The Word Versus the Image

Christ did not commission painters or sculptors. He commissioned preachers.

"Go ye into all the world, and preach the gospel to every creature." Mark 16:15
Not, *"Build me a monument,"* but *"Bear my message."*

236

The Word, not the image, reveals God.

"Faith comes by hearing, and hearing by the Word of God." *Romans 10:17*
And yet, as literacy faded in medieval Europe, pictures replaced preaching, and icons replaced instruction.
The Church told the poor they could not read the Bible, but they could look upon saints.
In doing so, it replaced revelation with representation.

The Reformers cried out against it:
Luther tore down relics. Calvin thundered against idols.
The Puritans stripped sanctuaries bare to return the focus to Scripture and Spirit.
And though centuries have passed, the warning remains the same:
God cannot be confined to art, nor contained in architecture.

"Heaven is My throne, and the earth is My footstool: what house will you build for Me? says the Lord." — *Acts 7:49*

The Spirit Beyond the Statues

The Church must remember that beauty without presence is vanity.
The splendor of the Vatican cannot save a soul.
A thousand candles cannot replace the light of the Holy Spirit.
And the painted eyes of saints cannot see, nor can their sculpted lips speak.

"Their idols are silver and gold, the work of men's hands." — *Psalm 115:4*

"They have mouths, but they speak not; eyes have they, but they see not." — *Psalm 115:5*

True worship is not found in cathedrals but in communion.
Not in incense, but in intimacy.
Not in relics, but in repentance.

When the Church returns to the simplicity of the Spirit,
when she stops polishing her idols and starts proclaiming her Savior, the glory will return.
Because God will not dwell in temples built by pride, he resides in the hearts of those built by grace.

"Know ye not that ye are the temple of God, and that the Spirit of God dwelleth in you?" — *1 Corinthians 3:16*

A Call to Return

The Church must no longer confuse beauty for holiness, or art for anointing.
The same Spirit who filled the upper room will not fill a museum of marble hearts.
He is calling His people back from icons to intimacy, from liturgy to life, from religion to relationship.

Let the Church tear down her gilded altars and rebuild the altar of the heart.
Let every believer say again, as Isaiah said, *"My eyes have seen the King, the Lord of hosts." — Isaiah 6:5*
Not an image, not an idol, but the living God.

Then the Spirit will return, and the Church will once again become what it was meant to be:
not a gallery of saints, but a gathering of servants.
Not a monument of history, but a movement of holiness.
Not the art of man, but the image of Christ.

"We all, with unveiled face, beholding as in a mirror the glory of the Lord, are being transformed into the same image." — *2 Corinthians 3:18*

Modern Idols in a Modern Church

Today, we live in a different kind of temple, one filled with technology, convenience, and self-importance. Yet the idols remain.

Some worship *success* in God's name.
Others worship *denomination* more than doctrine.
Many worship *pastors and personalities*, turning faith into fandom.

We've made idols out of celebrity preachers, church brands, and even emotions — mistaking goosebumps for the presence of God.

Our altars may glow with LED lights instead of candles, but they still serve the same human hunger: to see, to feel, to control.

But the Spirit cannot be controlled. He doesn't live in buildings made by human hands. He lives in hearts that are yielded, humble, and still enough to listen.

Curses anyone who makes a carved or molten image and sets it up in secret. Deuteronomy 27:15

That verse wasn't written to pagans. It was written to believers.

The Idol of Religion Itself

Religion can become the greatest idol of all when it replaces relationships.

When people defend their denomination more passionately than they defend the Gospel, they have built an idol.
When pastors fear losing members more than losing the truth, they have built an idol.
When we worship the *idea* of holiness more than we practice love, we have built an idol.

Idolatry isn't always visible; it often hides behind noble words. We tell ourselves we're being "faithful" when in reality, we're being fearful. We cling to systems because they make us feel secure.

But faith was never meant to be secure. It was meant to be surrendered.

Jesus didn't die to give us comfort; He died to set us free.

Freedom terrifies religion, because you can't control a person who's been set free by grace. That's why religion builds idols because it's easier to control what can be seen than to trust the unseen Spirit of God.

God's Jealous Love

The Bible says that God is *jealous* not in the petty human sense, but in the way a husband loves a bride. He doesn't want to share our hearts with substitutes.

"For you shall worship no other god, for the Lord, whose name is Jealous, is a jealous God." (Exodus 34:14)

God's jealousy is not about possession; it's about passion. He knows idols can't love us back. He knows that when we put anything above Him, even good things like family, tradition, or church, we slowly lose the intimacy He created us for.

That's why He keeps calling His people back from the temple to the tent, from ritual to relationship, from noise to stillness.

He doesn't want performance. He wants presence.

The Mirror of the Heart

If you really want to find your idols, don't look at your hands look at your heart.

Ask yourself:

- What do I defend more than I defend truth?
- What could I not give up, even if God asked me to?
- What draws more of my attention than He does?

Those answers reveal the idols we've built without even realizing it.
And the good news is this: **God doesn't destroy idols to punish us, He removes them to free us.**

When we lay down our idols, we don't lose anything of eternal value; we gain everything we were meant for. We begin to experience God not as *religion*, but as *reality*.

When Religion Becomes an Idol

Many people think idols are carved from wood or gold, but the most dangerous idols are invisible.
They are not on our mantels; they are in our minds.

When we defend our **denomination**, our **tradition**, or our **pastor** more fiercely than we defend truth, we are practicing idolatry in the name of faith.
If your loyalty to a religious system is stronger than your obedience to the Holy Spirit, that system has become your god.

Describes idols as lifeless and the work of human hands, and states that those who worship them become just as lifeless. Psalm 115:4-8:

Religion can become a golden calf, shiny, respectable, and utterly lifeless.
It promises security, but it steals intimacy.
It replaces the living presence of God with the comfort of habit and the pride of belonging.
But faith was never meant to be a membership card; it was meant to be a **mirror**.

Looking in the Mirror

When you stand before the mirror of the heart, you don't see what's wrong with the world you know what's wrong within yourself.

That's where true repentance begins.

I've had to look into that mirror many times.
When I examine my life, I can see how often I've built my own idols without even realizing it.
For me, one of those idols was the **desire for companionship**.

From my younger days up to now, I've longed deeply for connection to be loved, to share life with someone. And that's not evil; God Himself said, *"It is not good that man should be alone." — Genesis 2:18*

But even something good can become an idol when it takes the place where God belongs.
There were seasons when I sought the affection of a woman more than the presence of God.
I would pray for love, yet neglect the One who *is* love.

It wasn't until later that I realized my frustration with God, my questioning, my feeling of being forgotten was not because He denied me, but because He was refining me.
He was waiting for me to love Him first, not as a condition, but as a foundation.

Describes the customs of nations that carve idols and warns against adopting them. Jeremiah 10:1-5

Abraham and the Altar of the Heart

The story of **Abraham and Isaac** teaches us what the mirror reveals.
God tested Abraham's faith not to take his son away, but to show what and *who* came first in his heart.

"And He said, Take now thy son, thine only son Isaac, whom thou lovest... and offer him there for a burnt offering." — *Genesis 22:2*

Abraham obeyed. But as he lifted the knife, God intervened not because He wanted blood, but because He wished to *obey.*

Every believer faces a similar test.
God may not ask for your child, but He might ask for your comfort, your ambition, your reputation, even your relationships if they stand between you and Him.

For me, that realization came as a painful realization. I once put my marriage, my dreams, and my desires before God. When those things fell apart, I blamed Him. But now I understand that sometimes God allows idols to collapse so that He can rebuild us on solid ground.

"No man can serve two masters." — *Matthew 6:24*

What You Cannot Give Up

The second question: *What could I not give up, even if God asked me to?* pierces deeply.
For some, it's money—for others, fame, or comfort. For me, it was companionship.

God tested Abraham through Isaac; He tests us through whatever we hold dearest.
If God asked you to surrender it today, could you?
Would you trust that He has something better, not instead of what you love, but beyond it?

That is the real meaning of sacrifice: not loss, but **exchange**.
We give up what we cannot keep to gain what we cannot lose.

244

"He that findeth his life shall lose it: and he that loseth his life for My sake shall find it." — *Matthew 10:39*

What Draws Your Attention

The third question: **What draws more of my attention than He does?** exposes the everyday idols that slip into our lives unnoticed.
When I was young, football was my idol. I couldn't wait for church to end so I could see the game.
Others might replace that with golf, work, entertainment, or social media.

The problem isn't the thing itself; it's the *priority* we give it. **Anything that consistently takes more time, focus, or affection than God becomes a false altar.**

"For where your treasure is, there will your heart be also." — *Matthew 6:21*

Sometimes God removes these things, not to hurt us, but to heal us.
He prunes the branches that bear no fruit so that the tree may live.
It's better to lose what distracts you than to miss what defines you.

"Every branch in Me that beareth not fruit He taketh away: and every branch that beareth fruit, He purgeth it, that it may bring forth more fruit." — *John 15:2*

The Arrogance of the Educated Elite — When Knowledge Becomes an Idol

The world has always had its "high society" men and women, polished by institutions, decorated with letters beside their names, and convinced of their own brilliance.

They often live above the people they claim to understand. They speak of the common man from a distance, study poverty without ever tasting it, and discuss morality as though it were a theory rather than a spiritual reality.

They pride themselves not on wisdom, but on accomplishment in human achievement, not divine revelation.

Yet Scripture warns us plainly:

"Professing themselves to be wise, they became fools." — Romans 1:22

These elites, whether trained in secular universities, Christian colleges, or private academies, often emerge with a subtle but deadly belief:
That education equals superiority, and that superiority equals authority.

But education without humility becomes nothing more than sanitized pride.

When Education Replaces Illumination

Many of the so-called "intellectuals" of our day are highly trained and deeply indoctrinated, yet shockingly disconnected from reality. They have mastered theories but cannot navigate life. They excel in etiquette but lack empathy. They possess degrees but have no discernment.

They are the new Pharisees, people who know everything except the truth.

"Ever learning, and never able to come to the knowledge of the truth." — 2 Timothy 3:7

The tragedy is not their education.
The tragedy is that they worship it.

A university does not grant true intelligence; it is forged through humility, awareness, self-study, vigilance, and the fear of the Lord.

David was a shepherd.
Peter was a fisherman.
Amos was a fig farmer.
Jesus Himself was a carpenter from Nazareth.

God specializes in using the lowly to humble the lofty.

"For God has chosen the foolish things of the world to confound the wise." — 1 Corinthians 1:27

Etiquette, Superficiality, and the Mask of Pride

The elite pride themselves not only on education, but on etiquette—those external cultural codes that make them feel refined, superior, and polished. But etiquette is simply a costume that conceals insecurity.

Jesus was not moved by polished manners; He was moved by surrendered hearts.

The early church did not shake nations with aristocrats. It shook the world with the humble, the broken, the repentant, the bold.

"Man looks on the outward appearance, but the Lord looks on the heart." — 1 Samuel 16:7

In the Kingdom of God, superficial brilliance is useless.

How This Connects to Religious Power Structures

This is where this book, Religion Killed Jesus, becomes crystal clear:

Religion didn't just kill Jesus
The religious *elite* killed Jesus.

The most educated men in Israel, scribes, scholars, Pharisees, Sadducees, were the same ones who:

• **misinterpreted Scripture**
• **dismissed the poor**
• **worshiped their own intellect**
• **weaponized their status**
• **and placed their traditions above truth**

Their education became a wall that separated them from the God they claimed to serve.

Today's religious leaders, seminary-polished, degree-heavy, etiquette-rich, often mirror the same spirit. They have knowledge, but no power. Theology, but no relationship. Training, but no revelation.

They build churches like corporations.
Preach sermons like TED Talks.
Stand above the people rather than among them.

The elite blinded Israel to their Messiah.
The elite blind the modern Church to His voice.

"You nullify the word of God for the sake of your tradition." — Matthew 15:6

The Collapse of the Ivory Tower

The Lord is exposing the pride of intellectual empires.
He is tearing down every tower built on human brilliance rather than the fear of God.

248

Many who trusted in:

- their degrees
- their intellect
- their polished image
- their academic credentials

…will soon discover that these things cannot save them, guide them, or protect them in the shaking that is coming.

For God is raising up a new generation
a humble people, filled with fire, not theory, revelation, not rhetoric, wisdom, not vanity.

The last will become first.
The meek will confront the mighty.
And the simple will confound the scholars.

Reflection & Prayer

Reflection Questions

1. Have I mistaken education for wisdom?

2. Do I seek human approval more than God's revelation?

3. Have I adopted elitist thinking without realizing it?

4. Am I willing to learn from the humble, the broken, and the overlooked?

5. Do I judge others by worldly standards, appearance, vocabulary, degrees, status?

Prayer for Humility and True Wisdom

Father,
Strip me of every prideful thought.
Deliver me from the spirit of the Pharisee—
from the arrogance that exalts human knowledge over
divine truth.
Give me the courage to seek Your wisdom above man's
applause.
Teach me to value revelation over reputation,
and humility over intellect.
Open my eyes to see the world as You see it:
with compassion for the lowly,
respect for the simple,
and discernment to recognize deception in high places.
Make me a vessel of truth,
unshaken by the spirit of this age.
In Jesus' name Amen.

When God Rearranges the Order

In God's divine order, the sequence is precise: **God** →
Man → **Woman** → **Child.**
When that order is reversed, confusion and frustration take
root.
It's not that God despises love or family; He created them.
But He must remain first.

If pleasing your spouse comes before obeying God, the
marriage itself becomes an idol.
If ministry comes before prayer, even your calling becomes
a distraction.
If religion comes before relationship, you have built a
golden calf out of your own faith.

God wants your worship, not your performance.
He wants your surrender, not your routine.

"Thou shalt love the Lord thy God with all thy heart, and with all thy soul, and with all thy mind." *Matthew 22:37*

Refining Through Reflection

When things fall apart, whether relationships, careers, or dreams, we must ask not **"Why did God let this happen?"** but **"What is God teaching me through this?"**

Every loss has a lesson.
Every silence has a message.
Every idol that crumbles is an invitation to rebuild on truth.

"For whom the Lord loveth He chasteneth, and scourgeth every son whom He receiveth." *Hebrews 12:6*

We all fall short of God's glory. But grace isn't about perfection; it's about perspective.
The purpose of the mirror is not to shame you; it's to **show you where God still wants to heal you.**

When you see the idols in your heart, don't run from the reflection; run toward the Redeemer.
Because He never shows you what's wrong without offering to make it right.

"Create in me a clean heart, O God; and renew a right spirit within me." *Psalm 51:10*

Closing Reflection: The Mirror Cleansed

To see yourself clearly before God is not condemnation; it's freedom.
The idols we defend are the chains that bind us.
But when God breaks them, we find that the pain of surrender becomes the peace of restoration.

"And ye shall know the truth, and the truth shall make you free." *John 8:32*

Religion tells us to hide behind stained glass; God calls us to look through it.
He doesn't ask for perfection. He asks for honesty.
The mirror of the heart doesn't lie, but neither does the mercy of God.

When we finally see ourselves as we are, we begin to see Him as He is
and that is the beginning of true worship.

"The Lord seeth not as man seeth; for man looketh on the outward appearance, but the Lord looketh on the heart." — *1 Samuel 16:7*

The Priesthood of Every Believer

One of the greatest deceptions of religious history is the idea that man needs another man to reach God.
For centuries, priests have stood between the people and the Presence not as intercessors of compassion, but as gatekeepers of grace.
The faithful were taught that access to God must come through the Church, through confessionals, through sacraments, through men clothed in holy garments.

But the veil was torn.
When Christ gave up His spirit on the cross, the curtain that separated man from God was ripped from top to bottom, not by human hands, but by divine declaration.

"Having therefore, brethren, boldness to enter into the holiest by the blood of Jesus..." — Hebrews 10:19

That moment marked the end of the age of earthly mediators.
No priest, no pope, no pastor can now stand between the soul and its Creator.
There is only one High Priest who intercedes forever, Jesus Christ.

"For there is one God, and one mediator between God and men, the man Christ Jesus." — 1 Timothy 2:5

The Call to Personal Relationship

The tragedy of modern faith, particularly within the Catholic system, is that many have traded personal relationships for institutional dependence.
They wait for a priest to read the Word instead of opening it themselves.

They confess to men rather than communing directly with God.
They ask saints for favor while ignoring the One who already gave them access to the throne of grace.

"Let us therefore come boldly unto the throne of grace, that we may obtain mercy." — Hebrews 4:16

The Word of God was never meant to be chained to a pulpit or translated only by clergy.
Jesus came to make disciples, not dependents.
He came to fill every believer with His Spirit so that each heart could become a temple, each voice a prayer, each life a ministry.

No one can pray on your behalf better than the Spirit who dwells within you.
And no one can interpret Scripture more faithfully than the Author who lives in your heart.

The same Spirit who inspired the apostles now dwells in the believer who kneels beside their bed and opens the Word for themselves.

Breaking the Chains of Dependence

For generations, Catholics have been taught that holiness is conferred through sacraments, confession, baptism, and communion controlled by the Church.
But holiness is not a ritual; it is a relationship.
It is not earned by repetition, but born through revelation.

God never desired a people who rely on priests to hear Him.
He desires people who hear Him personally, daily, intimately.

That is why Jesus said,

"My sheep hear My voice, and I know them, and they follow Me." — **John 10:27**

The true Church is not a hierarchy; it is a household, a living body where every member is called, anointed, and equipped.
When we depend on others to pray for us, read for us, and believe for us, we remain children in faith.
But when we take ownership of our walk with God, we grow into sons and daughters who reflect His glory in the world.

This is not rebellion against leadership; it is the restoration of liberty.
Christ freed the Church from priestly control so that the Spirit could fill every believer with priestly power.

"Ye are a chosen generation, a royal priesthood, a holy nation..." — **1 Peter 2:9**

The Spirit of God does not dwell behind the altars of institutions.
He dwells in the hearts of His people.
And when believers begin to pray directly, study intensely, and live boldly, the fire that once fell in Acts will fall again.

Closing Reflection

The idols of today wear crosses, not crowns.
They quote Scripture, not spells.
They smile from pulpits and stand beneath stained glass,
preaching in the name of the One they've replaced.
And yet, they draw men's hearts away from the living God
just the same.

The question is no longer, *"Do we worship idols?"*
It is, *"Which ones have we baptized?"*

The Rise of the Pastoral Throne

In the early Church, Christ alone was called the Head. The
apostles taught that the Church was a **body** in which every
joint supplied strength and every believer carried
responsibility.
But over centuries, the ministry became a monarchy. The
shepherd's staff became a scepter.

What was once a fellowship became a franchise.
The pulpit became a pedestal.
And the pastor who was meant to equip the saints became
the saint to be served.

*"And He gave some apostles, and some prophets, and
some evangelists, and some pastors and teachers; for
the perfecting of the saints, for the work of ministry,
for the edifying of the body of Christ."* — Ephesians
4:11-12

The purpose was never to create one man who preaches
while a thousand watch.
It was to awaken a thousand who preach wherever they
walk.

But today, many churches have built altars to personalities.
The Body has become an audience.
And the Word has been reduced to a weekly performance
instead of a daily practice.

When the people of God depend on one man's sermon to hear from Heaven, idolatry has taken root.
Because the Spirit who speaks from the pulpit is the same Spirit who whispers in the pew.

Idolatry isn't just a sin of the past; it's the quiet battle of every believer. The enemy doesn't need to make us evil; he just needs to make us distracted.

That's why the Church today must repent not only of its sins, but of its substitutes, the things we have loved more than God Himself.

The Spirit of God still whispers through the ages:

"You shall have no other gods before Me."

Not because He demands control, but because He desires connection.

When we worship Him in Spirit and in truth, the idols fall, the noise fades, and love becomes the only thing left standing.

Closing Prayer

Lord Jesus, the true Head of the Church,
We come before You as one body, not as spectators, not as followers of men, but as members of Your living temple.
Forgive us, Lord, for the times we have exalted the pulpit above Your presence,
for the times we have crowned leaders and silenced the laity.
Forgive us for building platforms where You meant to build people.

Tear down every idol that bears Your name but hides Your face.

Remove from us the pride that seeks position, and give us the humility that seeks service.

Awaken Your Church again, every hand, every voice, every heart.
Let the pastors lead by love, not by lordship.
Let the prophets speak with grace, not with glory.
Let the teachers teach truth, not tradition.

And let every believer rise into their calling.
not waiting for permission from men, but moving by the anointing of Your Spirit.

Restore the vision of the early Church,
where no one man held the light,
but where the fire of Pentecost burned upon all flesh.

Lord, make us again a body unified in Spirit, diverse in gifts,
where every joint supplies, every voice matters, and every heart burns for You.

May we never again worship the messenger more than the Message,
or the shepherd more than the Savior.

Raise up Your Church not in power, but in purity.
Not in hierarchy, but in harmony.

For You alone are the Head, and we are Yours.

**In Your holy name we pray,
Amen.**

Chapter Eight

The Quiet Voice of the Spirit

After all the noise of religion, after all the systems and sermons and ceremonies, there remains one truth that can't be taught in any classroom, the voice of the Holy Spirit.

I have learned that God rarely shouts.
He whispers.
And only those who quiet their souls can hear Him.

I didn't always understand that. For years, I looked for God in activity in church services, in preachers, in passionate worship. I thought the louder the praise, the closer He must be. But in time, I discovered that His presence doesn't depend on volume.

The Spirit doesn't compete with our distractions.
He waits for silence.

The Whisper That Changes Everything

When Elijah fled into the wilderness, terrified and exhausted, he hid in a cave on Mount Horeb. He wanted to die.

He had seen fire fall from heaven, but now he was running from fear.

God called him out of the cave and said,

"Go stand on the mountain before the Lord."

Then the wind tore through the rocks, but God wasn't in the wind.
The earth shook, but God wasn't in the earthquake.
Then came fire, but God wasn't in the fire.

Finally, a still small voice spoke, and Elijah wrapped his face in his cloak and listened.
(1 Kings 19:11–13)

That story has followed me through my life.
I've felt the wind, the shaking, and the fire of life, but I've only found peace in the whisper.
That's where the Spirit lives.
Not in the spectacle, but in the stillness.

The Cave and the Apartment

There was a time when I understood Elijah's cave more than I ever wanted to.
I wasn't hiding from a queen's army, but I was running from despair.
I was alone in an apartment, with no money, no food, and the power was cut off.
I remember lying in a tub of cold water with candles flickering around me, the silence thick as stone.
I had nothing left but breath.

Like Elijah, I wanted to disappear.
But God met me in that stillness.

There was no thunder, no angel, no earthquake, just a whisper that came into my heart: have **HOPE**

That word has never left me.
It became a lamp in my darkness.
From that moment, I understood that God doesn't always roar; sometimes He just *reminds you to keep living.*

"For I know the plans I have for you, saith the Lord, plans to prosper you, and not to harm you, to give you a future and a hope." — *Jeremiah 29:11*

Since that day, no matter how deep the struggle or how loud the storm, that whisper of the word **HOPE** has carried me through.

Elijah's Fire and My Fear

When I was young, I didn't have the fire of Elijah in me.
I believed in God, but I lacked boldness.
I worried too much about what people thought.
I wanted to please everyone, and in doing so, I often forgot to please the One who called me.

But Elijah wasn't built that way.
He didn't negotiate obedience.
He stood before kings and false prophets with the courage of heaven burning in his chest.
He didn't fear offense; he feared disobedience.

"Then Elijah said unto all the people, 'How long halt ye between two opinions? If the Lord be God, follow Him.'" — *1 Kings 18:21*

That kind of faith doesn't come from personality; it comes from presence.
And when God met me in my own wilderness, I began to understand that same fire.

Not the fire of judgment, but the fire of conviction, a holy boldness that sets you free from the opinions of men.

When the Whisper Becomes a Flame

In that bathtub of cold water, something in me died, the part that feared failure, the part that lived for approval. And something else was born, the part that listened for the whisper.

From that day forward, I found myself doing things I never would have done before speaking truth when silence would've been easier, standing firm when walking away would've been safer.
The whisper became a fire.
And like Elijah, I learned that courage isn't the absence of fear; it's obedience that burns through fear.

"But the word was in my heart as a burning fire shut up in my bones, and I was weary with forbearing, and I could not stay." — *Jeremiah 20:9*

God gave Elijah courage to face death without flinching. He gave me the courage to face life without running. And that same Spirit is still whispering to every believer willing to listen.

The Lesson in the Wilderness

Both Elijah and I learned that God often waits until everything else is stripped away before He speaks.
The cave isn't punishment, it's preparation.
It's where pride dies, where fear loses its voice, and where the whisper becomes the only sound you need to hear.

"Be still, and know that I am God." *Psalm 46:10*

When you're left with nothing, you discover the truth:
Nothing is everything when you still have God.
He is enough in the cave, enough in the silence, sufficient in the still small voice.

My Life After the Whisper

Since that night, my life has never been the same.
The same God who spoke to Elijah in the stillness spoke to me in mine.
He didn't give me riches or rescue me instantly. He gave me *resolve*.
He taught me that hope is a seed that grows in darkness before it blooms in light.

I've faced financial loss, heartbreak, loneliness, and rejection, but never again without hope.
That whisper became a lifelong conversation with God, one that continues to this day.

And now, like Elijah, I don't worry about who it offends when I speak truth.
I just speak what He gives me.
Because when you've heard the whisper of God, you no longer need the applause of men.

Closing Reflection

Elijah didn't find God in the fire he found Him in the stillness.
And that's where I found Him, too.
Not in the noise of religion, or the heat of emotion, but in the quiet surrender of a heart finally ready to listen.

263

That whisper changed everything.
It gave me courage where there was fear, purpose where there was confusion, and hope where there was despair.
It was the moment I stopped *trying to be religious* and started *walking with God.*

The whisper is still there, not shouting, not demanding, just waiting.
Waiting for you to be still long enough to hear it.

"And after the fire, a still small voice." — *1 Kings 19:12*

Learning to Listen

Listening to the Holy Spirit is not a skill; it's a surrender. It means setting aside your agenda, your fear, and your assumptions about what God *should* say.

There have been moments in my life when I tried to force God to speak, wanting an answer right away. But the Spirit doesn't respond to demand; He responds to desire.

Sometimes His silence is not absence, it's an invitation.

When I sit alone with my Bible open, whether in Raleigh, on a mountain, or by the sea, I've come to recognize His presence not by words, but by peace. A stillness settles over me, a deep knowing that I am not alone.

In that quiet, the Spirit begins to guide my thoughts, shape my understanding, and remind me of truth. Jesus promised that:

"But the Helper, the Holy Spirit, whom the Father will send in My name, He will teach you all things and bring to your remembrance all that I have said to you."
John 14:26

I've experienced that promise firsthand. When my mind is weary, He reminds me of Scripture I didn't even know I remembered. When my heart is heavy, He brings to mind words of comfort that feel tailor-made for that moment.

He doesn't always answer my questions; sometimes He changes them.
He doesn't always remove my burdens; sometimes He teaches me how to carry them with grace.

That's the quiet miracle of the Spirit: He transforms us without noise.

The Presence That Teaches

There's a difference between reading the Bible for knowledge and reading it with the Holy Spirit. Without Him, Scripture is ink on a page; with Him, it's living fire.

I've spent nights reading verses that I'd seen a hundred times before, but suddenly, they came alive. A single line would pierce my heart, as if God Himself were speaking directly to me.

That's not imagination; that's illumination.

The Spirit doesn't just help us understand God's Word; He helps us understand *ourselves* in light of it. He convicts, corrects, comforts, and confirms.

He's not an energy or a feeling. He's a Person, the very presence of God living within us.

And once you've felt Him move, no ritual or religion can replace it.

How the Spirit Speaks — The Power of Psalm 91

I've learned that the Holy Spirit speaks in many ways, not always through words, but through *moments.*

Sometimes He speaks through peace, the kind that doesn't make sense.
Sometimes He speaks through discomfort, a gentle check in your spirit that says, *"Don't go there."*
Sometimes He speaks through people, through creation, through timing, or through the quiet tug of conviction.

But most of all, He speaks through love.

When you feel a wave of compassion for someone who's wronged you, that's Him.
When you're reminded to forgive when every part of you wants revenge, that's Him.
When you feel drawn to open your Bible when you'd rather scroll your phone, that's Him.

The Spirit doesn't manipulate; He ministers.
He doesn't condemn; He calls you closer.

But one of the most significant ways I've learned to recognize the Spirit's voice is through **protection** when His unseen hand moves to keep me from harm, warn me of danger, or redirect my steps.

The Spirit and the Blood

The same Holy Spirit who convicts us also covers us. His action in a believer's life is tied to the **atonement** of Jesus Christ, the blood shed on Calvary. That blood doesn't just cleanse our sins; it *protects* our lives.

Before Christ came, animal sacrifices offered temporary atonement for sin and protection from judgment. But when

Jesus shed His blood, He became the ultimate sacrifice, the final covering.

"They overcame him by the blood of the Lamb, and by the word of their testimony." *Revelation 12:11*

The blood of Jesus is a spiritual weapon not just against sin, but against fear, danger, and the powers of darkness.

"How much more shall the blood of Christ, who through the eternal Spirit offered Himself without spot to God, purge your conscience from dead works to serve the living God?" — *Hebrews 9:14*

"If we walk in the light, as He is in the light, we have fellowship one with another, and the blood of Jesus Christ His Son cleanseth us from all sin." *1 John 1:7*

Through that blood, the believer receives access to divine authority, courage, and protection. That's why I *plead the blood of Jesus* every day before I leave my home, not as superstition, but as **spiritual submission** to the covenant that still speaks.

Angels on Assignment

God's protection often manifests through **angels**, sent as ministers to those who belong to Him.

"The angel of the Lord encampeth round about them that fear Him, and delivereth them." — *Psalm 34:7*

I've seen this in my own life many times. There were moments when I felt a divine warning not to go a specific route, and later found out that an accident had occurred there.
There were times I hesitated at a green light, only to see a car speed through the intersection.

That wasn't a coincidence. That was **covenant protection.**
The Spirit speaks not only in church pews, but at stoplights and crossroads wherever His people walk in obedience.

The Secret Place — The Power of Psalm 91

Of all the Scriptures on divine protection, **Psalm 91** is the cornerstone. It is both a prayer and a promise of a spiritual shelter for the believer who abides in God's presence.

**"He that dwelleth in the secret place of the Most High shall abide under the shadow of the Almighty.
I will say of the Lord, He is my refuge and my fortress: my God; in Him will I trust."** *Psalm 91:1–2*

This psalm is more than words, it's a declaration of trust, a spiritual covenant written in prayer. It speaks of pestilence, danger, and battle, yet promises supernatural safety to those who love and cling to God.

**"Surely He shall deliver thee from the snare of the fowler, and from the noisome pestilence.
He shall cover thee with His feathers, and under His wings shalt thou trust: His truth shall be thy shield and buckler."** *— Psalm 91:3–4*

To dwell in the *secret place* means to live in continual awareness of God's presence, not visiting Him occasionally, but abiding in Him daily.

When you recite Psalm 91, you are not reciting poetry; you are reaffirming divine reality.
You are speaking life over your home, your family, your mind, your health, your steps, and your future.

"For He shall give His angels charge over thee, to keep thee in all thy ways.

They shall bear thee up in their hands, lest thou dash thy foot against a stone." — *Psalm 91:11–12*

Even Jesus referenced this promise when Satan tempted Him in the wilderness (Matthew 4:6). The enemy knows the power of this psalm, but he twists it to remove the obedience behind it.
That's why it's not enough to quote it simply; you must *believe* it, live it, and dwell in it.

The Promise of Deliverance

The closing verses of Psalm 91 are not man's words, they are **God's voice** speaking directly to His people:

"Because he has set his love upon Me, therefore will I deliver him:
I will set him on high, because he hath known My name.
He shall call upon Me, and I will answer him:
I will be with him in trouble; I will deliver him, and honor him.
With long life will I satisfy him, and show him My salvation." — *Psalm 91:14–16*

Here, God Himself becomes the speaker, promising divine protection, answered prayer, long life, and salvation to those who love Him.
To "set your love upon Him" means to cling to God with your whole heart, not to visit Him on Sundays, but to make Him your dwelling every day.

"The Lord is my light and my salvation; whom shall I fear?" — *Psalm 27:1*

When you love God deeply and abide in His Word, His Spirit surrounds you. His angels guard you. His blood

covers you.
No evil can touch what God has already claimed.

The Spirit's Language of Protection

The Holy Spirit still speaks — and often, He speaks through *protection.*
When you sense a sudden pause in your heart, that quiet, internal check, listen. That's not paranoia. That's Providence.

The Spirit that once hovered over the waters now hovers over your life.
He guides your steps, shields your mind, and intercedes when you don't even know what to pray.

"Likewise the Spirit also helpeth our infirmities: for we know not what we should pray for as we ought: but the Spirit itself maketh intercession for us with groanings which cannot be uttered." — *Romans 8:26*

That's why I never leave the house without pleading the blood of Jesus and declaring Psalm 91.
It's not a ritual, it's a relationship.
It's not superstition, it's submission.
It's the daily reminder that I live under divine covering.

Even in a world filled with evil, chaos, and confusion, I walk in peace because I know the same Spirit that spoke to David, protected Daniel, and empowered Elijah still watches over me.

"The Lord shall preserve thy going out and thy coming in from this time forth, and even for evermore." — *Psalm 121:8*

Closing Reflection

The Spirit doesn't just speak through prophecy; He speaks through **protection**.
Through warnings, through peace, through delay, through deliverance.
Every time danger passed me by, I realized the Spirit had already spoken before I even knew I was in need.

Psalm 91 is more than a psalm, it's a *promise.*
And when you combine that promise with the blood of Jesus, you are wrapped in the armor of heaven.

The Spirit still speaks.
Sometimes through a whisper.
Sometimes through a warning.
Sometimes, through the shield of His wings, His protection becomes the message itself.

"He shall cover thee with His feathers, and under His wings shalt thou trust." — *Psalm 91:4*

Wisdom and Watchfulness — Working with the Spirit

God wants us to trust Him for protection, and He also expects us to *think.*
We are made in His image with a mind to reason. That difference between humans and animals isn't accidental: God gave us the ability to weigh risk, read a room, and choose prudence. Faith and foolishness are not the same thing. God calls us to both trust and wisdom.

When the Spirit warns you, the quiet tug that says "don't go," obey it. But don't mistake obedience for irresponsibility. There is a place for common sense:

• **Be sober and vigilant**. Scripture calls us to watchfulness: **"Be sober, be vigilant; because your adversary the devil, as a roaring lion, walketh about, seeking whom he may devour." — *1 Peter 5:8.***
• **Use your head: "Behold, the beginning of wisdom is:**

get wisdom: and with all thy getting get understanding." — *Proverbs 4:7.*
• Be wise as well as innocent: "Behold, I send you forth as sheep in the midst of wolves: be ye therefore wise as serpents, and harmless as doves." — *Matthew 10:16.*

Part of spiritual maturity is *working with* the Spirit's protection. That means you plead the blood, pray Psalm 91, and at the same time you don't walk into a dark alley alone at night, or put yourself into reckless situations hoping God will bail you out. You don't test the Lord by tempting danger; you honor Him by stewarding the life He's given you so you can serve longer and bear more fruit.

Do Not Be Conformed to This World — The Narrow Road of Resistance

"And be not conformed to this world: but be transformed by the renewing of your mind." Romans 12:2

The world has always demanded conformity. It was true in the days of ancient Israel, true under the Roman Empire, and it remains true now. Systems, whether political, religious, or cultural, are built on one expectation: **that people will obey without questioning.**

But the Kingdom of God has never been built by those who blend in.
It is built by those who *stand out.*

272

Jesus Himself warned His followers that the road to heaven would never be crowded:

"For wide is the gate, and broad is the way that leads to destruction… and many there be which go in thereat. Because narrow is the gate, and difficult the way which leads to life, and few there be that find it." Matthew 7:13–14

You have probably heard people say, " Oh, but everyone else does it," or "the majority of the people like him, so he must be a good man." These are only a few examples, but always apply the theory that broad way often leads to destruction.

Always bear in mind that most people don't know the word of God, and if they do know it, they don't apply it to their lives. Only a few people actually apply the word of God to their lives.

So the next time you see masses of people going in one direction, go the other way, the narrow way. It's better to be safe than sorry. Don't be afraid to be the only person in the group to venture out in a different direction than your associates, family, or friends, etc.

.

The Narrow Road Requires a Different Mind

Paul's command in **Romans 12:2** is not poetic language, it is *war language*.

To **"be not conformed"** means to **refuse the mold**, the pressure, the expectations of a world that crucified Christ and still rejects His truth.

While Rome demanded allegiance to Caesar as god… While the Pharisees demanded allegiance to tradition over

truth…
While crowds demanded a Messiah who fit their political agenda…

Jesus called His people to walk a path **few would dare to walk**.

A transformed mind is a rebellious mind, not rebellious against God, but against every system that tries to replace Him.

Jesus Taught Us to Question Authority

The early church did not survive because it obeyed Rome. It survived because it **questioned** Rome.

Jesus questioned the Pharisees:

- **"Why do you break the commandment of God for the sake of your tradition?" (Matthew 15:3)**

He questioned the Temple system:

- He overturned tables, rebuked corruption, and declared the house of prayer had become a den of thieves **(Matthew 21:12–13).**

He questioned the religious interpretations of Sabbath, purity, and law.

He questioned the motives of crowds.

He even questioned His own disciples, not because He doubted them, but to expose what was hidden in their hearts.

Jesus lived in a religious world that demanded conformity. But He showed us how to walk in divine freedom.

Everybody Has a Judas

Not everyone who walks beside you walks *with* you.

Jesus had a Judas, a man who followed Him, ate with Him, served in ministry, and yet carried betrayal in his heart.

The lesson?

Beware of proximity — it can imitate discipleship, but only obedience proves it.

Historical records and Scripture show Judas was trusted enough to carry the group's money bag **(John 12:6).** Betrayal didn't come from a stranger or an enemy; it came from a friend, a follower, a familiar face.

In every generation, God's people have had Judases:

- Israel had Korah.

- David had Ahithophel.

- Paul had Demas.

- Jesus had Judas.

The warning is timeless:

Do not be conformed to the expectations of people who are comfortable betraying everything God stands for.

Blind Following Is Not Faith — It's Idolatry

History proves that crowds are usually wrong:

- Israel followed the crowd into the worship of the golden calf.

- The crowd shouted for Barabbas instead of Jesus.

- The crowd cried "Hosanna!" one week and "Crucify Him!" the next.

- The crowd stoned Stephen.

- The crowd persecuted the prophets.

Jesus never called His disciples to follow the masses
He called them to follow **Him**, even if they walked alone.

Majority agreement does not equal divine approval.

Truth has never needed a crowd.

Biblical History Warns Us of Conformity

In the Old Testament, God repeatedly warned Israel not to imitate the nations:

- **"You shall not walk in the customs of the nations." — Leviticus 20:23**

- **"Be holy, for I am holy." — 1 Peter 1:16 (echoing Leviticus 11:44)**

Israel fell every time they blended in.

The early church was powerful only because it refused assimilation.
They would rather face lions than bow to Caesar.
They would rather suffer flogging than silence the gospel.

Their refusal to conform changed history.

Transformation Is the Mark of the True Believer

Paul didn't just say **"do not conform"** he said **"be transformed."**

Transformation means:

- thinking differently

- living differently

- questioning differently

- resisting differently

276

- loving differently
- obeying God differently

Transformation is not passive. It requires confrontation — first with ourselves, then with the world.

Modern Application — The Pressure to Conform

Today, conformity wears new masks:

- political correctness
- church traditions elevated above Scripture
- religious hype without holiness
- social media mobs
- cultural pressure to redefine sin
- pastors who demand loyalty instead of repentance
- institutions that punish truth-speaking
- systems that reward silence

But the command remains unchanged:

Do not be conformed.
Be transformed.
Walk the narrow road.
Question what the world calls normal.
Follow Christ — even if few follow with you.

The narrow road has always been walked by the few, not the many.

It is the road of prophets, reformers, apostles, and believers who refuse to bend.

And it is the only road that leads to eternal life.

Do Not Be Conformed to This World — The Narrow Road of Resistance

Expanded with Prophetic Warning, Scripture, and Historical Witnesses

"And be not conformed to this world: but be transformed by the renewing of your mind." — Romans 12:2

The world has always demanded conformity. Empires depend on it. Institutions thrive on it. Religion enforces it. But the Kingdom of God has always advanced through the few who refused the crowd.

Jesus warned that following Him was never meant to be popular:

"Enter by the narrow gate… because narrow is the gate and difficult the way which leads to life, and few find it." Matthew 7:13–14

The masses have never walked the narrow road.
The remnant walks it, the ones who hear God's voice above human applause.

I personally vowed to be a nonconformist many years ago, way before I accepted Jesus as my savior. I never trusted anyone, and I'm still cautious about trusting people. I believe this stance has helped my walk with God and strengthened my faith.

Prophetic Exhortation: A Warning to the Last Days Church

Hear the word of the Lord:

A generation is rising that calls evil good and good evil **(Isaiah 5:20).**
A culture is forming that rewards silence and punishes truth.
A religion is emerging that resembles the world more than Christ.

The Spirit of God says:

"My people are conforming to a world I called them to confront."

When pastors fear losing members more than losing their anointing,
when churches echo the culture instead of the cross,
when believers fear offending people more than offending God
then the spirit of the age has already infiltrated the sanctuary.

This is the hour to resist.
Not with arrogance, but with allegiance not to man, but to God.

For the spirit of this age still whispers:

- "Don't question."

- "Don't stand out."

279

- "Follow the crowd."

But the Spirit of the Lord is whispering something else:

"Come out from among them and be separate." 2 Corinthians 6:17
"Do not follow the crowd in doing wrong." Exodus 23:2
"If anyone loves the world, the love of the Father is not in him." 1 John 2:15

This is the separating season
a dividing of the wheat and the tares,
the sheep and the goats,
the conformed and the transformed.

A storm is coming,
and only those rooted in truth will stand.

Everybody Has a Judas — A Timeless Warning

Jesus was not betrayed by a Pharisee, a Roman, or a stranger.
He was betrayed by **a follower**, a trusted one, a familiar face.

History repeats this pattern:

- Samson had Delilah.

- David had Ahithophel.

- Paul had Demas.

- Jesus had Judas.

The warning is prophetic:

In the last days, betrayal will come from those who pretend loyalty but carry hidden agendas.
(see Matthew 24:10–11)

Do not conform to relationships God is trying to expose.

Historical Witnesses — Those Who Refused to Conform

1. The Early Church

The first believers could have avoided persecution by obeying Rome.
All they had to do was sprinkle incense before Caesar's statue and say, "Caesar is lord."

They refused.

Their refusal became their testimony.
They chose the narrow road, the road that led to coliseums, chains, and flames.

Tertullian recorded,
"The blood of the martyrs is the seed of the Church."

They grew **because** they refused conformity, not in spite of it.

---

2. The Martyrs

Perpetua, a young noblewoman, was told to abandon Christ to save her life and her child.

She replied:
"I cannot be called anything other than what I am, a Christian."

Polycarp, disciple of the Apostle John, was commanded to deny Christ to spare himself.

He answered:
"Eighty and six years have I served Him, and He has done me no wrong."

He chose flames over conformity.

---

3. The Reformers

A corrupted church demanded conformity.
But God raised men who would not bow:

- **John Wycliffe** translated Scripture into English, though the Church threatened death.

- **Martin Luther** stood before emperors and councils declaring,
  "My conscience is captive to the Word of God."

- **Jan Hus** preached truth, knowing it would cost him his life; he died singing as fire consumed him.

They tore down the idols of tradition and restored the authority of Scripture.

Their legacy is simple:

Truth survives only when someone refuses to conform.

Blind Following Is Not Faith — It Is Idolatry

The Bible records countless times the crowd was wrong:

- The crowd built the golden calf (Exodus 32).

- The crowd demanded a king instead of God (1 Samuel 8).

- The crowd tried to stone David.

- The crowd shouted for Barabbas.

- The crowd crucified Christ.

- The crowd persecuted prophets and apostles.

Crowds don't lead you to God.
Conviction does.

The Narrow Road in the Last Days

Scripture warns that in the final generation:

- Many will fall away **(2 Thessalonians 2:3)**

- Some will follow deceiving spirits **(1 Timothy 4:1)**

- People will accumulate teachers who tell them what they want to hear **(2 Timothy 4:3)**

- Lawlessness will increase **(Matthew 24:12)**

- The love of many will grow cold

Conformity is the enemy of holiness.

And the world is shaping believers more than believers are shaping the world.

But God still has a remnant
Those who refuse the broad road.

Do Not Conform to the World System — The Erosion of Personal Relationships

Conformity comes in many forms, and not all of them look sinful at first glance. Some come quietly, disguised as **"progress," "technology," or "convenience."** But every system of the world that pulls the heart away from God, away from community, and away from authentic connection is a system that reshapes the soul if we are not watchful.

I grew up in the 70s and 80s, when relationships were personal, warm, and lived. Friends called each other on the phone. People checked in. Neighbors talked across the fence. Even acquaintances felt close. There was a sense of community, a sense of presence, a sense of being *seen*.

But the world system has shifted.
And with it, so has the human heart.

Today, technology has replaced touch.
Communication has become abstract texting, social media, emails, emojis, and distant digital exchanges. The more "connected" we are online, the more disconnected we become in spirit.

The Cost of Digital Conformity

What used to be a relationship has become a reaction.
What used to be fellowship has become follow-backs.
What used to be conversation has become notifications.

This new form of conformity is subtle but deadly.

People feel alone.
People feel unseen.
People feel forgotten.

And when personal connection fades, mental health collapses. Isolation grows. Depression settles in. Loneliness becomes normal. And many turn to drug prescription, or illegal, it makes no difference, trying to numb a spiritual wound with a chemical solution.

This is the fruit of a world system that teaches people to communicate without caring, to speak without listening, and to "connect" without commitment.

The Spiritual Root

Drug dependency outside of extreme medical necessity is often rooted in spiritual deprivation.
Where the Word of God is absent, wounds remain unhealed.
Where God's presence is absent, loneliness grows.
Where truth is ignored, bondage increases.

The world offers pills.
God offers peace.

The world offers escape.
God offers deliverance.

The world offers numbing.
God offers healing.

Jesus said:

"You shall know the truth, and the truth shall make you free." John 8:32

When the Word of God enters the soul, it transforms from the inside out. It renews the mind. It softens the heart. It heals the broken spaces technology cannot reach.

When God alters your mind, miracles happen.
When God renews your mind, healing flows.
When your mind is submitted to God, love begins to rise.

For **God** *is* **love** (1 John 4:8).

And where God's love reigns, addiction loses its power.

Love as the Antidote to Isolation

When love enters one's life, everything changes.
God places His love into the heart, and suddenly you can love, be loved, and give love.
You reap what you sow, and when you sow love, you reap joy, connection, and spiritual life.

This is why relationships matter.
This is why affection matters.
This is why personal communication matters.

Conformity in Communication

When someone refuses to call but only texts, they have conformed to the new world system of communication.

When people who grew up before the digital age abandon meaningful connection in favor of superficial messaging, they surrender a gift they once knew how to hold.

Young people may not know better, they were born into this.
But older generations *do* know better.
And many have allowed technology to erode the very things that once made relationships sacred.

This is conformity — slow, quiet, and deadly to the soul.

The Call to Return

This is the moment to return to what was lost.
To rediscover personal connection.
To rebuild fellowship.

To value voice over text, presence over posts, prayer over performance.

God calls His people to:

- Fast
- Pray
- Reflect
- Repent
- Detox from the world's system
- Renew their mind in the Word
- Restore real relationships

Romans 12:2 commands:

"Do not be conformed to this world, but be transformed by the renewing of your mind."

To conform is to let the world think for you.
To be transformed is to let God renew you.

When we depend on God, we become free from the world's false dependencies.
When we cling to God, we loosen our grip on the addictions of the culture.
When God alters the mind, the heart follows.

And healing begins.

Scripture Commentary Sidebar: Romans 12:2

"Do not be conformed to this world, but be transformed by the renewing of your mind."
Commentary:
Paul warns the church that the *world will always attempt to shape the believer*. The Greek word for "conform" (συσχηματίζω, syschematízō) means "to be molded from the outside."
Technology molds behavior.
Culture molds values.
Isolation molds emotions.
Transformation only comes from the inside — by the Spirit of God renewing the mind through the Word.

Proverbs 18:1

"A man who isolates himself seeks his own desire; he rages against all wise judgment."
Commentary:
Isolation is not merely emotional; it is spiritual. It pulls a person away from wisdom, correction, and community. Satan thrives in separation. God moves in fellowship.

Prophetic Warning: "The Age of Silent Souls"

Thus says the Spirit of the Lord:
"A generation is rising that has a thousand digital voices but no spiritual sound.
Their words multiply, but their hearts grow quiet.
Their screens glow, but their spirits dim.
I warn My people: the enemy is using distance to destroy discernment,
and isolation to imprison identity."

"Return to one another.
Return to communion.
Return to the fellowship of the saints.
Return to the sound of prayer in homes,
the sound of compassion in conversations,
and the sound of My voice above the noise of technology."

"Those who conform to this world's system of isolation will wither,
but those who seek My presence and My people will flourish.
Choose connection over convenience,
love over laziness,
and fellowship over the false comfort of digital shadows."

Hebrews 10:24–25

"Let us consider one another to provoke unto love and good works; not forsaking the assembling of ourselves together... but exhorting one another."
Commentary:
The early church survived persecution because they assembled, connected, encouraged, prayed, and supported one another.
Satan attacks fellowship because fellowship strengthens faith.

Reflection : "Where Have I Conformed?"

Before moving forward, pause and let the Holy Spirit examine your heart.

Ask yourself:

1. **Have I allowed technology to replace true relationships?**
   Do I reach for the phone to text instead of call... or call instead of visit?

2. **Have I become emotionally distant while pretending to be digitally connected?**
   Am I "active" online but absent in real life?

3. **Has isolation become a habit instead of a warning sign?**
   Do I retreat inward instead of reaching outward?

4. **Where have I replaced prayer with distraction?**
   Do I numb myself with entertainment instead of seeking God's presence?

5. **Have I abandoned the spiritual discipline of fellowship?**
   Do I avoid community because it requires vulnerability?

6. **Where has the world system slowly shaped me without me realizing it?**
   Ask the Lord to show you the subtle ways conformity has crept in.

7. **Who have I neglected to love, call, visit, or encourage?**
   Whose loneliness could be healed by my obedience?

Quiet your heart.
Listen.
Write down what the Spirit reveals.

Transformation begins where honesty begins.

Early Church Community Practices — The Blueprint God Gave Us

The early church did not merely believe together **they lived together**.
Their practices stand as a rebuke to the isolation of modern Christianity and as a blueprint for Kingdom community.

1. They Met Daily (Acts 2:46)

"They continued daily with one accord... breaking bread from house to house."

The early believers didn't "fit God in" once a week.
they built their lives around fellowship.

2. They Prayed Together (Acts 1:14)

"These all continued with one accord in prayer and supplication..."

Prayer was not individual; it was corporate.
The power of God often fell when they were together.

3. They Carried Each Other's Burdens (Galatians 6:2)

They didn't let anyone walk through depression, fear, or need alone.
Community was a spiritual safety net.

4. They Shared What They Had (Acts 2:44–45)

"They had all things in common..."

Generosity flowed naturally because they saw themselves as one family.

5. They Confessed Their Faults to One Another (James 5:16)

Community created accountability and protection.
Isolation breeds hidden sin.
Fellowship breeds healing.

6. They Ate Together (Acts 2:46)

Meals were a ministry.
Breaking bread opened hearts and homes.
Food carried fellowship, and fellowship carried spiritual strength.

7. They Heard the Word Together (Acts 2:42)

"They devoted themselves to the apostles' teaching…"

**They didn't consume sermons alone online.
they gathered as one body to receive the Word.**

8. They Encouraged One Another Daily (Hebrews 3:13)

They refused to let sin, sadness, or suffering harden the heart.
Daily encouragement was a Kingdom lifestyle.

9. They Welcomed Strangers as Family (Romans 12:13)

Hospitality wasn't optional; it was ministry.

10. They Grew Spiritually Because They Grew Together (Acts 2:47)

The Lord added to the church **daily** because the church lived daily Christianity.

Why This Matters Today

The early church **thrived under persecution** because it was united.

Modern believers struggle with convenience because we are isolated.

The first-century church gathered in homes.
the modern church hides behind screens.

The early church risked imprisonment for fellowship.
many believers today won't risk discomfort.

God is calling His people back to the **ancient path**,
back to the power of community,
back to the fellowship that fueled revival.

Isolation kills.
Community heals.
And love, real, embodied, personal love, is the lifeblood of the Church.

Closing Prayer for the Restoration of Community

Father, in the name of Jesus,
we come before You, asking for restoration
Restoration of relationships, connection, compassion, fellowship, and love.

Lord, tear down every wall of isolation the enemy has built.
Break every chain of loneliness.
Heal every wound created by distance, neglect, or digital distraction.

Reignite in us the desire for genuine fellowship.
to call, to visit, to embrace, to pray together,
to share life the way the early church lived in unity.

Remove the spirit of indifference.
Restore a spirit of intentionality.
Replace selfish comfort with selfless compassion.

Let our homes become gathering places.
Let our phones become ministry tools, not hiding places.
Let our conversations become healing rivers.

God, restore what technology has stolen.
Rebuild what isolation has broken.
Renew what depression has drained.

Holy Spirit, fill Your people again.
Awaken us to love deeply,
to see the unseen,
to reach the lonely,
and to be the hands and feet of Jesus in a broken world.

Bind us together in perfect unity.
Make us one, as You and the Father are One.

In Jesus' name, Amen.

Group Discussion Guide For Churches, Small Groups, or Bible Studies

Use these questions to spark reflection, healing conversations, and community-building.

1. What part of this chapter impacted you most? Why?

2. How has technology affected your personal relationships?

- Has it helped?

- Has it harmed?

- Has it replaced real connection?

3. Do you see signs of spiritual or emotional isolation in your life?

What triggered it?

4. What is one relationship God may be calling you to restore or strengthen?

5. How can we imitate the early church's model of community in our modern world?

Which practice from the Acts 2 church speaks to you the most?

6. What practical steps can you take this week to break patterns of isolation?

Examples:

- Call instead of text

- Visit instead of scrolling

- Pray with someone instead of watching from a distance

7. What spiritual disciplines have you neglected because of busyness or digital distraction?

Fasting? Prayer? Fellowship? Bible study?

8. Where have you conformed to the world without noticing?

What does repentance look like?

9. How can this group (church, family, or class) support one another in rebuilding community?

10. What does God's love look like when expressed through real, intentional, personal relationships?

The Jezebel Spirit A Word of Warning

There is also a spiritual reality that the Bible warns us about, a controlling, seductive influence often called the spirit of Jezebel. In Scripture, Jezebel was a woman who led a nation into idolatry and immorality **(see *1 Kings 16– 21*)**. Jesus uses that same name symbolically in His message to the church in Thyatira: a woman who "calls herself a prophetess" and seduces servants into immorality and false teaching. He says plainly that allowing that spirit into the church brings deception and bondage. ***Revelation 2:20–23***.

What does that mean for us today? The Jezebel spirit is less about a single person and more about patterns of control and seduction that:

- Push people away from God's Word and into loyalty to a person, system, or charismatic voice.

- Use manipulation, sexual immorality, and power plays to control others.

- Blind judgment with flattery or twisted teaching so people stop reasoning and start following.

Jesus warns strongly because the cost is high: believers can be led into sin, confusion, and spiritual bondage when they substitute persons or systems for the voice of the Holy Spirit.

How to Respond — Practical Steps

1. **Pray and protect.** Continue pleading the blood of Jesus and praying Psalm 91 as a covenant of protection and a spiritual posture. Psalm 91 anchors you in God's shelter while you act wisely.

2. **Use your mind.** Don't romanticize danger. Avoid risky places and unwise companionships. Trust God but also lock your doors, set healthy boundaries, and cultivate discernment.

3. **Test every spirit.** The Bible says: **"Beloved, believe not every spirit; but try the spirits whether they are of God." *1 John 4:1.*** Test teachings against Scripture, not popularity or pressure.

4. **Guard your heart.** If someone pressures you into secrecy, sexual compromise, unbiblical allegiance, or controlling loyalties, step back and call trusted, mature believers for counsel.

5. **Call out abuse, not victims.** If you see manipulation or abuse, expose the pattern, but don't shame the one being controlled. Compassion goes with truth.

6. **Put obedience over bravado.** Courage is not always confrontation; often it's choosing what God calls you to do and refusing what He forbids.

A Final Balance

God's protection is absolute, angels guard His children, the blood of Christ secures us, and Psalm 91 gives voice to His promises. But the Spirit also calls us to participate we stay alert, think clearly, set boundaries, and refuse to be seduced by control or appetite. Faith makes you brave; wisdom makes your bravery faithful.

"Put on the whole armour of God, that ye may be able to stand against the wiles of the devil." *Ephesians 6:11.*
"The Lord shall preserve thy going out and thy coming in from this time forth, and even for evermore." *Psalm 121:8.*

God protects those who love Him, and He honors those who love Him with both heart and mind.

The Spirit Versus Religion

Religion often tries to contain what the Spirit wants to release. It gives you formulas for offering friendship. It measures worth by attendance, appearance, or position, while the Spirit measures by the heart.

The Spirit is not confined to a denomination, a doctrine, or a title. He flows where He is welcome.

That's why Jesus told Nicodemus, *"The wind blows where it wishes; you hear its sound, but cannot tell where it comes from or where it goes. So is everyone born of the Spirit."* (John 3:8)

You can't control the wind; you can only receive it.

I've learned that when we stop trying to *manage* God, He finally starts to move.

The Peace That Follows

Every time I leave the mountains or the sea and return to everyday life, I take one thing back with me: peace. Not the fragile kind that depends on quiet surroundings, but the kind that lives inside no matter where I am.

That's the Spirit's gift.

"Peace I leave with you, My peace I give to you; not as the world gives do I give to you." (John 14:27)

That peace has carried me through heartbreak, uncertainty, and loss. It's not the peace of understanding, it's the peace of trusting.

The Spirit doesn't erase pain; He redeems it.
He doesn't always change your circumstances; He changes you inside them.

When religion leaves you exhausted, the Spirit restores you.
When people fail you, the Spirit reminds you you're still loved.

When life becomes too loud, the Spirit calls you back to stillness to the whisper.

Closing Reflection

The quiet voice of the Spirit is the antidote to every idol, every ritual, and every distraction this world offers.

If you want to know God, don't just look for Him in churches or ceremonies; look for Him in the quiet corners of your heart. He's there, waiting, not with judgment, but with joy.

The Spirit doesn't demand; He invites.
He doesn't shout; He sings softly.
And when you finally listen, you'll realize He's been speaking all along.

It's in that stillness, the same stillness I find in the mountains and the sea, that I hear Him best.

And in that voice, I find everything religion could never give me:
truth, peace, and the presence of God Himself.

Chapter Nine

The Modern Crucifixion

The story of the cross didn't end two thousand years ago. The nails may be gone, but the spirit that drove them still lives.

Every time truth is silenced, every time love is mocked, every time faith is turned into a tool for power, Christ is crucified again. Not in flesh, but in spirit. Not by Romans, but by hearts that claim to serve Him while serving themselves.

We no longer hang Him on a wooden cross; we hang Him in hypocrisy.

Crucifying Him with Comfort

Modern Christianity has learned how to wear the cross without carrying it.
We've made faith fashionable, comfortable, and convenient.
We talk about blessing more than burden, success more than surrender.

But Jesus never said, **"Take up your comfort and follow Me."**
He said, *"Take up your cross."* (Luke 9:23)

The modern church often avoids that part. We prefer a Jesus who heals, not one who humbles. We praise His resurrection while ignoring His rejection. We want the crown without the cost.

And every time we choose comfort over conviction, we repeat the betrayal of Judas not with silver, but with silence.

We crucify Christ when we trade obedience for acceptance.
We crucify Him when we honor Him with our lips while our hearts chase everything else.
We crucify Him when religion becomes performance instead of presence.

The New Pharisees

The Pharisees of old wore robes and scrolls. The new ones wear microphones and platforms.

They preach power instead of repentance, prosperity instead of humility. They've built kingdoms in His name while forgetting His kingdom **"is not of this world."** (John 18:36)

Jesus warned about them long ago:

"Beware of the scribes, who desire to go in long robes, love greetings in the marketplaces, the best seats in the synagogues, and the places of honor at feasts." (Luke 20:46)

The danger of religion has always been the same: the desire to appear holy without actually being changed. Today, holiness has been replaced by branding, and repentance by marketing.

The temple has turned digital, but the idols are the same.
We follow influencers more than intercessors.
We chase applause more than anointing.
We want popularity without purity.

That's the modern crucifixion: truth pierced by pride, love suffocated by ego, and Jesus replaced by celebrity.

The Crucifixion of Truth

We live in a world that claims to love truth as long as it doesn't convict.
The moment truth demands repentance, it's canceled.

302

We've built a culture that preaches tolerance but practices idolatry. We tolerate sin but not conviction, comfort but not correction. And even in the church, we're more afraid of offending people than offending God.

The same spirit that shouted *"Crucify Him!"* still cries out today not against a man on a cross, but against the message of that cross.

Because the cross demands death to pride, ego death, death to sin.
And human nature will always resist dying.

So instead, the world reshapes Jesus to fit its image:
A Jesus who never judges.
A Jesus who never corrects.
A Jesus who asks for nothing but gives everything.

That's not the Christ of the Bible, that's the idol of the age.

When we reshape Him to suit our comfort, we crucify the real Jesus all over again.

The Crucifixion of Compassion

Religion also crucifies Christ through indifference.
When churches ignore the poor, the broken, and the lost, they repeat the same sin as those who passed Him by on the road to Calvary.

Jesus said, *"Whatever you did for one of the least of these brothers and sisters of mine, you did for Me."* (Matthew 25:40)

But modern religion often does the opposite. We build bigger sanctuaries while neglecting the suffering outside their walls. We pray for revival but ignore the hungry. We shout about morality while walking past need.

Every time love takes second place to image, Jesus is crucified again, not by nails, but by neglect.

He came to heal the sick, lift the poor, and forgive sinners. But religion still prefers order over mercy.

We forget that the cross wasn't built in a church; it was built on a hill outside the city, the place where outcasts go.

That's where Jesus still waits, not in the center of power, but on the margins of compassion.

The Crucifixion of Conscience

There's another way Christ is crucified today through the silence of conscience.

We see corruption and stay quiet.
We watch injustice and call it "not our problem."
We hear lies and choose convenience over truth.

Every time good men stay silent, the nails go in a little deeper.

In the days of Jesus, Pilate knew He was innocent. He said, *"I find no fault in this man."* **(Luke 23:4)** Yet he still handed Him over to be crucified, not because he believed it was right, but because he feared the crowd.

The modern world is full of Pilates people who know the truth but refuse to stand for it.
We wash our hands and call it peace.

But real peace never comes from compromise; it comes from courage.

To follow Jesus today means standing against the crowd when the crowd stands against truth.

When Religion Misses the Resurrection

The tragedy of modern Christianity is that many celebrate the resurrection while still living at the foot of the cross. They believe in the risen Christ, but still crucify Him daily with pride, judgment, and hypocrisy.

They carry crosses around their necks but not in their hearts.
They preach grace but deny mercy.
They proclaim victory while living in defeat.

The cross was never meant to be jewelry; it was meant to be a mirror.

When we look at it, we should see ourselves both the reason He died and the reason He rose.

The resurrection is not just proof of life after death; it's proof that love is stronger than hate, truth is stronger than lies, and God's grace still triumphs over man's failure.

Closing Reflection

The modern crucifixion isn't about nails and wood, it's about hearts hardened by pride. It happens every time religion forgets relationship, every time believers use Christ's name to build their own kingdoms instead of His.

But the story doesn't end there. It never has.

The same Jesus who rose from the grave still rises today in every heart that chooses truth over tradition, humility over pride, love over judgment.

Religion may crucify Him again and again, but grace resurrects Him every time.

And that is the hope of our age that even in a world of false prophets, fading morals, and broken churches, the Spirit of Christ still lives, still moves, and still saves.

Because you can crucify truth, but you can't keep it buried.

Chapter Ten

Redemption Beyond Religion

After everything man has done in the name of God, every war, every division, every corruption and betrayal, grace still stands.

That's the miracle that humbles me most.
Religion has failed countless times. People have fallen short. Churches have risen and fallen like empires. But the message of Jesus has never changed.

Love still wins.
Mercy still calls.
And redemption still reaches farther than religion ever could.

The Simplicity of the Gospel

Some truths are so simple that the world refuses to believe them.
One of them is this: *Salvation is not earned, it's received.*

It doesn't come from belonging to the right church, praying the right way, or memorizing the right verses. It comes from faith in Christ alone, from surrendering the heart rather than performing the ritual.

"For by grace you have been saved through faith, and that not of yourselves; it is the gift of God — not of works, lest any man should boast."
— Ephesians 2:8–9

That verse has set me free more times than I can count.
When religion told me I wasn't enough, grace told me I was loved.
When religion demanded perfection, grace reminded me that Jesus already paid for my imperfection.
When religion bound me with fear, grace broke the chains with forgiveness.

That is redemption beyond religion, a love that doesn't keep score, a mercy that doesn't need permission.

The God Who Meets You Where You Are

One of the most significant lies of religion is that you have to climb up to God.
But the truth of the Gospel is that God came down to us.

He found the prodigal son in a pigpen, not a temple.
He found the thief on a cross, not in a congregation.

He found Saul of Tarsus on a dusty road, blinded and broken, and turned him into Paul, the preacher of grace.

I've learned that God doesn't wait for us to be worthy. He meets us in the middle of our mess and makes us new.

Religion says, "Clean yourself up first."
Grace says, "Come as you are, I'll do the cleaning."

That's why Jesus came not to build another system, but to tear down the walls between God and man.
The veil in the temple wasn't just a curtain; it was a symbol of separation. When it tore in two at His death, God was saying, ***"You don't need a priest to reach Me anymore, I'm right here."***

A Relationship, Not a Ritual

I've spent years studying theology, listening to sermons, and observing denominations — but nothing compares to the moments I've had alone with God.

The most significant revelations in my life haven't come from pulpits, but from prayer.
They haven't come through argument, but through stillness.

I've learned that God doesn't want religion from me; He wants a relationship with me.
He doesn't need perfect prayers. He wants honest ones.

When I talk to Him now, I don't try to impress Him with words. I speak from my heart, and I feel His Spirit respond in peace.

Religion tells you *how* to pray.
Relationship teaches you *why*.

It's not about repeating memorized words; it's about communion with the living God who knows you better than you know yourself.

Grace Stronger Than the Church

Throughout history, churches have fallen into error, pride, and corruption. But grace has never failed.

It reached the thief on the cross.
It reached Saul the persecutor.
It reached me, a sinner who once confused religion with righteousness.

Grace does what no institution can: it transforms from the inside out.
It doesn't need a title, a robe, or a pulpit. It just needs a willing heart.

The same Spirit that raised Christ from the dead still breathes into broken people today, into those disillusioned by religion, betrayed by hypocrisy, or tired of pretending.

He whispers, *"Come to Me, all who are weary and heavy laden, and I will give you rest."* (Matthew 11:28)

The Church God Intended

I believe there's still hope for the Church, not as an empire, but as a family.
Not as an institution, but as a living body of believers joined by love, not law.

The true Church isn't defined by denomination or doctrine.
It's defined by the presence of the Spirit and the practice of love.

When Jesus said, *"Where two or three are gathered in My name, there am I in the midst of them,"* (Matthew 18:20)
He wasn't talking about a cathedral. He was talking about connection.

The Church God intended was never meant to control; it was meant to care.
It was never meant to judge; it was meant to heal.
It was never meant to crucify, it was meant to carry the cross.

That's what redemption beyond religion looks like, not the death of the Church, but its rebirth.

When Love Becomes the Law

If religion tends to complicate, love simplifies.

Love fulfills every commandment, every prophecy, every law.
It's the heartbeat of heaven and the foundation of genuine faith.

Jesus said it plainly:

"A new commandment I give unto you, that you love one another; as I have loved you." (John 13:34)

That's the command religion forgot and the one that will save it.

When love becomes the law again, grace will flow, truth will heal, and the Church will shine like it was meant to.

Until then, God keeps calling individuals, not institutions, to live out that love one heart at a time.

Closing Reflection

I wrote *Religion Killed Jesus* not to condemn, but to awaken.
To remind anyone who has ever been hurt by hypocrisy or turned away by judgment that **God still loves you.**

He doesn't live in the stained glass or the rituals. He lives in the hearts of those who seek Him.

Religion killed Jesus, but it couldn't keep Him dead. Love resurrected Him, and that same love is still resurrecting hearts today.

If you've ever doubted your worth, if you've ever felt like you don't belong in the church, remember this:
You were never called to a religion; you were called to a relationship.

And in that relationship, you will find everything the world and religion could never give you:
peace, forgiveness, and a love that will never let you go.

Chapter Eleven

When Truth Threatens Power

Every age has its prophets, men and women who carry light into dark systems. Some wore robes, others, rags. Some preached from pulpits, others from prison cells.

What they all shared was this: they refused to trade truth for acceptance.

Religion fears that kind of faith because it cannot control it. A man or woman who walks with God directly needs no permission from hierarchy, no blessing from bureaucracy. That kind of freedom terrifies systems built on control.

It's easier to call such people heretics than to admit they might be right.

Then came the moment when the refusal to compromise was answered with the ultimate cost. On September 10, 2025, Charlie Kirk was speaking at an outdoor event at a college when a single shot ended his life. This was no private dissent; this was a public act. And the price paid for standing in the open was real.

Kirk's ministry was built on the conviction that faith must *not* be sanitized by comfort. He insisted, in speeches to youth and students, that **"I want to be remembered for courage for my faith. That would be the most important thing. The most important thing is my faith in my life."**

He also declared that **"If you believe in something, you need to have the courage to fight for those ideas, not run away from them or try and silence them."**

He argued that **"Without faith, freedom cannot survive. A society without God will always search for something else to worship."** He planted himself in the open field of youth, culture, politics, and ideology. To many of the systems, religious, secular, and institutional, that is a threat. Because once a follower of God engages directly, hierarchy loses its monopoly on authority, and control structures tremble.

In his words: **"The truth is that while those on the left, particularly the far left, claim to be tolerant and welcoming of diversity, in reality many are quite intolerant of anyone not embracing their radical views."** And he warned plainly: **"When people stop talking, that's when you get violence. That's when civil war happens, because you start to think the other side is so evil, and they lose their humanity."** What systems, religious, secular, institutional fear is someone who walks with God and does so without seeking the imprimatur of a hierarchical structure. A man or woman who refuses to trade truth for acceptance needs no permission from bureaucracy; no blessing from a denomination or governing board. And that kind of freedom terrifies systems built on control.

When Kirk refused to moderate truth for comfort's sake, he invited the full power of the system's reaction. The religious institution may vilify such a person, the political institution may demonize them, the media may caricature them, but the ultimate response comes when control is threatened so profoundly that the system aims to silence the voice altogether. In his assassination, we see the fear laid bare: the cost of prophetic dissent, when the prophet stands in the open and refuses to hide.

And yet, the prophet persists. Kirk's ministry reminds us that you need not wear a clerical robe to be prophetic; you need not belong to the pulpit to carry the light. He engaged young people, visited campuses, entered debate trenches not just about politics, but about ultimate things: truth, faith, meaning, freedom. That is precisely what this book traces: prophets in rag or robe, but all refusing to trade truth for acceptance.

In the reactions to his death, we see the system speak in its own tongue: not simply condemnation of violence, but a hardened sense of reinforced boundaries. Many leaders described his shooting as the inevitable product of a culture that silences truth-speakers. The culture's guardians looked on, some shocked, some dismissive; some suggested his rhetoric had made him a target. That is the power's answer: not simply to call him heretic, but to make his voice impossible.

Yet the final word is not power's reaction, but the prophet's endurance. Kirk did not begin his work seeking popularity among the establishment; he started by engaging young people, by building a network of influence outside traditional church hierarchies (through Turning Point USA). He trusted that his walking with God gave him the authority he needed. He spoke even when the culture insisted on silence. He stood even when the institution demanded conformity.

And so we return to the central question: what happens when truth threatens power? The answer: power will respond, it may call you a heretic, it may vilify you, it may try to kill the voice. But the truth-carrier persists. And by persisting, the truth-carrier draws the line between the system and the living voice of God. Because the truth they refused to trade for acceptance is not theirs alone, it is the Lord's.

What systems, religious, secular, institutional, is someone who walks with God and does so without seeking the imprimatur of a hierarchical structure. A man or woman who refuses to trade truth for acceptance needs no permission from bureaucracy, no blessing from a denomination or governing board. And that kind of freedom terrifies systems built on control.

.

His death becomes a testimony that freedom needs no blessing from bureaucracy, that faith which fears no institution becomes the greatest threat to those who depend on obedience. And thus in every age, when truth threatens power, the prophet will stand — and the system will realise it cannot help but react. The question is: will we, the watchers, recognise the reaction for what it is? Will we see the system tightening its chokehold, or will we see freedom that walks without asking permission?

A WAKE-UP CALL FROM GOD

My awakening to the danger of offense did not come from a sermon or a book; it came from a moment that shook my spirit to the core, the Charlie Kirk Assassination. I spoke about this publicly on my fitness channel, **Run-Fitness.com**, because I knew it wasn't just a news event; it was a spiritual wake-up call.

Life is short.
Whether someone is an evangelist, an atheist, a believer, or someone still searching, our life is a breath compared to eternity **(James 4:14)**. I realized I had been drifting, procrastinating my calling, hesitating in my obedience, and allowing seasons of inconsistency to shape my ministry. Sometimes I was sensitive to God's voice… sometimes I wasn't. But the walk of a disciple requires **persistence**, not spiritual autopilot.

Then the assassination of Charlie Kirk hit the nation like a bolt of lightning, and it shook me. I didn't know him personally, but when I heard his widow speak of life, conviction, courage, and unshakable faith in the midst of tragedy, something pierced me. In her voice, I heard strength, purpose, and Christ Himself.

It wasn't just political, it was **prophetic**.

Political opinions can divide us, but the spiritual battle behind politics is real. We have seen these patterns before. When President John F. Kennedy was assassinated, though I was only an infant, the nation shifted. Many believe a prophetic national voice was silenced. Whether one agrees or disagrees is their right, but the lesson for me was this:

We cannot afford to live in a state of offense.
We cannot waste time arguing.
We cannot delay our calling.

The Holy Spirit showed me:
Offense is proof that pride is still alive.
Arguments don't win souls, **love** does.

My calling isn't to argue my convictions; it is to stand on the Word of God, love people without partiality, and minister truth in compassion (**James 2:1; Ephesians 4:15**).

Yes, politically, I personally align with the values of life, justice, free speech, the right to bear arms, marriage is solely exclusive for a man and a woman, and God-honoring morality. I do have traditional values. But **I minister equally to every person, liberal, conservative, independent, or undecided.** No political stance should ever outweigh the command of Christ:

"Love one another as I have loved you." John 13:34

The mature Christian recognizes that differences of opinion, political, religious, or cultural, are not grounds for offense. They are opportunities to show Christ.

The moment I witnessed the aftermath of Charlie Kirk's assassination, I felt God telling me:

**"Time is short.
Stop drifting.
Stop delaying.
Stop taking offense."**

A believer who lives offended cannot live effectively

And so I say this to you, the reader:

**Do not let the enemy bait you into offense.
Do not let political opinions divide the Body.
Do not let arguments steal your peace.**

Stand firm in the truth.
Stand firm in love.
Stand firm in Christ.

Because the only way to win a soul is love
and the surest way to lose one is offense.

"THE SPIRIT OF OFFENSE AND THE PROOF OF SPIRITUAL MATURITY"

Religion Killed Jesus was written out of passion, love, and obedience to Christ, but also out of wisdom forged through Scripture. One lesson the Holy Spirit taught me early is this: **a believer who is easily offended is not yet rooted in Christ.**

Jesus never took offense at the accusations thrown at Him. He confronted evil actions with righteous anger, yes, but People's words never wounded him. Actions and words are not the same, and spiritual maturity requires us to learn the difference.

When I was in middle school, kids often called each other names. I remember hearing the old saying:
"Sticks and stones may break my bones, but words will never hurt me."

As simple as it sounds, that phrase is profoundly biblical. Scripture confirms this truth over and over again. Today, I still live by it. I am not offended by personal attacks, political opinions, abstract criticisms, or differences in worldview. People have opinions, and they have the right to express them even when I disagree.

But here is the revealing part:
People who are easily offended usually are not secure in God.
It is a spiritual giveaway that they don't honestly know Him.

Even Christians fall into this trap. **Offense exposes a heart still tied to pride, insecurity, and the approval of man. Where offense lives, identity in Christ does not.**

ACCUSATION — THE DEVIL'S FIRST LANGUAGE

Accusation is not a fruit of the Spirit; it is the language of Satan.

The book of Job makes this painfully clear. It was Satan who accused Job before God, claiming Job only served Him because of the blessings. God allowed Job to be tested, not because He was cruel, but because He knew Job's heart. Job was a man who would remain faithful even in suffering.

And yes, **Job got angry with God.**
That is not a sin.

- **Biblical examples:**

Several biblical figures openly expressed their struggles and anger toward God.

- **Job:** Suffered immense pain and questioned God's justice.

318

- **Jonah:** Became angry with God for showing mercy to the people of Nineveh.

- **Moses:** Asked God, "Why have you brought this trouble on your servant?".

- **Jeremiah:** Expressed his feelings of being deceived by God, stating, "You are stronger than I, and you have prevailed" **(Jeremiah 20:7).**

- **Psalm 89:46:** David questions, **"How long, Lord? Will You hide Yourself forever? Will Your anger keep burning like fire?".**

You can express frustration, confusion, or heartbreak before God. He already knows. What He opposes is *pride,* the belief that our perspective is higher than His.

If you are prideful about your accomplishments…
If you boast in your value, income, position, or reputation…
If you elevate yourself above anyone else…

That is not of God.
Those things belong to the world, not the Kingdom.

GIVE GOD THE GLORY — PUBLICLY AND WITHOUT FEAR

Scripture teaches that when we give God credit **before** we give ourselves credit, it becomes one of the most powerful forms of witnessing.

If your testimony causes even *one* person to come to Christ, heaven rejoices. God promises that your works for Him are never in vain.

Works do not earn salvation, but your **position and reward in the Kingdom** *are* connected to your faithfulness.

King David sits at the right hand of Christ not because he was perfect, but because he was a man after God's own heart, a worshiper, a witness, and a warrior who lived for something bigger than himself.

THE CALL OF EVERY BELIEVER — NOT JUST THE PASTOR

One reason I never felt content sitting in a pew listening to a single man preach week after week is that Scripture plainly teaches:

Every believer is called to be a disciple.
Every believer is called to be a witness.
Every believer is called to preach the Word of God.

Not one.
Not two.
Not three.
ALL.

Church was never meant to be a weekly gathering of people listening to one man's opinion. That system is built on religion, not relationships.

Bible study and fellowship are essential, yes.
But your personal relationship with God cannot be outsourced to a pastor. If you are depending on a preacher to hear God for you, you will remain spiritually weak.

THE QUIET PLACE — WHERE GOD ACTUALLY SPEAKS

"Study to show yourself approved unto God" (2 Timothy 2:15).

The busier you are, the less you know God.
People today stay constantly distracted socially, politically, digitally, and even religiously.

But the Kingdom of God is found in the secret place.
In stillness.
In solitude.
In intimacy with Christ.

To walk in power, you must spend time **alone** with God.

That is where revelation comes.
That is where identity is formed.
That is where you become unoffendable.

FINAL EXHORTATION

Do not live offended.
Do not live pridefully.

Do not live dependent on another man's revelation.
Seek first the Kingdom of God, and everything else will fall into place.

"THE OFFENSE TEST" — A WORD FROM THE LORD

My people have embraced offense more than My presence.
They defend their pride more than their faith.
They hear the voices of men louder than My whisper.
But I am raising a remnant who cannot be shaken.
A people who refuse offense, who walk in humility, and who know Me in the secret place.
Come away with me, and I will give you a heart that words cannot wound,
a spirit unmoved by accusation,
and a faith unshaken by storms.
Return to Me, and I will remove the spirit of offense from your life."

SCRIPTURE REFERENCES ADDED

On Offense

- Psalm 119:165
- Luke 17:1
- Proverbs 19:11

On Accusation

- Revelation 12:10
- Job 1–2

On Humility vs Pride

- James 4:6
- 1 John 2:16
- Proverbs 16:18

On Witness

- Matthew 5:16
- Luke 15:7
- 1 Corinthians 3:12–15

On Every Believer's Calling

- Mark 16:15
- Matthew 28:18–20
- Acts 1:8
- 1 Timothy 2:5

On the Quiet Place

- Matthew 6:6
- 2 Timothy 2:15
- Matthew 6:33

REFLECTION & DISCUSSION QUESTIONS

(For readers, small groups, or end-of-chapter use)

Reflection

Are you unoffendable?
Do people's words wound you more than God's truth fills you?
The Spirit of Offense reveals a deeper need:
the need to return to intimacy with God and to find identity in Him alone.

Discussion Questions

1. What are the areas in your life where offense rises quickly?

2. Do negative words affect you more than God's Word strengthens you? Why?

3. How does focusing on the actions of Christ help distinguish between offense and righteous anger?

4. Do you rely too heavily on pastors, leaders, or personalities for spiritual growth?

5. What steps will you take this week to enter the "secret place" and be alone with God?

6. Where is pride hiding in your life, and how can humility replace it?

7. Whom can you witness to by publicly giving God the glory for your story?

A Disciple Even Behind the Wheel — Driving as a Reflection of Christ

Most people think of driving as a simple daily task, commuting to work, running errands, or traveling for leisure. But for the follower of Christ, even this act becomes a place of witness, character, and spiritual discipline.

Jesus did not divide life into "holy" and "ordinary."
Everything we do reflects who we truly are.
Even the way we handle a motor vehicle reveals our relationship with God.

Driving Responsibly Because You Honor Life

A true Christian drives responsibly not out of fear of a ticket, but out of reverence for life and obedience to God.

"Obey the governing authorities... for the authorities are God's servants." — Romans 13:1–4

Obedience to the law is obedience to God.
Reckless driving is more than foolish; it is sin, because it risks the lives of those God created in His image.

"Thou shalt not kill." Exodus 20:13

When someone speeds dangerously, tailgates, weaves between lanes, blows through lights, or ignores crosswalks, they gamble with someone else's life.
God does not take that lightly.

"An eye for an eye, and a tooth for a tooth." Exodus 21:23–25

This is not about revenge; this is about the value God places on human life.
To take a life carelessly is to condemn one's own life in the eyes of God.

**The law may treat vehicular homicide as an "accident," but heaven does not.
God holds humans accountable for the lives they endanger.**

Respecting the Lives Inside Your Own Vehicle

Recklessness in a car is also a betrayal of those riding with you.
A Christ-follower does not endanger their own family or passengers to prove a point, rush somewhere, or indulge impatience.

You may take risks with your own life, but **you have no right to take risks with theirs**.

"Look not every man on his own things, but every man also on the things of others." Philippians 2:4

If you drive fast alone, that is your choice. Also, driving recklessly voids the blood of Christ, protecting you. Christ will not protect you if you don't value your own life and the lives of others. If you speed and drive recklessly, it means you don't place a value on your life and are being disobedient to God. The Blood of Jesus will not protect fools who live dangerously.
And when someone else is in your car, their life becomes your responsibility before God.

Overcoming Road Rage: The War Within the Car

Anger behind the wheel is one of the most revealing mirrors of the heart.
Impatience with strangers on the road exposes spiritual immaturity.

"Be angry, and sin not." Ephesians 4:26
"The anger of man does not produce the righteousness of God." James 1:20

A Christian does **not**:

• lay on the horn to shame someone
• yell, curse, or gesture
• take offense at a mistake
• tailgate to intimidate
• speed past someone to "teach them a lesson."

The horn exists as a safety device, not **a weapon of anger**.

When you burst into rage on the road, you have surrendered your emotions to the enemy.

"Blessed are the peacemakers." Matthew 5:9
"Be not overcome with evil, but overcome evil with good." Romans 12:21

Why You Must Not Judge Other Drivers

Everyone has mental lapses.
Everyone makes mistakes.
Everyone has moments of absent-mindedness, **including you**.

When you judge a stranger's mistake more harshly than you would judge your own, you reveal a lack of mercy.

Jesus confronted this spirit:

"With the measure you use, it will be measured to you." Matthew 7:2

Before reacting, visualize this:

What if the person who made that mistake was your wife?
Your mother?
Your son?

Would you blast your horn?
Tailgate them?
Scream at them?

No because love covers mistakes.

So why is a stranger any different?
They are flesh and bone, just like your own family.
They are someone's child, someone's spouse, someone's parent.

Your anger reveals that you value your own circle, but not your neighbor.
Jesus condemns that divided heart.

"Love your neighbor as yourself." Mark 12:31

Driving as a Mark of Your Discipleship

Your behavior behind the wheel preaches a sermon louder than words:

• Respecting others → humility
• Obeying laws → submission to God
• Driving defensively → valuing life
• Controlling anger → living by the Spirit
• Showing mercy → walking like Christ

People who drive recklessly, speeding, tailgating, and weaving through lanes demonstrate more than bad habits. They demonstrate that **they do not know Christ**.

A true disciple honors God in all things, even on the highway.

"Whatever you do… do it for the glory of God." 1 Corinthians 10:31

Reflection & Prayer

Reflection Questions

1. Do I drive in a way that reflects Christ or my flesh?

2. Do I value the lives around me as much as my own schedule?

3. Does anger rise quickly when I am behind the wheel?

4. Am I patient with strangers the same way I am patient with loved ones?

5. Does my driving honor the God who commands me to love my neighbor?

Prayer for Driving with the Character of Christ

Father,
Teach me to reflect Your love in every part of my life, even in how I drive.
Remove anger, pride, impatience, and frustration from my heart.
Please fill me with humility, compassion, and self-control.
Let me value the lives around me as You value them.
Guard my mind, guide my reactions, and keep me in perfect peace.
May every mile I travel be a testimony to Christ in me.
In Jesus' name

Amen.

 Fire Became the Weapon of Faith: The Trial and Triumph of Joan of Arc

When Fire Became the Weapon of Faith

Centuries after the Cross, religion found new ways to silence its prophets through councils, prisons, and flames. The Church, now clothed in Roman power, turned its judgment outward, branding those who questioned authority as heretics.

One of the darkest symbols of that era was the stake, the place where truth and fear collided.

In 1431, Joan of Arc, a young woman from France who claimed divine visions, was burned alive by the Church she professed to serve. Her crime wasn't sin; it was obedience. She had heard God's voice and followed it, and that terrified the men who thought they controlled Him.

They called her a witch. Centuries later, the same Church that condemned her, the Roman Catholic Church, would canonize her as a saint, proving that truth, though buried, always rises again.

She wasn't the first, and she wasn't the last. Countless others were tortured, exiled, or executed for daring to say what God put on their hearts.

Religion's history is written not only in ink, but in ashes.

A Girl Who Heard Heaven

Joan of Arc was not born into power or privilege. She was a shepherd's daughter from Domrémy, a small French village battered by the Hundred Years' War. While kings plotted and priests debated, Heaven whispered to a teenage girl.

At thirteen, she began to see visions of the Archangel Michael, St. Catherine, and St. Margaret — calling her to deliver France from English domination. She wept, prayed, and resisted the call, but the voice grew stronger:

"Go, daughter of God. I will be with you."

Faith became her armor, and obedience her sword.

While men argued about politics, Joan obeyed her visions. And with that obedience, she frightened every hierarchy built on fear.

"While bishops argued and kings hesitated, a peasant girl believed."

When Religion Fears Faith

The Church of her day, intertwined with political power, could bless a king's war but not a girl's faith. Joan's authority did not come from Rome or royal decree; it came from divine encounter. And that made her dangerous.

Institutions love loyalty but fear intimacy with God. Joan bypassed the hierarchy. She didn't ask for permission to hear His voice, she simply listened.

"Institutions can bless you for serving them — but they will burn you for hearing God without their permission."

The same spirit that crucified Christ built the stake that burned Joan.

They called her disobedient, defiant, delusional. But Joan's faith was simple:

"I am not afraid… I was born to do this."

That statement could have been spoken by any prophet, any reformer, any believer who chose obedience over acceptance.

The Trial – A Court of Wolves

In Rouen, 1431, Joan stood before her accusers — a tribunal of priests, scholars, and judges sent by the English Crown but sanctioned by the Church.

Her judges quoted Scripture to trap her; they demanded that she submit to their interpretation of God's will. Yet, like Jesus before Pilate, she remained calm, confident, and unshaken.

When asked if she was in a state of grace — a trick question meant to condemn her — she answered with divine simplicity:

"If I am not, may God put me there; and if I am, may God so keep me."

That answer silenced theologians. It revealed her unshakable awareness that grace comes from God, not from men in robes.

They could not comprehend that this teenage girl, uneducated in theology, understood grace better than the council assembled to destroy her.

Fire as the Weapon of Faith

332

On May 30, 1431, in the market square of Rouen, the Roman Catholic Church, which claimed to serve Christ, became the executioner of His servant.

They tied her to a wooden post, surrounded by kindling and fear. The flames that rose around her meant to erase her name — but they only engraved it into history.

"The same fire they lit to silence her became the torch that carried her story into eternity."

As the smoke climbed toward heaven, witnesses said they saw her lips move in prayer, her eyes lifted toward the sky. She died crying the name of Jesus.

The crowd wept. Even hardened soldiers trembled. The fire they meant for judgment became an altar of glory.

"Fire became her weapon — not because it destroyed her, but because it revealed what could not be burned."

The Purification of Truth

Years later, the Roman Catholic Church realized what Heaven already knew: that Joan was innocent.
A retrial in 1456 declared her not guilty, calling her death a **"martyrdom of faith."**

Almost five hundred years later, in 1920, the same Church canonized her as **Saint Joan of Arc.**
The irony is staggering: the institution that condemned her for her visions later sanctified her for them.

"Religion repented centuries after it burned the saint. But Heaven had vindicated her the moment her spirit rose."

This is the rhythm of religious history persecution first, repentance later.
The Church always recognizes its prophets too late.

The Fire Still Speaks

The flames that consumed Joan did not die. They became a symbol of faith unbroken, courage uncorrupted, and obedience uncompromised.

Every generation faces fire. For some, it is persecution, for others, rejection, ridicule, or exile. But the principle remains:

True faith always passes through fire.

In Joan's ashes, God planted a seed of awakening. Her story reminds us that religion can wound, but truth resurrects.

"Somewhere today, another Joan is hearing the voice of Heaven trembling not from fear, but from calling."

And perhaps God still looks for such faith, a faith that walks into the fire not to die, but to reveal what can't be destroyed.

Closing Reflection

The fires of the past still burn, not in judgment, but in memory.
They remind us that the Church is never at its best when it controls, but when it believes.
That God never needed permission from councils or kings to speak, only a willing heart to listen.

"The fire that killed her also purified her, and in that flame, faith was reborn."

Prayer

Lord, give us the faith that fears no flame.
Let obedience become our courage, and truth our weapon.
Forgive us for every altar where fear was stronger than faith.
And if we must walk through fire, let Your presence be the light that carries us through.
As You were with Joan, be with all who dare to obey You.
In Jesus' name, Amen.

The Revolutionaries: When the Word Broke the Chains

There are moments in history when the Spirit of Truth bursts through the walls of tradition — when God raises voices that shake thrones and challenge the idols of religion.
The sixteenth century was one of those moments.

For nearly a thousand years, the Church had wrapped itself in power, wealth, and ritual. The Word of God, once preached freely in the streets of Jerusalem, had been locked away in Latin and guarded by priests. The gospel became property, grace became merchandise, and the people were taught to buy what Christ had already paid for.

"Freely ye have received, freely give." Matthew 10:8

The Dark Age of the Word

From the fall of Rome to the dawn of the Renaissance, the Western Church reigned supreme. Kings bowed before popes, and nations trembled under papal decrees. Forgiveness could be purchased through indulgences. Salvation was administered through sacraments. Religion had replaced relationship; ceremony had silenced conviction.

The Scriptures warned long before:

"My people are destroyed for lack of knowledge."
Hosea 4:6

And indeed, ignorance was the weapon of control. The Bible was chained to cathedral pulpits, its truth restricted to priests and scholars.
The common man was told to obey, not to read, to listen, not to question.

But the Spirit of God cannot be chained.
And in time, He stirred men who dared to read the forbidden Word for themselves.

Martin Luther The Hammer That Shook the Church

In 1517, a German monk named **Martin Luther** walked to the doors of the Castle Church in Wittenberg and nailed to it a parchment of protest, **his Ninety-Five Theses.**
He did not seek to destroy the Church but to cleanse it. Yet his hammer echoed through all of Europe.

Luther's revelation was simple, yet revolutionary:

"The just shall live by faith." Romans 1:17

Not by works, not by payment, not by papal decree, but by faith in Christ alone.

The Church had sold forgiveness; Luther preached that Jesus' blood had already bought it.
*The Church exalted priests; Luther declared that every believer was a priest unto God. **(1 Peter 2:9)***
The Church elevated the Pope as the voice of heaven; Luther reminded the world that the Scriptures are the voice of God.

When Rome demanded his silence, Luther stood firm:

"My conscience is captive to the Word of God. Here I stand, I can do no other."

That stand cost him everything: his title, his safety, his home, but it gave the world something greater: the open Bible.

Before the hammer ever struck the church doors of Wittenberg, it first hit the heart of a young monk searching for God.

The Making of a Reformer

Martin Luther was born in 1483 in Eisleben, Germany, the son of Hans and Margarethe Luther. His father, a hardworking miner, dreamed of his son becoming a lawyer. Luther obeyed, studying philosophy and law at the University of Erfurt, one of Europe's finest schools.
He was brilliant, disciplined, and driven, but also tormented by the question that haunted his soul: *"How can a man be right with God?"*

Then, in 1505, everything changed.
Caught in a violent thunderstorm on his way home,
lightning struck near his feet. Terrified, Luther cried out,

"Help me, St. Anne! I will become a monk!"

True to his vow, he abandoned his law books and entered
the Augustinian monastery in Erfurt.
He fasted, prayed, confessed, and punished his body, yet
peace escaped him.
He later wrote,

"I was a good monk, and kept the rule of my order so
strictly that I may say: if ever a monk got to heaven by his
monkery, it was I. Yet my conscience found no rest."

The Light in the Darkness

In 1507, Luther was ordained a priest. A few years later, he
was sent to the University of Wittenberg to teach theology.
There, as he studied the Scriptures, particularly the Book
of Romans, the veil began to lift.

One verse pierced his heart like lightning:

"The just shall live by faith." *Romans 1:17*

Luther realized that salvation was not earned through good
works, indulgences, or rituals — but received by grace
through faith in Christ alone.
This revelation became the fire that would ignite a
revolution.

**"For by grace are ye saved through faith; and that not
of yourselves: it is the gift of God."** *Ephesians 2:8–9*

No longer bound by fear, Luther began to see God not as
a harsh judge but as a loving Father.
That revelation of grace was the breaking of chains, and
those chains would soon fall across all of Europe.

The Spark That Lit the Reformation

In 1517, Luther's outrage reached its peak.
A Dominican friar named Johann Tetzel was selling indulgences near Wittenberg, promising that the souls of the dead could escape purgatory for a price.
His slogan was blasphemous:

"As soon as a coin in the coffer rings, a soul from purgatory springs."

Luther could not stay silent.
On **October 31, 1517**, he walked to the Castle Church door in Wittenberg, the community bulletin board, and nailed his **Ninety-Five Theses**, challenging the corruption and spiritual deception of the Church.

He did not intend to divide Christianity, but to call it back to truth.
Yet his hammer's echo became the sound of spiritual rebellion against centuries of tyranny.

"Thy word is a lamp unto my feet, and a light unto my path." *Psalm 119:105*

Rome demanded his recantation, but Luther's conscience had been anchored in Scripture, not in the decrees of men. Standing before Emperor Charles V at the **Diet of Worms in 1521**, Luther declared,

"My conscience is captive to the Word of God. I cannot and will not recant anything. Here I stand, I can do no other. God help me."

With that stand, Luther shattered the illusion of papal infallibility and placed the Bible, not the Pope, at the center of faith.

The Bible for the People

Branded a heretic and excommunicated, Luther went into hiding at Wartburg Castle, protected by Frederick the Wise.
There, in solitude and secrecy, he performed one of history's most significant acts of faith, translating the **New Testament into German** so that ordinary people could read the Word of God for themselves.

"The entrance of Thy words giveth light; it giveth understanding unto the simple." *Psalm 119:130*

That translation, completed in 1522, became the cornerstone of the Reformation.
The Bible, once chained in Latin, now spoke in the language of the people.
The printing press carried Luther's words like wildfire through Europe.

From Germany to Switzerland, England to Scandinavia, the Protestant Reformation reshaped civilization.
It taught nations that truth was not bound to Rome, and that salvation was not purchased through priests but through personal faith in Christ.

The Legacy of Freedom

Luther's courage opened the floodgates for men like **John Calvin**, **Ulrich Zwingli**, and **John Knox**, who expanded the Reformation across Europe.
Education flourished, literacy spread, and Western thought shifted from blind obedience to spiritual discernment.

"Ye shall know the truth, and the truth shall make you free." *John 8:32*

340

Out of Luther's defiance came the **Protestant Church**, grounded in five eternal truths —

1. **Sola Scriptura** – Scripture Alone

2. **Sola Fide** – Faith Alone

3. **Sola Gratia** – Grace Alone

4. **Solus Christus** – Christ Alone

5. **Soli Deo Gloria** – To the Glory of God Alone

The movement Luther began was not simply theological; it was a spiritual revolution.
It birthed freedom of conscience, the right to read the Bible, and the conviction that no man stands between God and His people but Christ alone.

"For there is one God, and one mediator between God and men, the man Christ Jesus." *1 Timothy 2:5*

The Faith That Still Speaks

Luther died in 1546, but his echo still resounds.
He gave the world not a new religion, but a reminder that the gospel had never changed.
He broke not the Church of Christ, but the chains of religion that bound it.

"Stand fast therefore in the liberty wherewith Christ hath made us free, and be not entangled again with the yoke of bondage." *Galatians 5:1*

Martin Luther was not perfect, but he was prophetic.
He did not create truth; he rediscovered it.
And through his faith, God reopened the floodgates of grace to a world drowning in ritual.

The hammer that struck the door of Wittenberg still strikes today, not against wood, but against the hearts of believers who must once again remember:
The shall live by faith.

John Calvin The Mind of the Reformation

*If Martin Luther was the hammer that broke the chains of religion, **John Calvin** was the architect who built the framework for faith's renewal.*
While Luther's fire ignited reform, Calvin's mind refined it, shaping a movement that would redefine Christianity, government, and culture for centuries.

*After Luther, another voice rose, **John Calvin**, a French scholar exiled for his faith.*
Calvin's pen became as powerful as Luther's hammer. While Luther struck the chains, Calvin forged the foundation, returning theology to the sovereignty of God and the supremacy of Scripture.

"All Scripture is given by inspiration of God, and is profitable for doctrine, for reproof, for correction, for instruction in righteousness." 2 Timothy 3:16

Calvin taught that salvation is the work of grace alone, not the achievement of man.
He emphasized that no priest, pope, or bishop could stand between the believer and God, for the veil was torn from top to bottom when Christ died. (Matthew 27:51)

His writings shaped nations. Geneva became a refuge for believers fleeing persecution, and from there, the flame of reformation spread across Europe to England, Scotland, and eventually to the New World.

The Early Years of a Scholar

John Calvin was born on **July 10, 1509**, in Noyon, France, to a devout but ambitious family. His father, Gérard Cauvin, served as an administrative official for the Catholic Church, and from a young age, Calvin was marked for the priesthood.
He was a prodigy, reserved, brilliant, and deeply disciplined.

At just 14, he was sent to **the University of Paris**, the greatest center of learning in Europe at the time. There he studied **theology, philosophy, and Latin**, immersing himself in the scholastic traditions of medieval Catholicism.

But even as he studied the logic of men, the Spirit began to stir questions in his soul. He saw that the Church of his day was rich in ceremony but poor in truth, ornate in ritual but empty of power.

When his father fell out with the clergy, Calvin shifted his studies to **law at the University of Orléans and Bourges**, mastering Greek and Hebrew the very languages in which the Scriptures were written.
That divine redirection, though political in appearance, would become providential for God was preparing the scholar to become a reformer.

"The preparations of the heart in man, and the answer of the tongue, is from the Lord." Proverbs 16:1

A Scholar Meets the Savior

*By his early twenties, Calvin had mastered philosophy and jurisprudence, but his heart remained bound by religion. Then, sometime around **1533**, God intervened. Calvin later described his conversion in quiet but powerful words:*

"God subdued and brought my heart to docility, which was more hardened than was proper for such a young man."

Like Luther, Calvin came face-to-face with grace.
He discovered not the wrath of God, but the mercy of God, not salvation earned through penance, but salvation given through promise.

The same Word that had set Luther free now awakened another generation.
Calvin began to study the Bible as divine revelation rather than human philosophy. He saw in its pages the sovereignty of God, the authority of Scripture, and the simplicity of salvation.

"For by grace are ye saved through faith; and that not of yourselves: it is the gift of God." Ephesians 2:8

In that revelation, the young scholar was reborn as a servant.

Exile and Calling

In **1535**, persecution swept France under King Francis I. Believers were arrested, tortured, and burned for reading or preaching the Bible.
Calvin, branded a heretic, fled Paris in the night carrying little but his manuscripts and his faith.

He found refuge in **Basel, Switzerland**, where he published his masterpiece:
"The Institutes of the Christian Religion."

It was first printed in 1536 when Calvin was only **26 years old**, and became the defining theological work of the Protestant Reformation.

In it, Calvin declared that Scripture alone reveals the will of God, that salvation is by grace alone, and that the entire world exists under God's sovereignty.
He wrote not merely as a theologian, but as a man who had seen the idols fall and the Word rise.

"All Scripture is given by inspiration of God, and is profitable for doctrine, for reproof, for correction, for instruction in righteousness." 2 Timothy 3:16

Geneva The City on a Hill

Calvin eventually settled in **Geneva**, a small city-state in Switzerland that would become the heart of the Reformed faith.
There, he organized the Church around biblical principles rather than papal decrees.
He established schools, trained pastors, and instituted what he called a "theocracy of grace" — a city governed by Scripture rather than superstition.

Geneva became a beacon for believers fleeing persecution, a refuge for reformers from France, England, Scotland, and beyond.
From Geneva's printing presses flowed sermons, commentaries, and Bibles that spread the flame of faith throughout Europe.

"Ye are the light of the world. A city that is set on a hill cannot be hid." Matthew 5:14

Through his leadership, Geneva earned the name "the Protestant Rome. But unlike Rome, a man did not rule it; the Word governed it.

The Theology That Shaped the West

Where Luther had emphasized justification by faith, Calvin emphasized the sovereignty of God.
Luther broke from Rome; Calvin built a framework that would guide the Church for generations.

He taught that:

- **God's grace, not human merit, determines salvation.**

- **The believer's entire life is lived before the face of God "Coram Deo."**

- **The Church must be governed by the Word, not by the will of man.**

- **Every vocation, farmer, merchant, scholar, is a sacred calling under Christ's lordship.**

This last idea reshaped Western civilization.
*It birthed what came to be known as the **Protestant Work Ethic**, the belief that all labor done unto God is holy.*

From it sprang the foundations of modern education, democracy, and personal liberty.

Calvin's teaching helped shape nations such as **Scotland** through **John Knox**, **England** through the Puritans, and eventually **America**, where his ideas of divine calling and covenant would echo in the founding vision of a people "under God."

"Whether therefore ye eat, or drink, or whatsoever ye do, do all to the glory of God." — 1 Corinthians 10:31

Different Flames, One Fire

Martin Luther and John Calvin were different men forged by the same fire.
Luther was the bold reformer, emotional, passionate, and often defiant.
Calvin was the thinker precise, disciplined, methodical.
Luther shattered the chains; Calvin systematized the truth.
Luther lit the match; Calvin built the lamp.

Together, they transformed Europe from the darkness of medieval superstition to the light of biblical revelation. Their work was not perfect, but it was prophetic, a divine interruption in a world that had forgotten its God.

"For the word of God is quick, and powerful, and sharper than any two-edged sword." — Hebrews 4:12

Calvin died in **1564**, worn from labor but rich in legacy. He had lived quietly, refused titles, and requested to be buried in an unmarked grave so that glory would belong to God alone.

The Mind That Still Shapes Faith

John Calvin's influence did not end in Geneva.
From his teachings came the great Protestant denominations, Presbyterian, Reformed, Congregational, and Puritan.
His vision of a God-governed people laid the moral and intellectual foundation for the modern West.

His life reminds us that true reformation begins not in rebellion, but in revelation.
He did not fight to destroy a Church, but to restore its soul.

And his voice still calls to us today:
Return to the Scriptures.
Return to the sovereignty of God.
Return to the faith that stands on grace alone.

"The grass withereth, the flower fadeth: but the word of our God shall stand forever." — Isaiah 40:8

The Birth of the Protestant Church

The Reformation was not a rebellion against faith; it was a return to it.
It was a movement to bring the Church back to the cross, back to the Word, back to the simplicity of Christ.

The Protestants were named not because they hated the Church, but because they protested corruption in the name

348

of truth.
They proclaimed Sola Scriptura, Scripture alone, as the final authority.
Sola Fide: faith alone for salvation.
Sola Gratia, grace alone as the means.
Solus Christus Christ alone as mediator.
Soli Deo Gloria to the glory of God alone.

"Ye shall know the truth, and the truth shall make you free." John 8:32

The printing press became the pulpit of reformation, and the Bible, once hidden in Latin, was now printed in the language of the people.
The Word walked again among men.

The Spirit That Still Speaks

But every reformation is a reminder, not a relic.
The same Church that once hid the Scriptures now risks hiding them again behind entertainment and comfort.
The same spirit that once sold indulgences now sells inspiration.
The same idolatry that once worshiped statues now worships personalities.

The reformers cried for purity, not popularity.
They longed for repentance, not revenue.
And they still remind us that truth must always be defended, even when it costs everything.

"Earnestly contend for the faith which was once delivered unto the saints." Jude 1:3

The Church of today must not merely celebrate the reformers but continue their work, not reform for the sake of history, but revival for the sake of eternity.

The Reformation was never finished.
It was not the victory of men, but the voice of God calling His people once again:
"Come out of Babylon, My people. Return to Me."
(Revelation 18:4)

And until the Church bows again to the Word above all words, the revolution must continue.

A Heart Shaped by Service

My heart for Christ didn't grow in the safety of religion; it grew in the rawness of serving others.
I didn't find God in a sermon; I saw Him in the streets, in broken eyes, in trembling hands, and in whispered prayers from souls who thought Heaven had forgotten them.

I remember praying with a man outside a convenience store one night.
He smelled of alcohol and loneliness.
When I shared Christ with him, tears carved paths through the dirt on his face.
He said, "I thought God stopped caring about me a long time ago."
In that moment, I realized something: church isn't a building. It's wherever a believer carries God's love.

"The Spirit of the Lord is upon Me, because He hath anointed Me to preach the gospel to the poor;
He hath sent Me to heal the brokenhearted..." Luke 4:18

That night, I learned that faithful ministry doesn't wait behind stained glass; it walks into the places the world avoids.
It listens to stories others ignore.
It touches wounds that others judge.
That's where Jesus is among the broken, the forgotten, and the desperate.

A Visit to the Mental Institution

Some time later, I visited a mental institution.
There, behind the locked doors and white walls, I met a young girl who had lost her will to live.
Her eyes were dim, but her words were sharp with truth.
She said, *"I don't want to live outside these walls anymore. The world is too evil. There's no love out there."*

Her words pierced my heart like a prophet's cry.
In that sterile room, I saw the reflection of a broken world one that had traded compassion for convenience, and truth for pleasure.
And I realized something profound: she was right.
The world is dark because it is no longer ruled by love but by lies.

"The whole world lieth in wickedness." — 1 John 5:19

That moment solidified my faith in a way no sermon ever could.
It reminded me that the world indeed belongs to the evil one, but also that God has not left us powerless.
When I prayed for that young girl, I asked God to give her courage to live — not in fear of the world, but in faith in His power.
And in that moment, Heaven's peace filled the room.

I prayed, *"Lord, give her strength to walk in your light even when the world around her is dark. Teach her to seek you first and let your spirit empower her to overcome evil in an evil world."*

As I prayed, I felt Heaven move not in thunder or lightning, but in peace.
I saw tears form in her eyes, and in that moment, I knew God was there.
It wasn't about saving a soul for the sake of statistics or counting conversions.
It was about love — the kind that sees beyond diagnosis, beyond despair, and touches the eternal part of a person that still longs for God.

That encounter deepened my calling.
It confirmed that my purpose was never to build a name, but to build the Kingdom one hurting heart at a time.
It renewed my commitment to press forward with my ministry, **Livingstone's Spiritual House** (livingstonesspiritualhouse.org),
Where the mission remains sacred and straightforward: to reach the lost, to love the broken, and to remind a dying world that Christ still lives.

I learned that day that faithful ministry is not about being safe it's about being sent.
And when we walk into the darkest places, carrying the light of Christ, even Hell has to tremble.

"Ye are the light of the world. A city that is set on a hill cannot be hid." Matthew 5:14

A Miracle at the Assisted Living Facility

Another time, while serving food to the poor at an assisted living facility, I saw the Spirit of God move again.
Most of the residents were quiet, grateful, and weary souls

whose time had forgotten.
As I handed out meals, a young woman suddenly fell to her knees, trembling, tears flooding her face.
She cried out, saying she felt God's presence.
Right there, amid paper plates and plastic forks, Heaven came down.

I knelt beside her, prayed with her, and invited her to one of our services.
A few weeks later, she walked through the doors of **Livingstone's Spiritual House** and surrendered her life to Christ.
That day, the angels rejoiced proof that the Gospel still changes hearts, one encounter at a time.

The Woman with Cancer

God's work also followed me into my daily business.
There was a woman — a faithful customer of mine for years who was dying of cancer.
As her body weakened, her spirit began to reach for hope.
One day, she invited me into her home to pray.

As I stood by her bedside, asking God to comfort her, her husband suddenly entered the room — angry, grief-stricken, and misunderstanding my intentions.
He shouted at me, accusing me and demanding that I leave.
But instead of reacting in fear or anger, a divine calm came over me.
I placed my hand gently on his shoulder and said,
"It's going to be all right. God sent me to pray for her, and He's about to give you peace and understanding."

Immediately, his rage dissolved.
His words stopped mid-breath.
He stared at me in silence, then turned and quietly walked

away.
The Holy Spirit had entered that home, calming the storm with nothing but peace and presence.

The Ministry of Compassion: Visiting the Forgotten

My Living Stones Spiritual House Ministry led me to visit nursing homes regularly—
Not by ambition, but by divine assignment.
God placed it upon my heart to walk into places where loneliness often lingers like a shadow,
to carry His light into forgotten rooms, and to remind those who felt abandoned that Heaven still knew their name.

**"Pure religion and undefiled before God and the Father is this,
to visit the fatherless and widows in their affliction,
and to keep himself unspotted from the world." —
James 1:27**

A Calling to the Margins

From the beginning, I knew this ministry was not about preaching from a pulpit,
but about sitting at the bedside of the broken.
I developed rapport with staff and residents alike learning their names, their stories, their struggles.
Many of these men and women were nearing the end of their earthly journey.
Some smiled when I spoke of Jesus; others wept silently as old memories resurfaced.
A few turned away, their hearts hardened by pain.
But most listened, curious—yearning for a word of hope.

Each time before visiting, I would pray:

"Lord, let Your anointing rest upon me.
Let me see them as You see them—through eyes of mercy."

As I entered those halls, I sensed the weight of eternity pressing upon ordinary conversations.
In every room, I found the presence of Christ among the suffering.

"For I was hungry, and you gave Me food;
I was thirsty, and you gave me a drink.
I was a stranger, and you took me in...
I was sick, and you visited me." Matthew 25:35 36

The Soldier Without Legs

Among the many souls I met, one man's story still lingers deeply within me.
He was a veteran—a soldier who had lost both legs in war.
His body bore the scars of battle, but his heart carried deeper wounds.
He had been a resident of the nursing home for two or three years,
Placed there by his family, who lived less than an hour away.

When he told me that no one had visited him since he arrived, his voice trembled.
Tears welled in his eyes and fell like confessions onto his folded blanket.
It was almost unbearable to hear—a man who had given everything for his country, now forgotten by his own.

"When my father and my mother forsake me,
Then the Lord will take me up." Psalm 27:10

I prayed with him often. We spoke about heaven how in God's kingdom,

The lame would leap like a deer, and every tear would be wiped away (Isaiah 35:6, Revelation 21:4).
He told me he could almost see that day coming.
When he died, I felt the loss like that of a brother.
Yet I knew his faith had been rekindled before his final breath.
He reminded me that even in the quiet halls of neglect, God's mercy moves.

The Ministry of Presence

Faithful ministry is not measured in sermons preached but in hearts touched.
When Jesus walked this earth, He spent more time healing, feeding, and comforting than addressing crowds.
He knelt beside the broken, touched the lepers, and wept with the grieving.
He was moved with compassion.
and that same compassion still moves through those who carry His Spirit.

"When He saw the multitudes, He was moved with compassion on them,
Because they fainted, and were scattered abroad, as sheep having no shepherd." Matthew 9:36

The early Church understood this.
Historical records show that by the second century, Christians were known for their works of mercy.
While Rome abandoned its sick and elderly, believers cared for them.
Dionysius of Alexandria (A.D. 260) wrote that Christians **"visited the sick fearlessly…**
and died joyfully beside them."
Even pagan emperors, like Julian the Apostate, complained that "the Christians not only care for their own poor but ours as well."

That was true religion, faith that took on flesh and walked into suffering.

The Forgotten Generation

In every nursing home, I saw a reflection of a greater spiritual truth:
the world forgets what it no longer finds useful.
The elderly, the sick, the poor, those who once built families and communities, are often left to fade in solitude.
But the Kingdom of God operates in reverse.
The least become greatest; the forgotten become beloved.

"The last shall be first, and the first last." Matthew 20:16

I saw the gospel alive in wrinkled hands that trembled when they prayed.
I saw forgiveness in the eyes of those whose own blood had been neglected.
I learned that revival doesn't always happen in crowded auditoriums—it happens in quiet rooms filled with pain and prayer.

A Ministry that Changed Me

My visits to those nursing homes didn't just minister to others; they transformed me.
Their stories became parables, their resilience became sermons, their gratitude became worship.
When one resident passed away, I would return home in tears,
feeling both grief and holy conviction
A reminder that we are all but a breath, and only what we do for Christ will last.

"Teach us to number our days, that we may apply our hearts unto wisdom." — Psalm 90:12

Through Living Stones Spiritual House Ministry,
God taught me that compassion is the purest form of evangelism.
It's the kind of faith that doesn't demand attention but draws heaven's applause.

"Bear ye one another's burdens, and so fulfil the law of Christ." Galatians 6:2

Every handshake, every whispered prayer, every tear shed beside a bed.
Became an altar where Christ was present.
And though I entered those nursing homes as a minister,
I often left as the one who had been ministered to.

Reflection: The True Religion of the Cross

The cross is not only a symbol of salvation but also the pattern for our lives.
It reminds us that real ministry is sacrificial, that love costs something,
and that compassion is not a sermon but a lifestyle.

**"Let this mind be in you, which was also in Christ Jesus:
Who, being in the form of God… made Himself of no reputation,
and took upon Him the form of a servant." Philippians 2:5–7**

When we kneel beside the forgotten,
we kneel beside Christ Himself.
Every tear we wipe, every prayer we whisper,
Becomes a reflection of the heart of God.

And one day, when we stand before Him,
the Savior will say to those who loved the least of these:

**"Inasmuch as ye have done it unto one of the least of these My brethren,
ye have done it unto Me." Matthew 25:40**

A Closing Prayer

Lord, make me a vessel of Your compassion.
Teach me to see the lonely as You see them,
to touch the forgotten with Your love,
and to bring hope where despair has taken root.
Let every nursing home, hospital, and broken heart.
Become a sanctuary where Your presence abides.
For Yours is the Kingdom, and the power, and the glory
forever.
Amen.

The Man with the Gun

Yet there was another time when the danger was more
physical.
After finishing a food delivery, I was approached by a man
wearing a coat in the heat of summer.
He pulled a gun, pointed it at me, and demanded all my
money.

I told him the truth: *"All I have is a twenty-dollar bill."*
He snatched it angrily and shouted, **"You must have more than that!"**

Then his tone changed. His voice cracked.
He said, *"I just got out of prison. I don't even want to live anymore."*
I looked at him, unafraid, and said,
"You have every reason to live. God loves you. He sent His Son for you. He wants to forgive you and give you a new life."

He froze. His hand trembled.
Then, without saying another word, he turned and walked away.
Only later did I realize how close I had been to death and how near God had been to me.
It wasn't courage that saved me. It was grace.

**"Yea, though I walk through the valley of the shadow of death, I will fear no evil:
for Thou art with me; Thy rod and Thy staff they comfort me." Psalm 23:4**

Archie A Brother in Christ

And then there was **Archie**. I acknowledge him at the beginning of the book.
I met him one afternoon when he came into my office seeking a job.
He had a ponytail, a wrinkled shirt, and a restless look in his eyes.
During the interview, I told him, *"You're welcome to work here, but you'll need to dress better and you'll have to cut the ponytail."*

He left disappointed, and as soon as the door closed, conviction fell on me like a weight.
I realized I had judged by appearance, not by heart.
I had acted in the flesh — not in the Spirit.
That night I prayed, *"Lord, give me another chance to show Your grace."*

Two weeks later, Archie returned — clean-cut, neatly dressed, no ponytail, and humbled.
He looked me in the eye and said, **"I'm ready to work."**
I hired him on the spot.
During his two-week training, I learned that he was an alcoholic.
He reeked of alcohol most days, slurred his words, and struggled to function.
But God told me to keep showing grace.

Every day as we worked, I talked to him about faith — about the God who changed my life and could change his.
We prayed together, we talked about the cross, and before long, Archie accepted Jesus Christ as his Savior.
Not long after, we were baptized together — two broken men washed in the same grace.

Over time, Archie quit drinking.
We became best friends. We talked daily, and even started a podcast together.
He couldn't conquer every battle — cigarettes took a toll on his body.
He placed them on the altar once, trying to quit, but the withdrawal was too painful.
Eventually, the cigarettes claimed his life.

When he passed from a stroke, my heart broke, but then came the dream.
In that dream, Archie appeared to me smiling, radiant, alive.
He said, *"I'm still here. I never died."*

And I knew in my spirit what he meant; he was alive with God.

"Jesus said unto her, I am the resurrection, and the life:
he that believeth in Me, though he were dead, yet shall he live." — John 11:25

Archie's friendship changed me.
He taught me that ministry isn't about perfection — it's about persistence.
It's about loving people through their weaknesses, not around them.
Archie didn't just find Christ; Christ found him.
And through him, I learned again what it means to have a heart shaped by service.

Prayer for Courage, Compassion, and Friendship

Heavenly Father,
Thank You for every soul You've placed on my path
For the broken, the lost, the angry, and the afraid.
Thank you for the girl in the hospital, the woman in the nursing home,
The man with the gun, the husband filled with rage, and my brother Archie.

Each one reminds me that You are always near
In danger, in sorrow, and even in the quiet moments of regret.
You turn weakness into witness, fear into faith, and strangers into friends.

Lord, let Your Spirit continue to use my hands to feed,
my voice to comfort, and my life to testify that **the power of God is real**.
Bless the memory of Archie
my friend, my brother in Christ, my fellow traveler in grace.
Thank You for assuring me that he lives with You still,
Whole, healed, and free.

Let my ministry, **Livingstone's Spiritual House**,
Remain a place of refuge and revival,
A house built not by religion but by Your Spirit.

In Jesus' mighty and merciful name,
Amen.

When Obedience Divides but God Unites

Not all spiritual battles are fought in public.
Some take place in living rooms, around kitchen tables, or in the unseen chambers of the heart.
The war between faith and fear does not always shout; it often whispers.
And sometimes, the battlefield is our own home.

**"For we wrestle not against flesh and blood,
but against principalities, against powers,
against the rulers of the darkness of this world,
against spiritual wickedness in high places."
Ephesians 6:12**

The Kitchen Table Conversion

363

It was a quiet evening in our small cul-de-sac neighborhood when my neighbor, **Ray**, came to my door. He was trembling, his eyes heavy with guilt, his spirit crushed under the weight of sin.
Ray had worked for me for a while, and like **Archie** before him, he struggled with alcoholism.
But that night, he wasn't just a man battling a bottle; he was a soul searching for salvation.

He told me about his arrest for DWI, the car he'd wrecked, the jail cell he'd just left,
and the emptiness he carried home with him.
My heart broke for him.

I invited him to sit down at our **kitchen table**, a place that would soon become an altar.
My wife, Michelle, sat across from us, quiet at first, listening.
As Ray poured out his story, the atmosphere grew heavy, but not with despair.
It was as though the Holy Spirit had entered that little kitchen, waiting for a decision.

When Ray finished, I looked him in the eyes and asked,
"Ray, are you tired of living this way? Are you ready to try Jesus?"

He hesitated, then whispered, **"Yes."**

In that moment, heaven opened.
I reached for his hand and prayed the sinner's prayer with him,
Leading him to confess Christ as Lord and Savior.

**"That if thou shalt confess with thy mouth the Lord Jesus,
and shalt believe in thine heart that God hath raised Him from the dead,
thou shalt be saved." Romans 10:9**

As we prayed, tears streamed down Ray's face.
He wept with a depth that only true repentance can bring.
I felt the Holy Spirit's presence so strongly that I could hardly speak.
It was as if the entire room was glowing with grace.
Heaven rejoiced that night, and I rejoiced with it.

A Strange Withdrawal

But as I opened my eyes, I realized something unsettling.
My wife had quietly slipped out of the room.
I called her name softly, but there was no response.
When I looked down the hallway, I saw her peering out from behind the bedroom door—her face pale, her expression troubled.

It was a strange sight, almost chilling.
She wasn't angry—she was afraid.
Something about that moment, about the Spirit moving so powerfully in our home, seemed to disturb her deeply.
It was as though she had seen something unseen,
as though light had entered the room and darkness retreated from it.

"And the light shineth in darkness; and the darkness comprehended it not." John 1:5

I turned my focus back to Ray, who was still weeping and thanking God.
But in the back of my mind, a question burned:
Why would my wife leave the room when the presence of God was so strong?
That thought lingered long after Ray went home that night.

Ray's Redemption and My Wife's Rebellion

After that day, Ray began attending the same church my wife and I attended. The church embraced him wholeheartedly. The pastor, deeply moved by the testimony, welcomed him with open arms. I explained to the pastor what had happened at our kitchen table — how Ray had accepted Christ, how decisive the moment had been and the pastor rejoiced.

The church understood Ray's struggles and even helped him rebuild his life. Ray had lost his car in the accident and was struggling financially. The pastor and congregation gathered funds to help him get another vehicle. It was the church being the Church — living out Galatians 6:2:

"Bear ye one another's burdens and so fulfil the law of Christ." — Galatians 6:2

The congregation celebrated the miracle of a new soul coming to Christ.
But in my own home, the celebration turned to conflict.

My wife grew bitter. She mocked the church for helping Ray and accused the pastor of favoritism. Her words became harsh, her heart hardened. She resented others' joy, and anger began to consume her.

When Ray's baptism day arrived, the pastor invited me to attend as the man who had led him to Christ. But that morning, before I could leave, my wife confronted me in the kitchen. Her voice was sharp, her face filled with rage. She snarled,
"If you go to Ray's baptism, consider our marriage over."

I froze. Fear and confusion overtook me. I allowed her threat to silence my obedience to God.
That morning, I stayed home.

The following Sunday, I went to church alone. As I approached the building, Ray came out to meet me. His eyes were full of pain and disappointment.

He looked up at me and said, *"James, you of all people — the one who led me to Christ didn't come to my baptism."*

Those words pierced my heart like a blade. I apologized, but my spirit was crushed.

I knew I had failed not just Ray I had failed God.

As I stood there in the church walkway, the Holy Spirit convicted me. I had allowed fear to rule me. I had put my wife above God just as Adam once did with Eve.

The Battle Within the Marriage

Over time, my wife and I faced our own spiritual battles. I tried to lead our home in prayer and in the Word, but her heart was distant. There were moments of coldness that went beyond misunderstanding moments that felt spiritual in nature.

At one point, I confronted her about intimacy in our marriage. The Bible teaches that withholding love from a spouse opens the door for the enemy. Scripture says:

"Defraud ye not one the other, except it be with consent for a time, that ye may give yourselves to fasting and prayer; and come together again, that Satan tempt you not for your incontinency." 1 Corinthians 7:3-5

This verse makes it clear that intentionally withholding affection or intimacy from one's spouse is not just emotional neglect — it becomes a spiritual weapon of manipulation. Any time love is replaced with control, resentment, or withholding, it borders on the very rebellion that Scripture calls **witchcraft**:

"For rebellion is as the sin of witchcraft, and stubbornness is as iniquity and idolatry." 1 Samuel 15:23

When I showed her these passages with an open Bible, she threw it across the room and shouted, *"Get out of my room!"*
It wasn't anger I felt — it was sorrow. Because in that moment, I saw how hard the enemy works to divide what God has joined together.

Marriage was never meant to be a battlefield of control; it was meant to be a covenant of unity. When passion dies, so does connection. When prayer dies, so does peace. A marriage without spiritual intimacy will soon lose emotional and physical intimacy, too.

The Battle Within the Marriage: Lessons from the Song of Solomon

The first night after my marriage to Mitchell, my heart was full of spiritual intention.
Our honeymoon wasn't just meant to celebrate our union; it was meant to honor God.
I wanted our first evening together to reflect the beauty of Christ's love for His Church, and for us to begin our marriage centered on the Word.
So I opened my Bible to the **Song of Solomon**, that poetic masterpiece of love and intimacy, which has long been understood as both a celebration of marital affection and a symbolic image of the divine Bridegroom's love for His bride.

"Let him kiss me with the kisses of his mouth: for thy love is better than wine." Song of Solomon 1:2

To me, this passage was more than romantic poetry it was spiritual music.
It echoed Christ's desire for His Church: pure, passionate, and eternal.
Since my wife was my bride, I saw this connection as sacred I was the bridegroom, she the bride.
Just as Christ's love sanctifies His Church, I wanted our love to be sanctified in Him.

Yet, that night would become a lesson I would carry for years.

The Intellectual Divide

As I began reading aloud, I noticed her expression change.
The beauty that filled my heart wasn't being shared.
Where I felt reverence, she felt discomfort.
Where I saw spiritual imagery, she saw confusion.

It was at that moment I realized something vital
intellectual harmony in marriage matters.
Love cannot thrive where minds do not meet.
Faith can unite, but understanding sustains.

"Can two walk together, except they be agreed?"
Amos 3:3

I am, by nature, an eccentric person creative, symbolic, sometimes abstract.
To me, romance is as much **intellectual** as it is physical.
Conversation stimulates me; shared thought deepens attraction.
But that night, I was so caught up in my own meaning that I failed to meet her in hers.

When Solomon's words failed to resonate, I stopped reading and turned my attention to her.
I wanted her to feel loved, not lectured.

369

Still, something sacred in that moment had been lost and though I didn't know it then, **that fracture would widen over time.**

The Divine Blueprint of Marriage

The **Song of Solomon** celebrates the wholeness of love physical, emotional, and spiritual.
It builds upon the ancient design from **Genesis 2:24:**

"Therefore shall a man leave his father and his mother, And shall cleave unto his wife: And they shall be one flesh."

Marriage, in its purest form, is a trinity **God, man, and wife.**
Just as the Father, Son, and Holy Spirit exist in perfect unity, so should husband and wife under God's authority.
If that order is disrupted if the intellectual, spiritual, or emotional balance breaks the harmony falters.

Peter later called marriage *"the grace of life."*

"Likewise, ye husbands, dwell with them according to knowledge,
giving honour unto the wife, as unto the weaker vessel,
and as being heirs together of the grace of life." 1 Peter 3:7

Knowledge not dominance, not emotion sustains the grace of marriage.
It requires mutual understanding.
Looking back, I see that I had assumed we were equally yoked because we shared the same faith.
But spiritual yoking is more than shared belief it is shared depth.

It is an agreement not only in salvation but in the *interpretation* of love itself.

The Poetic Reflection of the Bride and Groom

The **Song of Solomon** opens with passion, but it also models partnership.
The Shulamite and Solomon speak to one another, praising rather than competing.
He says,

"Behold, thou art fair, my love; behold, thou art fair; thou hast doves' eyes." Song of Solomon 1:15

And she responds,

"Behold, thou art fair, my beloved, yea, pleasant: also our bed is green." Song of Solomon 1:16

The word *"our"* dominates this passage *our bed, our house, our rafters.*
It is not *mine* or *yours*, but *ours.*
That's the essence of harmony a shared pronoun.

In marriage, when *"our"* becomes *"I"*, unity begins to crumble.
Solomon revered his bride as both sister and spouse,

"Thou hast ravished my heart, my sister, my spouse." Song of Solomon 4:9
He honored her purity, comparing her to a garden enclosed a symbol of both sacredness and trust:
"A garden enclosed is my sister, my spouse; a spring shut up, a fountain sealed." Song of Solomon 4:12

That was the kind of love I longed to reflect on, holy, respectful, eternal.

371

But what I saw as spiritual poetry, she saw as strangeness. And where I expected intimacy to bloom from intellectual union, she withdrew.

The Morning After

The next morning, as sunlight poured through the balcony doors, she stood gazing toward the sea.
Her first words pierced the air like ice *"Annulment."*
It was as if the bond of marriage had vanished in a breath.
I was stunned.
In my heart, I knew that no marriage rooted in Christ could break so easily.
It felt as though **something spiritual had spoken through her** not reason, not love, but defiance.

"What therefore God hath joined together, let not man put asunder." Mark 10:9

In that moment, I recognized the deeper war at work not between husband and wife, but between the Spirit and the accuser.
Satan had sought to destroy what God had begun,
and he found an opening through emotional division and intellectual disconnect.

What began as a gesture of love reading Scripture became a spark of misunderstanding.
It wasn't her fault or mine alone; it was the enemy's design to divide what was meant to reflect divine unity.

"For where envying and strife is, there is confusion and every evil work." James 3:16

The Spiritual Lesson

That experience became a revelation.
Marriage is not sustained by passion alone it must be grounded in understanding.
It is not secured by emotion, but by shared revelation.
It is not merely a covenant of bodies, but of minds and spirits under God's order.

If we are not intellectually and spiritually yoked before marriage,
the weight of life will make the imbalance evident after.
This was my lesson: I had sought harmony, but I had mistaken belief for balance.

Still, even in failure, the Word of God stood true:
The **Song of Solomon** remains a reminder that marriage in its purest form
is a sacred song of devotion, written not for man's pleasure but for God's glory.

"Many waters cannot quench love, neither can the floods drown it." — Song of Solomon 8:7

Love that is born of God survives misunderstanding, surpasses intellect, and endures beyond wounds.
And though my marriage did not last, the spiritual revelation did:
Marriage mirrors the eternal union between Christ and His Bride.
a love that forgives, redeems, and never lets go.

Reflection and Prayer

Father,
You created marriage as a reflection of Your covenant with us.
Teach us to love not only in passion but in purpose
not only in emotion but in understanding.
Deliver every husband and wife from the spirit of division and accusation.
Let our homes echo the harmony of heaven.
And when misunderstanding comes, let Your Word be the bridge that unites.
In Jesus' name, **Amen.**

The Test of Obedience

Not long after, my grandmother suffered a massive stroke. One Sunday morning, my wife and I sat in church together, planning a rare romantic getaway to the mountains. But during the service, I heard the voice of God so clearly it startled me:

"Go see your grandmother today. This will be the last day she lives."

I turned to my wife and told her. She scoffed, angry and dismissive.
I pleaded gently, "We can go to the mountains after I visit her I just need to see her today."

She refused. The words that came out of her mouth that morning were sharp and full of bitterness.
But I knew what I had to do.

374

When I arrived at my grandmother's bedside, the Lord placed **John 14:2-4** in my heart:

"In my Father's house are many mansions: if it were not so, I would have told you.
I go to prepare a place for you. And if I go and prepare a place for you, I will come again and receive you to myself, so that where I am, there you may be also. And that where I go, you know, and the way you know—
John 14:2-4

I read it aloud to her. She smiled faintly, took my hand, and I felt the peace of Heaven fill that room. I knew she had received her final comfort.
The next day, she passed away.

If I had chosen to put my wife over God and obedience, I would have carried that guilt for the rest of my life. Instead, I took peace the peace that comes only when you obey the voice of God, even when it costs you something you love.

What God Taught Me Through It All

That season of my life taught me something vital:
When a marriage stops honoring God, it begins to dishonor itself.
When we stop praying together, we start drifting apart.
And when one spouse refuses to walk in the Spirit, the other must walk alone but never without Christ.

Obedience to God may cost you relationships, comfort, even companionship but it will never cost you His presence.

"But seek ye first the kingdom of God, and His righteousness; and all these things shall be added unto you." — Matthew 6:33
"What therefore God hath joined together, let not man put asunder." — Mark 10:9
"A threefold cord is not quickly broken." — Ecclesiastes 4:12

Even though that marriage ended, my faith did not.
God used the breaking to build me stronger.
He showed me that true love is not born out of convenience, but out of covenant.
And even when a covenant fails, God's promises never fail.

Prayer for Obedience and Spiritual Unity

Father God,
Thank You for teaching me that obedience to You must come before obedience to anyone else.
Please help me to walk in humility and truth, even when it brings separation.

Protect every marriage where the enemy is sowing division, coldness, or manipulation.

Remind husbands and wives that love is not control, that intimacy is sacred,
and that to withhold affection is to open a door for darkness.
Heal those wounds, Lord. Restore what rebellion has broken.

And when obedience to You costs us something dear,
give us peace that passes understanding
The kind of peace that comes from walking in Your will, no matter the cost.

In Jesus' name,
Amen.

The Adam Parallel — When Men Lose Spiritual Headship

I thought back to the garden.
God had walked with Adam, spoken to him directly, and given him dominion and instruction. Adam's relationship with God came **before** Eve was ever formed.

But when the serpent deceived Eve, Adam stood silent. He watched her take the forbidden fruit, and then he took it himself, not out of ignorance, but out of misplaced loyalty. Adam's sin was not eating the forbidden fruit; it was **putting Eve above God**.

"And Adam was not deceived, but the woman being deceived was in the transgression." — 1 Timothy 2:14

Eve's deception opened the door to sin, but Adam's disobedience opened the floodgates.
He was supposed to cover her to lead her away from the temptation, but instead, he followed her into it.

That's what I did. I put my wife's demands above God's command.
I allowed manipulation to replace leadership. I surrendered my spiritual authority to appease her emotions.
And in that moment, my home fell out of divine order.

"For the husband is the head of the wife, even as Christ is the head of the church:
and He is the savior of the body." — Ephesians 5:23

I learned that day that a man who refuses to lead his home spiritually allows confusion to reign.
God's order is clear: God first, then husband, then wife, then children.
When that order is broken, chaos enters.

The spirit of Jezebel thrives where the man of the house forfeits his authority in God.
That spirit doesn't wear horns or breathe fire; it operates through manipulation, pride, and rebellion against godly leadership.
It seeks to control, divide, and destroy the very structure God designed.

And like Adam, I had yielded to it.
But once I saw it for what it was, I repented.
I vowed never again to let fear silence obedience.

What God Taught Me Through It All

From Ray's redemption to my own repentance, God revealed something eternal:
A man's love for his wife must be profound, but his loyalty must always belong to God.
When a husband chooses God's voice over worldly peace, God restores order and covers the home with blessing.

"But as for me and my house, we will serve the Lord."
— Joshua 24:15
"Except the Lord build the house, they labour in vain that build it." — Psalm 127:1

Even though my obedience cost me that marriage, it saved my soul from compromise.
I learned that God must always remain first.
Because when you choose God, even what you lose becomes a seed for something eternal.

Prayer for Spiritual Order and Obedience

Heavenly Father,
Thank You for the lessons You've taught me through pain, failure, and redemption.
Thank You for showing me that obedience to You is greater than the approval of man or the comfort of peace.

Lord, restore divine order in every household that has fallen out of alignment.
Raise up men who will lead in humility, prayer, and love.
Remove the spirit of rebellion that seeks to destroy marriages and silence truth.
Give wives hearts that honor their husbands as they honor You,

and give husbands the courage to love their wives as Christ loved the Church with truth, sacrifice, and protection.

Help me always to remember that my first covenant is with You.
May I never again choose fear over faith, or flesh over Spirit.
Let my home, my heart, and my ministry always reflect Your order and Your love.

In Jesus' name,
Amen.

When Love Fails but Faith Remains

There are moments in life when love fails not because it wasn't real, but because it wasn't rooted in God.
A marriage can begin in affection and end in ashes when one heart walks in the Spirit and the other walks in the flesh.

When my first marriage fell apart, I grieved not just the loss of a companion, but the death of something sacred.
For a time, I asked God *why* He allowed the one I loved to turn against the very light we once shared.
But the Lord spoke to me through His Word, gently reminding me:

"If any man come to Me, and hate not his father, and mother, and wife, and children, and brethren, and sisters, yea, and his own life also, he cannot be My disciple." — Luke 14:26

This wasn't a command to stop loving others it was a call to love God *more.*
To make Him first in everything.
Because the love that survives eternity is not the love built on emotion, but the love built on obedience.

When I lost that marriage, I found my calling.
The silence of that house became the altar where I learned to listen to God again.
The heartbreak that could have destroyed me became the seed of my ministry.
And I realized: sometimes God allows something to break so something greater can be born.

"And we know that all things work together for good to them that love God,
to them who are the called according to His purpose."
— Romans 8:28

The Lord used that season to purify my faith.
He stripped away the comfort, the companionship, the illusion of control and what remained was Him.
When the dust settled, I was no longer the same man.
I was broken, but I was usable.
And in that brokenness, the anointing began to flow.

I found strength in prayer, purpose in pain, and power in His presence.
I realized that faith doesn't begin when everything is perfect it starts when everything falls apart.

"My grace is sufficient for thee: for My strength is made perfect in weakness." — 2 Corinthians 12:9

Every tear became oil for the lamp.
Every rejection became a revelation.
Every loss became a lesson.

God showed me that love without faith is fragile, but faith without love is dead.
And even when human love fails, divine love never does.

So I chose to forgive.
I chose to release.
I chose to walk forward in the ministry God gave me,
Livingstone's Spiritual House.
Because I now understand what it means to be a living stone,
Shaped by pressure, refined by fire, and built upon the Chief Cornerstone, Christ Himself.

**"To whom coming, as unto a living stone, disallowed indeed of men, but chosen of God, and precious…
Ye also, as lively stones, are built up a spiritual house." — 1 Peter 2:4–5**

I learned that obedience will sometimes cost you relationships,
but it will never cost you God's favor.
The hands that once wounded you will fade,
but the hand of the Lord will never let you go.

And when love fails, faith remains
Because faith is born not in comfort, but in surrender.
It's in the surrender that your purpose is revealed.
And in that purpose, the Kingdom advances.

Prayer for Healing and Renewal

Father in Heaven,
Thank You for turning my mourning into ministry,
for transforming heartbreak into holiness,
and for showing me that what I lost was never greater than what You were preparing.

Heal those who have walked through the fire of betrayal and loss.
Teach them that Your love never fails.
Help them forgive the ones who could not walk with them into their next season.
And remind them that the calling is greater than the comfort.

Make us faithful even when love fails,
steadfast even when others leave,
And strong enough to walk alone because we are never truly alone when You are with us.

Lord, let every broken home, every broken heart, and every broken promise.
Become a place where Your glory can dwell.
And let every reader who carries pain from a failed relationship.
find peace in Your presence and strength in Your promise.

In the name above all names
Jesus Christ,
Amen.

INTRODUCTORY BRIDGE — WHEN RELIGION CONDEMNS BUT JESUS RESTORES

The story of my second marriage is not just a personal testimony, it is a living illustration of the central message of *Religion Killed Jesus*. Religion takes accusation and turns it into condemnation. Religion hears a misunderstanding and rushes to judgment. Religion takes Scripture out of context and uses it as a weapon instead of a healing balm. That is precisely what happened during the collapse of my marriage. Instead of restoration, counsel, and forgiveness, the very things Jesus embodies, religion stepped in with legalism, suspicion, and finality. The spirit of religion always kills what Jesus came to save: relationships, mercy, unity, and hope.

But Jesus does the opposite. Jesus restores the broken. Jesus heals the insecure. Jesus stands between the accuser and the accused and says, **"Neither do I condemn thee—go and sin no more."** The same Christ who defended the woman caught in adultery would have urged forgiveness, grace, and reconciliation, not spiritual policing or weaponized Scripture. My experience shows how quickly good people can become instruments of the Accuser when they follow religion instead of the Holy Spirit. And it shows how Christ, even in our deepest failures, still teaches us, refines us, and redeems our story for His glory. My marriage testimony may be painful, but it is also proof that the voice of religion destroys, but the voice of Jesus restores.

When Trust Is Tested: Lessons from My Second Marriage

My second marriage was nothing like the first.
The first had been a war of rebellion, a clash between divine order and defiance.
The second began with tenderness, prayer, and the hope of peace.
She was not defiant like the first; she was loving, kind, and obedient to God's design for marriage.
But insecurity became the thief that entered through an unguarded door.

I loved her sincerely, and as Paul wrote,

"It is better to marry than to burn." 1 Corinthians 7:9

I believed that love and faithfulness would overcome any fear.
We courted briefly and chose to honor God by keeping ourselves pure until marriage.
She came from a Catholic background and was unfamiliar with ministry, but she followed my lead as I taught her to serve.
For a time, we worshiped together, prayed together, and I thought I had finally found peace.
But what I didn't see was how subtle insecurity can be when it's not surrendered to God.

The Test of Misunderstanding

Shortly before the wedding, I wrestled with unease, not knowing if it came from God or the enemy.
I prayed and fasted for clarity.
The feeling passed, and I chose faith over fear.
But after we married, that same uncertainty began to rise in both of us.
I was focused on finishing my degree and providing for our future.
She struggled with doubt, thinking I no longer desired her.

My heart still loved her, but I found myself weighed down by a strange heaviness.
A spiritual oppression that dulled my affection and stole my joy.
Unlike my first marriage, this time *I* became the one who withdrew.
What I had once suffered, I now inflicted.

It was a painful reminder that what we sow can return to us, and that even the obedient can stumble.

The Moment Everything Changed

During this difficult time, a message came from an old acquaintance, a woman I had known online years before, from Canada.
Our conversations were not physical; she only called to wish me a Happy Birthday, but it became a source of suspicion.
When my wife found the text, she was furious.
She struck me, we argued, and she left.
We later went to Christian counseling, but the counselor sided with her, saying my behavior was "adultery of the heart."

They cited the words of Jesus:

"Whosoever looketh on a woman to lust after her hath committed adultery with her already in his heart."
Matthew 5:28

If your right eye causes you to sin, pluck it out and cast it from you, for it is more profitable for you that one of your members perish, than for your whole body to be cast into hell. -Matthew 5:29

And if your right hand causes you to sin, cut it off and cast it from you; for it is more profitable for you that one of your members perish, than for your whole body to be cast into hell. Matthew 5:30

I explained that Christ used hyperbole, strong, graphic language to show how deadly sin can be if left unchecked.

He did not command literal self-mutilation, but repentance of the heart.
Even so, they refused to see nuance.
My attempt to reason with Scripture only hardened their stance.

I reminded them of what James wrote:

"Every man is tempted, when he is drawn away by his own lust, and enticed. Then when lust hath conceived, it bringeth forth sin." James 1:14 15

Temptation is not sin until it is conceived and acted upon.
But reason could not win a battle that was spiritual at its core.
The marriage that began in obedience ended in accusation.

The Moment Everything Changed: The Spirit of Accusation

Accusation has always been Satan's oldest weapon.
From the Garden to Gethsemane, the enemy has never ceased doing what **Revelation 12:10** calls him by name, *"the accuser of the brethren."*
He doesn't simply attack with violence; he attacks with whispers of guilt, condemnation, and doubt.
He knows how to twist truth into torment.
And in marriage, in ministry, in friendship, those whispers can divide what God has joined.

**"And I heard a loud voice saying in heaven,
Now is come salvation, and strength, and the kingdom of our God, and the power of His Christ:
for the accuser of our brethren is cast down,**

**Which accused them before our God Day and night."
— Revelation 12:10**

Accusation: Satan's Oldest Tactic

In the Book of **Job**, Satan appeared before God, not to tempt first, but to accuse.

"Doth Job fear God for nought?" Job 1:9
The devil sought to redefine Job's faith as hypocrisy, to turn righteousness into suspicion.
That same spirit still works today, twisting motives, poisoning perceptions, and turning love into distrust.

In **Zechariah 3:1**, we see the same pattern:

"And he shewed me Joshua the high priest standing before the angel of the Lord, and Satan standing at his right hand to resist him."
The Hebrew word for "resist" there means *to accuse, to oppose in court.*
Satan acts like a prosecutor but without mercy.
He builds a case from fragments of truth, removing context, exaggerating weaknesses, and presenting shame as evidence.

When my wife Tiffany found the message from that old acquaintance, the Accuser entered the room unseen, but very much present.
What began as a misunderstanding became spiritual warfare.
What was simply temptation became interpreted as betrayal.
What was confession became condemnation.

And just as he did in Eden, Satan did not shout; he whispered.
He whispered to my wife's heart: *"You've been*

deceived.”
He whispered to mine: *“You've been disqualified.”*
And between those whispers, he built a wall.

“For we are not ignorant of his devices.” 2 Corinthians **2:11**

When the Enemy Comes After You — Why Temptation Intensifies After Salvation

One of the first realities a believer must accept after coming to Christ is this: the enemy will come after you. Salvation awakens a spiritual war you may not have recognized before. Jesus Himself, who is entirely God, endured relentless temptation. But unlike us, He possessed extraordinary spiritual resilience. He was the Son of God, appointed from before the foundation of the world to be the Lamb without blemish, the perfect sacrifice for sin **(John 1:29; 1 Peter 1:19-20).** His divine assignment gave Him supernatural resolve, yet He still felt temptation through a real human body of flesh and bone **(Hebrews 4:15).**

We, on the other hand, are not the Son of God. We are human, flawed, and fragile. Scripture reminds us plainly: **“All have sinned and fall short of the glory of God.” — Romans 3:23**
Not one person reading this book, not your parents, not your grandparents, not your pastor, not even Billy Graham, lived a sinless life. Only Jesus walked in absolute perfection.

Because of this, when we fall, we should feel momentary conviction, but never prolonged condemnation. Conviction comes from the Holy Spirit. Condemnation comes from the enemy.

Once you ask God for forgiveness, lingering guilt is no longer from heaven but from hell.

Responding When You Fall Short

The very moment you recognize you've sinned, stop and pray. Do not continue with daily life without realigning your heart. Ask God to:

- **Reveal the root of what happened**

- **Strengthen you in your weakness**

- **Purify your motives and desires**

- **Keep His Spirit close so you won't fall again**

One scripture that has carried me through every failure is **Psalm 51**, a prayer David cried out after his darkest sin. I have memorized it because it lives in my heart:

**"Have mercy upon me, O God, according to Your lovingkindness;
According to the multitude of Your tender mercies, blot out my transgressions…" Psalm 51:1**

When I pray **Psalm 51**, **I *personalize it*.** I name the **specific sin**. I ask God for the strength not to return to it. This is not empty, vain repetition; it is targeted spiritual surgery. God desires sincerity, not generic prayers.

Rejecting the Enemy's Lies

After repentance, if guilt still tries to cling to you, understand this:
that guilt is not from God.
Satan wants you to feel unworthy, dirty, and disqualified. His goal is to convince you that God only loves "religious" people, or strong people, or perfect people.
That is a lie from the pit of hell.

Forgiveness is one of the most powerful forces in the Christian life, both giving and receiving it. When you call on God with a sincere heart, He forgives instantly. God does not shame you.
God restores you.
God equips you to try again.

You can create your own pattern of repentance, but mine always includes **Psalm 51**. In it, I confess specifics, ask for strength, and invite the Holy Spirit to transform me. This is how a believer stays aligned with God while walking in a human body that is prone to weakness.

Temptation will come. The enemy will attack. But forgiveness and restoration belong to God, and He gives them freely to all who call upon Him.

Twisting the Word to Wound

The enemy even uses Scripture to accuse.
When Jesus fasted in the wilderness, Satan quoted Psalm 91, twisting God's Word to provoke sin (**Matthew 4:6**).
In that same way, the verse in Matthew 5 about **"adultery in the heart"** was used against me, not for conviction, but for condemnation.

Jesus did not give that teaching to crush the repentant; He gave it to expose the self-righteous.
He used hyperbole to reveal how sin begins in the heart, not to arm religion with legalism.
But the Accuser knows how to turn revelation into regulation.
He knows how to weaponize holiness.

"The letter killeth, but the Spirit giveth life." 2 Corinthians 3:6

In that counseling room, I felt the weight of the letter cold, rigid, and final.
Every explanation I offered from Scripture about temptation versus sin, about the process described in **James 1:14-15**, was dismissed.
Reason could not penetrate what was already spiritually poisoned.
It wasn't my wife or even the counselor who stood against me, it was the spirit of accusation itself, hiding behind religion.

Accusation Versus Intercession

Where Satan accuses, **Christ intercedes.**
While the enemy points to our failures, Jesus points to His finished work.

"Who shall lay anything to the charge of God's elect? It is God that justifieth.
Who is he that condemneth? It is Christ that died, yea rather, that is risen again,
who is even at the right hand of God, who also maketh intercession for us." Romans 8:33-34

Satan wants believers to believe that failure is final, that grace has limits, that forgiveness ends where accusation begins.
But the blood of Jesus speaks a better word than the voice of condemnation.

"And they overcame him by the blood of the Lamb, and by the word of their testimony." Revelation 12:11

Even when my marriage fractured under suspicion, God was still teaching me that no accusation can stand against a repentant heart.
Religion may accuse, but redemption restores.
The accuser builds walls, the Redeemer opens doors.

The Psychology of Accusation

Accusation is not always loud; often it masquerades as discernment.
It disguises itself as moral superiority or "righteous anger."
But its fruit is always the same division, shame, and fear.

Jesus faced this spirit continually.
The Pharisees accused Him of breaking the Sabbath **(John 9:16).**
They accused Him of blasphemy **(John 10:33).**
They even accused Him of being demon-possessed **(Matthew 12:24).**
Yet in each instance, Jesus responded not with defense, but with truth and silence.

"He was oppressed, and He was afflicted, yet He opened not His mouth." Isaiah 53:7

The accuser demands reaction, but the Spirit demands stillness.
Because accusation feeds on energy, the more you defend yourself, the more it multiplies.
Only when we anchor ourselves in the righteousness of Christ do those arrows lose their power.

"No weapon that is formed against thee shall prosper; and every tongue that shall rise against thee in judgment thou shalt condemn." Isaiah 54:17

When Religion Blinds the Heart — The Spirit of Accusation and the Death of Grace

Religion has a way of blinding people, hardening their hearts, and turning sincere believers into gatekeepers of judgment rather than vessels of grace. I have seen this repeatedly, especially within the Catholic circles I knew growing up: friends, coworkers, an ex-wife, a mother-in-law, a father-in-law, and many others. Though each person was different, they all shared one tragic trait: **unforgiveness.**

Unforgiveness is one of Satan's greatest weapons. It paralyzes spiritual growth and distorts one's view of God. And in many religious environments, if your lifestyle does not conform to their traditions, you are instantly labeled: An outsider, a sinner, an outcast.

A Friendship Destroyed by Religion

I once worked with a skilled carpenter, and together we remodeled a home. From that project, we developed a genuine friendship. One evening, he invited me to dinner with his wife. They prayed over the meal, and everything felt peaceful. While enjoying the steak his wife had prepared, I asked for a glass of wine, because I enjoy wine with steak.

What happened next exposed the power of religious blindness.
My friend stood up, yelled at me, and ordered me out of his house, all because I asked for wine.

This was not the heart of Christ; this was the spirit of religion.

Jesus Himself turned water into wine at a wedding. Not to promote drunkenness, but to bring joy, celebration, and **hospitality. Yet here was a man who claimed to love Christ, unable to show basic hospitality or understanding.**

His wife calmed him down, and we finished the meal, but the friendship died that night, not because of sin, not because of alcohol, but because of religious judgment rooted in fear and pride.

Another Example: A Pastor Bound by Tradition

I once spoke with a pastor friend who was tending a grapevine. I asked if he planned to make wine from the grapes. Instead of answering, he condemned me instantly. He shouted**, "Alcohol has destroyed many lives, including my brother's!"**

I told him gently:
"It was not alcohol that destroyed your brother. It was the condition of his heart."

That statement enraged him, and he told me to leave his presence.

Even sincere, well-meaning pastors can be blinded by religion.

The Heart of Christ vs. The Heart of Religion

**Religion condemns. Christ restores.
Religion accuses. Christ intercedes.
Religion shames. Christ forgives.
Religion elevates the self. Christ elevates the broken.**

When someone takes the position of the accuser, they have stepped into the role of Satan himself. The Bible says:

"The accuser of our brethren… accuses them before God day and night."
Revelation 12:10

Satan accused Job before God, insisting Job wouldn't love God if his blessings were removed. That is what the spirit of accusation does: it questions motives, attacks character, and destroys relationships.

Why Religion Fails

Religion is dangerous when it:

- Distorts Scripture through man-made rules

- Replaces compassion with condemnation

- Elevates tradition over truth

- Produces pride instead of humility

- Creates outcasts instead of disciples

This is why Scripture commands us:

"Study to show yourself approved unto God…" 2 Timothy 2:15

Your faith must rest on God, not on a pastor, not on a friend, not on a church tradition.
Humans, even good people, are vulnerable to deception.

My carpenter friend was not evil.
My pastor neighbor was not evil.
They were blinded. Blinded by religion, not led by the Spirit of Christ.

What Christ Actually Demonstrates

Jesus ate with sinners.
Jesus sat at tables with the broken.
Jesus accepted invitations from tax collectors, outcasts, and people the religious elite despised.

He did this not to approve their sin, but to demonstrate:

- Love

- Grace

- Relationship

- Redemption

- Mercy

If Christ Himself was not afraid to sit among sinners, then surely we must question a religion that cannot even tolerate a question about wine.

The Truth You Must Hear

Religion can corrupt the heart if left unchecked.
It can twist righteous concern into judgment.
It can transform passion into pride.
It can turn believers into Pharisees without them ever realizing it.

And worst of all, religion can make you believe you are defending God while you are actually opposing His heart.

When Accusation Enters a Marriage

In marriage, accusation can become the greatest destroyer.
Satan does not need adultery or abuse to ruin a covenant; suspicion is enough.
He knows how to take half-truths and fill them with fear.
He uses miscommunication to sow distrust, and distrust to invite division.

"What therefore God hath joined together, let not man put asunder." Mark 10:9

That night, when anger replaced grace and misunderstanding replaced mercy,
the enemy rejoiced.
But God, even in that broken moment, began to teach me
that love without forgiveness cannot survive,
and forgiveness without humility cannot begin.

The marriage that started in obedience ended in accusation
but God used even that collapse to strengthen my discernment.
I learned to recognize the voice of the accuser,
And to silence it not by argument, but by the authority of Christ's blood.

"The Lord rebuke thee, O Satan; even the Lord that hath chosen Jerusalem rebuke thee." — Zechariah 3:2

Reflection: When Accusation Meets Grace

Satan accuses.
Christ advocates.
The difference between the two voices is eternal.

The accuser says, *"You are finished."*
The Advocate says, *"It is finished."*

And though accusation may destroy relationships,
it can never destroy redemption.
Because the cross silenced every charge that could ever
stand against a child of God.

**"Blotting out the handwriting of ordinances that was
against us,
Which was contrary to us, and took it out of the way,
nailing it to His cross." — Colossians 2:14**

The moment everything changed was not the day my
marriage fractured
it was the day I understood that my righteousness comes
not from defending myself,
But from being defended by the blood of Christ.

The Seeds of Division

As I reflected, I saw how the enemy had worked again, not
through rebellion this time, but through fear, doubt, and
misunderstanding.
Tiffany's mother, still rooted in Catholic tradition, opposed

much of what I taught.
We debated about Scripture, about truth, about idols and mediators,
and I realized too late that our union had never been fully *yoked* in faith.

"Be ye not unequally yoked together with unbelievers: for what fellowship hath righteousness with unrighteousness?" 2 Corinthians 6:14

Even though my wife claimed faith in Christ, her heart was still divided by family influence and insecurity.
Her mother's counsel often contradicted Scripture,
and as the serpent whispered to Eve, so the enemy whispered into our home through half-truths and wounded pride.

Eventually, Tiffany left me.
And just like the first time, I found myself alone with God.
But this time I did not feel shame, only sorrow, and the steady conviction that the Lord was still refining me.

A TESTIMONY OF ACCUSATION, MINISTRY, AND A MARRIAGE UNDER ATTACK

There was a season in my life when I experienced firsthand how accusation can enter a marriage with the force of a storm and unravel something God intended to use powerfully. This was during my second marriage, with my wife Tiffany, a woman gifted, anointed, and compassionate. Together, we carried a ministry that touched heaven and moved hearts.

Once a week, Tiffany and I visited a retirement home to minister to the elderly.
Her spiritual gift was singing, pure, beautiful, and anointed. Her voice resonated like healing, and I watched tears fall from many as the presence of God filled the room. My own gift of exhortation complemented hers. After she sang, I prayed, encouraged, and spoke life over each person.

It was a powerful combination.
A faithful marriage ministry.
A union that carried the power of Christ.

I believe Satan recognized the spiritual potential in our partnership.
He knew the impact we could make if our gifts continued to operate in unity. For Scripture says one can chase a thousand, but two can put ten thousand to flight (**Deuteronomy 32:30**). And married couples who minister together often carry a special grace a synergy a divine harmony that is difficult for the enemy to withstand.

But Satan found an entry point.
He planted a seed of doubt in Tiffany's mind, a whisper of suspicion that opened the door to accusation.

One moment.
One whisper.
One seed.

Accusation entered our marriage.

I acknowledge my part: I engaged in a conversation I should not have entertained while married. I told her I was married, and the conversation started with her wishing me a happy birthday. I had no intention of pursuing anything. I never cheated, emotionally or physically. I never planned on visiting her, especially not in another country. But the conversation itself was unwise.

Yet the consequence of it was far greater than the action. Tiffany interpreted the message as an act of adultery, and the enemy used that moment to deepen the insecurity already in her heart. Satan often attacks the place where we are weakest, and when he finds insecurity, he amplifies the accusation.

It was technically wrong for me to converse with someone else in that way — but it did not merit the destruction of a marriage.

I asked God for forgiveness.
I asked Tiffany for forgiveness.

And I believe God would have loved to see forgiveness extended, because forgiveness breaks curses, heals wounds, and restores destinies.

Our ministry together was short, but it was anointed.
I still remember the power of God in those services, the tears, the joy, the healing, and the unity. I believed then, and still think now, that if we had continued ministering together, we could have brought hundreds, if not thousands, to Christ. The enemy knew that.

And so he targeted our marriage.

Not because of our weaknesses,
but because of our **calling**.

He attacked us not because of who we were,
but because of who we could have become.

Tiffany is still a woman I cherish deeply.
She has a tender soul, a beautiful voice, and a kind spirit.

And though our marriage fell under spiritual attack, the love and respect I hold for her remain.

I also acknowledge my own shortcomings, seasons of doubt, vulnerability, and oppression that clouded my thinking. None of these justified divorce, and none of these diminished the calling God placed on our lives as a couple.

If one day God ever chooses to bring restoration, and forgiveness ever finds its way back into her heart, I would welcome it. Because what Satan steals, God can restore. What the enemy tears apart, God can rebuild.

But I release the outcome to Him.
Only God knows the future of that story.

What I do know is this:
Accusation destroys.
Forgiveness restores.
And unity in marriage is one of the most powerful tools in the Kingdom of God.

What the Lord Revealed

Through prayer and fasting, God showed me three truths:

1. **Love must be anchored in truth, not emotion.**
   A marriage built on affection but not shared faith will drift like a ship without a rudder.

"Except the Lord build the house, they labor in vain that build it." Psalm 127:1

2. **Temptation is not defeated until it's taken captive.**
   Even righteous men face thoughts that must be brought under Christ's authority.

"Casting down imaginations, and every high thing that exalteth itself against the knowledge of God, and bringing into captivity every thought to the obedience of Christ." 2 Corinthians 10:5

3. **Forgiveness is the doorway to freedom.**
   No one wins by proving who was right. Victory comes when we release bitterness.

**"Be ye kind one to another, tenderhearted, forgiving one another,
even as God for Christ's sake hath forgiven you." — Ephesians 4:32**

When Two Marriages End but Faith Endures

Both my first and second marriages ended the same way, not because God failed me,
but because the enemy sought to destroy what God was building in me.

Each battle taught me something different:
The first is about authority; the second, about humility.

And together they taught me that marriage is not the highest calling, obedience is.

I now understand why Paul said:

"He that is unmarried careth for the things that belong to the Lord, how he may please the Lord." — 1 Corinthians 7:32

I once prayed for a partner to share ministry with; now I thank God for teaching me how to stand alone if I must.

Because sometimes God removes what you think you need so you can become what He called you to be.

Prayer for Wisdom and Restoration

Father God,

Thank you for teaching me through both loss and love. Thank You for showing me that no failure is wasted when it brings me closer to You.

Forgive me where I faltered in discernment, where fear clouded my hearing,
And where my need for companionship overshadowed my need for Your counsel.

Lord, heal the hearts of those who have faced divorce or betrayal.
Remind them that you still have purpose beyond pain.

Give them wisdom to discern Your voice from the voice of the enemy,
And strength to walk in purity and patience as they wait upon You.

Let Your Spirit cover every marriage under attack.
Let every believer remember that obedience is love,
and love without obedience cannot stand.

In Jesus' mighty name,
Amen.

When Forgiveness Is Refused

When the misunderstanding with the woman from Canada surfaced, it became the breaking point.

I tried to explain that no affair had taken place, that my heart had not wandered, that I had been careless but not unfaithful.

Still, anger filled the air. My wife struck me in her rage, left the home, and later returned with a counselor.

In that session, I tried to bring Scripture into the light.

I stated, **"Assuming, for the sake of argument, that I had committed a transgression." Let's say I did what you accuse me of. Even then, forgiveness must still be the foundation of love."**

King David committed adultery with Bathsheba. He fell. But when Nathan the prophet confronted him, David repented, and God forgave him.

"Then David said to Nathan, 'I have sinned against the Lord.'
And Nathan said to David, 'The Lord also hath put away thy sin; thou shalt not die.'" — 2 Samuel 12:13

Forgiveness doesn't excuse sin, it redeems it.
It takes the ashes of failure and gives them to the Potter to shape again.

Jesus made forgiveness the cornerstone of His teaching:

"For if ye forgive men their trespasses, your heavenly Father will also forgive you:
But if ye forgive not men their trespasses, neither will your Father forgive your trespasses." Matthew 6:14–15

Forgiveness is not a choice; it's a command.

Even in marriage, especially in marriage, forgiveness is sacred.

How can we claim to love God, whom we have not seen, if we cannot forgive our spouse, whom we have?

"Beloved, let us love one another: for love is of God." 1 John 4:7

Had she chosen to forgive, our marriage might have been restored.

So many marriages have survived betrayal, even infidelity, through the power of grace.

But the world teaches retaliation; the Word teaches reconciliation.

"God hates divorce." — Malachi 2:16
"Above all things have fervent charity among yourselves: for charity shall cover the multitude of sins." — 1 Peter 4:8

When a husband or wife stumbles and repents, the heart of Christ calls for restoration, not rejection.

Forgiveness can heal adultery. Grace can rebuild trust. It is the very heartbeat of God's covenant love.

The Moment Everything Changed: When Satan Attacks Through Accusation

Accusation has always been one of Satan's sharpest weapons.
From Eden to the early Church, he has used suspicion, misunderstanding, and half-truths to divide what God unites.

Scripture calls him "the accuser of the brethren" (**Revelation 12:10**), and his method has never changed; he twists truth just enough to turn believers against each other, especially those who are effective in ministry.

The enemy knows that if he can divide the home, he can derail the mission.
He knows that if he can plant doubt between husband and wife, he can stop the prayers that move heaven.

**"If two of you shall agree on earth as touching any thing that they shall ask,
it shall be done for them of my Father which is in heaven." Matthew 18:19**

That agreement, the unity of faith, is what he fears most.

A Marriage Built on Ministry

Before the accusations, before the counseling sessions, Tiffany and I had a beautiful ministry together through **Living Stones Spiritual House**.
At first, she was reluctant, shy, and unsure if she could speak or sing in front of others.
I remember vividly our first day driving to a local retirement home for a service.
She was so nervous that her hands trembled like leaves in a storm.

I reassured her, praying as we drove:

"God has not given us the spirit of fear, but of power, and of love, and of a sound mind." 2 Timothy 1:7

When we arrived, something divine happened.
The Holy Spirit took hold of that moment.
Her voice, soft and trembling at first, grew into a melody that filled the entire room.

She sang hymns of hope and grace. Her voice was pure, angelic, anointed.

I had experience in public performance from my entertainment days, Elvis tributes, and community events. but this was different.
This wasn't entertainment; it was an encounter with God.

While she sang, I moved among the people, many of them elderly residents, gathered in what felt like a grand hotel lobby, with chairs lined in rows and faces full of expectation.
I prayed over them, laid hands on them, and spoke words of encouragement.
I felt my gift of exhortation come alive.
We watched the Spirit move tangibly, people weeping, raising their hands, some rededicating their lives to Christ, others accepting Him for the first time.

**"Is any sick among you? Let him call for the elders of the church, and let them pray over him,
anointing him with oil in the name of the Lord." James 5:14**

For months, we served faithfully together in harmony.
Our ministry grew stronger each week.
Together, we prayed for healing, comfort, and salvation for those the world had forgotten.
The devil took notice.
Satan cannot stand when a couple moves in spiritual agreement, because a unified marriage reflects Christ and the Church.

"A threefold cord is not quickly broken." Ecclesiastes 4:12

The Strategy of the Enemy

Looking back now, I see what was really happening.

Satan targeted our marriage because of our ministry.
He saw the souls being saved, the hearts being healed,
and the light we carried into dark places.

He knew he couldn't destroy us through simple temptation,
so he used accusation.
He had to break the marriage to break the ministry.

He began subtly, whispering lies into my wife's heart,
sowing seeds of fear and suspicion.

When the text message from an old acquaintance
surfaced, he seized the opportunity.
The moment was human, but the warfare behind it was
spiritual.

**"Be sober, be vigilant; because your adversary the
devil, as a roaring lion, walketh about,
seeking whom he may devour." 1 Peter 5:8**

Our marriage, once full of prayer and praise, became
clouded by doubt and distrust.

The same enemy who once tempted Eve with **"Did God
really say?"**
now whispered to my wife, **"Did he really mean it?"**

He used emotion to twist perception.
He used shame to turn love into suspicion.
He used Scripture itself to justify separation.

Just as he quoted **Psalm 91** to Jesus in the wilderness
(Matthew 4:6),
Satan quoted truth out of context to turn hearts away from
each other.

He took Jesus' words in **Matthew 5:28**

410

"Whosoever looketh on a woman to lust after her hath committed adultery with her already in his heart."

and twisted them into condemnation.

The counselor and my wife, both sincere but spiritually deceived, stood on the side of accusation rather than intercession.

Accusation Always Seeks to Divide

Accusation is Satan's counterfeit of conviction.

Conviction draws us closer to God; accusation drives us further from Him and from each other.

Conviction says, **"Repent and be restored."**
Accusation says, **"You are condemned and beyond repair."**

"There is therefore now no condemnation to them which are in Christ Jesus." Romans 8:1

The enemy knows that when two people pray together, heaven listens.
but when they accuse one another, hell celebrates.

He has always used this strategy:

- In the garden, he divided Adam and Eve.

- In Job's story, he accused Job before God.

- In Zechariah 3, he accused the high priest Joshua.

- In Revelation 12, he accuses the brethren "day and night."

He accuses, isolates to weaken, and weakens to destroy.

Our marriage fell into that pattern.

What began as a partnership in purpose turned into spiritual warfare behind closed doors.

We both loved God, but one of us listened to His Spirit, and the other listened to lies.

The enemy had succeeded, for a time, in dividing what God had ordained.

When Satan Breaks, God Rebuilds

Even after the separation, I could see clearly what had happened.

Satan had attacked not just a relationship but a calling. He couldn't silence the ministry outright, so he silenced it through strife.

But God reminded me that even when the accuser wins a battle, he never wins the war.

"And the God of peace shall bruise Satan under your feet shortly." Romans 16:20

The souls saved through our ministry remain eternal fruit. The prayers we prayed together were not wasted; they are memorials before God.

The devil broke the vessel, but he could not erase the oil that was poured out.

Now I understand why Jesus told Peter,

**"Simon, Simon, behold, Satan hath desired to have you, that he may sift you as wheat:
But I have prayed for thee, that thy faith fail not." Luke 22:31–32**

Satan may sift, but Christ sustains.

What was lost in division can still be redeemed in destiny.

The same God who allowed the storm will use it to strengthen the survivor.

Reflection: When the Accuser Comes

Accusation will always come where anointing flows.

The enemy fears nothing more than a marriage in which the couple ministers together, because such unity mirrors Christ and His Bride, the Church.

So when accusation rises, we must remember who stands behind them.

"The thief cometh not, but for to steal, and to kill, and to destroy." John 10:10

He steals peace, kills unity, and destroys trust.

But Christ came that we "might have life, and have it more abundantly."

Every attack on our marriage became an education in spiritual warfare.
Every tear became a seed of discernment.

And though the accuser sought to destroy, God used it to deepen my understanding of grace and truth.

Marriage A Covenant Before God, Not the State

One of the deeper conflicts in that relationship was over the meaning of marriage itself.

We had exchanged vows before witnesses, before God, but we had not yet registered our marriage with the state.

Her mother and family saw this as illegitimate.

But I explained to them that marriage is not defined by paperwork, but by covenant.

**"Therefore shall a man leave his father and his mother and shall cleave unto his wife:
and they shall be one flesh." Genesis 2:24**

Marriage was God's creation long before governments existed.

The state did not begin regulating marriage until the 19th century.
but from the beginning, God ordained it as a sacred bond witnessed by heaven itself.

Jesus reaffirmed this in Matthew 19:6:

"Wherefore they are no more twain, but one flesh. What therefore God hath joined together, let not man put asunder." Matthew 19:6

The marriage covenant belongs to God, not Caesar.
A license may record it, but only God can sanctify it.

That truth became another source of division between my wife, her mother, and me.
They valued man's approval over God's ordinance.

This showed that she and her family placed greater trust in the Certificate of Marriage than in God's trinitarian marriage covenant. Essentially, they valued the state's marriage certificate above their faith in God, making it a revealing test of their beliefs.

But the Lord reminded me that my vows to Him were greater than any signature on paper.

Lessons Learned

Looking back, I realize that both of my marriages revealed different aspects of my spiritual growth:

- The first taught me to lead.
- The second taught me to forgive even when forgiveness was not returned.

Forgiveness is not about keeping a relationship; it's about keeping your soul free.

Even Jesus, betrayed by His closest friends, still said,

"Father, forgive them; for they know not what they do." Luke 23:34

And in every heartbreak, God has drawn me closer to Him, shaping me, refining me, preparing me for the ministry He called me to.

Because obedience, humility, and forgiveness are not separate virtues, they are one.
And they are the only soil where love can grow.

Prayer for Forgiveness and Covenant Restoration

Heavenly Father,

Thank you for showing me that forgiveness is the key that unlocks every prison.
Thank You for teaching me that marriage is defined by Your covenant, not by man's contract.

Lord, teach every husband and wife to forgive as You forgive.

Where there has been betrayal, bring repentance.
Where there has been anger, bring understanding.
Where there has been separation, bring peace.

Remind us that love keeps no record of wrongs,
That grace covers sin,
and that mercy rebuilds what pride destroys.

May every couple who reads this remember that what You
have joined, no man can divide
not anger, not fear, not the voice of the enemy.

You alone are the center of every covenant.

In Jesus' name,
Amen.

The Power of Forgiveness and the True Covenant of Marriage

As I spoke to Tiffany and the psychologist, I made one final appeal, an appeal not of defense, but of truth.

I said to them both, **"Let's just say, hypothetically, I did sin. Let's say I had done what you believe. Would forgiveness not still be the command of Christ?"**

That question hung heavy in the room. Because forgiveness is not based on whether a person deserves it, it's based on obedience to God.

**"For if ye forgive men their trespasses, your heavenly Father will also forgive you:
But if ye forgive not men their trespasses, neither will your Father forgive your trespasses." Matthew 6:14–15**

Jesus didn't make forgiveness optional. He made it foundational.

Even in the deepest wounds of marriage, even in betrayal, God calls for forgiveness first, not retaliation.

I told them that even King David, anointed by God, fell when he looked upon Bathsheba and took her to himself. His sin cost him dearly.

Yet when David repented, the Lord forgave him.

**"Then David said unto Nathan, I have sinned against the Lord.
And Nathan said unto David, The Lord also hath put away thy sin; thou shalt not die." 2 Samuel 12:13**

David's sin brought consequence, yes, but not condemnation.
And that same grace still flows to this very day.

God's mercy never justifies sin, but it redeems the sinner who repents.

That was the truth I wanted my wife to see: that even if I had fallen, grace was still greater than failure.

But forgiveness was something she could not extend. Her heart hardened, and with time, distance grew.

In marriage, forgiveness is not a luxury; it's a lifeline.

It is the very essence of the covenant we make when we stand before God and vow "for better or for worse."

Because love without forgiveness will not endure, and forgiveness without love cannot heal.

"Above all things have fervent charity among yourselves: for charity shall cover the multitude of sins." — 1 Peter 4:8

When the World Defines What God Ordained

Another trial in that marriage stemmed from a misunderstanding of what truly makes a union sacred.

My wife and her mother accused me of not being truly married because we hadn't yet registered our marriage with the state.

I explained that in God's eyes, marriage is not defined by a government office or a document; it is characterized by a covenant made before Him.

"Therefore shall a man leave his father and his mother, and shall cleave unto his wife: and they shall be one flesh." Genesis 2:24

That Scripture alone establishes God's divine order.

Marriage is not man-made; it is heaven-ordained.

The state did not begin to regulate marriage until centuries after God instituted it.
When two people make vows before God, witnessed by others, that bond becomes sacred.

The state can record it, but only God can recognize and sanctify it.

"What therefore God hath joined together, let not man put asunder." — Matthew 19:6

I told my wife and her family, **"Our marriage is not bound by ink and seal, but by Spirit and covenant."**

But the world no longer sees it that way.

We live in a time when legality matters more than loyalty, and paperwork outweighs promise.

Forgiveness Is the Heartbeat of Covenant

If marriages are to survive, whether through conflict, misunderstanding, or even betrayal, forgiveness must remain at the center.

The refusal to forgive is what turns love cold and gives Satan his foothold.

"Neither give place to the devil." Ephesians 4:27

Forgiveness is not forgetting what happened; it's remembering that God is bigger than what happened.

Even when a partner has sinned, genuine repentance can mend what sin has marred.

I told the psychologist and my wife, **"There are countless marriages that have endured adultery, and through forgiveness, those marriages became stronger than before."**

Because forgiveness is not weakness, it is spiritual warfare.

It breaks curses, heals wounds, and closes the door to bitterness.

**"Be ye kind one to another, tenderhearted, forgiving one another,
even as God for Christ's sake hath forgiven you."
Ephesians 4:32**

My wife couldn't understand that at the time.
To her, forgiveness looked like surrender.

But to God, forgiveness is victory because it makes room for restoration.

Reflection: The Lesson of Grace

Looking back, I know the Lord allowed me to walk through that second marriage not to break me, but to teach me how deeply His grace runs.

He wanted me to see that love without forgiveness cannot reflect Christ, because Christ Himself **is** forgiveness.

Even though that marriage ended, I hold no bitterness.

I pray for her often, because I know she, too, was under spiritual attack the same way Satan came against Adam and Eve, the same way he comes against every marriage rooted in the truth.

Forgiveness was the lesson God wrote on my heart through her.

And if this book reaches even one person standing on the edge of divorce,
I pray they hear this: **choose forgiveness first.**

Because God hates divorce, but He blesses those who forgive.

He rebuilds what others throw away.
And He turns every wound into wisdom for those who trust Him.

The first Marriage Adam and Eve

Adam's Accountability Was Greater — Not Equal to Eve's

Scripture makes it unmistakably clear that **humanity fell through Adam**, not Eve. Though Eve ate first, God never placed the weight of original sin on her shoulders. The responsibility lies squarely with Adam, not Eve; it was Adam **who stood in a covenant relationship with God before she was created.**

Adam walked with God *personally.*
Adam received the command directly from the Lord **(Genesis 2:16–17).**
Adam was given authority, dominion, and responsibility over the garden, over creation, and ultimately over his household.

When Eve sinned, she disobeyed.
When **Adam** sinned, creation fell.

That distinction matters.

The Bible does *not* say we inherited the sin of Eve. It says:

"By one man sin entered into the world, and death by sin."
Romans 5:12

Paul doesn't say **"by one *woman*."**
He doesn't say **"by the couple."**
He says **by one man**.

Why?
Because God held **Adam** responsible as the covenant head.

Adam Failed to Cover His Wife

The modern Church often teaches that Adam and Eve were "equal culprits," but Scripture shows something different. In marriage, the husband is charged with covering, **guarding**, and **leading** his wife spiritually. Even Peter reflects this order:

"The husband is the head of the wife."
— 1 Corinthians 11:3

"Husbands, love your wives as Christ loved the Church, and gave Himself for her."
— Ephesians 5:25

Headship is not superiority — it is **responsibility**.

So when Eve was deceived, she sinned, but the **greater accountability** fell on Adam because he:

- Received the command directly

- Was not deceived

- Was entrusted with covering his wife

- Chose to follow her rebellion instead of leading in obedience

Paul states clearly:

"Adam was not deceived, but the woman being deceived was in the transgression."
1 Timothy 2:14

Eve was deceived.
Adam made a willful choice.

That is why **God calls out Adam first (Genesis 3:9).**

That is why **sin nature flows through Adam**, not Eve.

That is why **the whole creation fell under his disobedience**, not hers.

The Weight of Responsibility Falls on the Husband

In a biblical marriage, both husband and wife are responsible for their actions, but when it comes to divine accountability, **God holds the husband answerable first**. Eve sinned, yes, but Adam failed in his God-given duty to *cover, protect, instruct, and lead*.

This doesn't remove Eve's guilt, but it does place **the heavier burden** where God placed it:
On the man whom He formed first and entrusted with covenant headship.

Equal Guilt Theology

Many modern preachers teach that Adam and Eve share equal blame for humanity's fall. This view claims:

- Both sinned, therefore both carry equal responsibility.

- Eve's deception is treated as equal to Adam's disobedience.

- The Fall is viewed as a "joint failure," implying symmetrical accountability.

The Problem:
This perspective ignores the biblical order of responsibility. It treats marriage as a partnership without hierarchy, disregarding that God held Adam accountable *first* and *primarily*. Scripture never says humanity fell through Eve's sin.

Federal Headship (Biblical View)

Federal Headship teaches that God appointed Adam as the covenant representative of the human race. This means:

- Adam received God's command directly (**Gen. 2:16–17**).

- Adam was responsible for protecting, covering, and instructing Eve.

- Adam was not deceived; his sin was willful **(1 Tim. 2:14)**.

- Sin entered the world through *one man*, not through the couple **(Rom. 5:12)**.

- God called for **Adam** first after the Fall **(Gen. 3:9)**.

Key Truth:
Eve sinned first, but Adam's rebellion caused the Fall because Adam was the head of humanity, the covenant keeper, and the one God held responsible.

Why This Matters Today

Misunderstanding headship leads to:

- Weak men who abdicate spiritual responsibility

- Marriages where no one leads, or the woman leads, in this case, the man has surrendered his authority granted to him by God to his wife. Which is doom in the making.

- Churches that preach equality of blame but not equality of accountability

- A culture that rejects God's divine order

Federal Headship restores the biblical truth:
The man bears the weight of spiritual covering in the home.

Prophetic Commentary: Responsibility, Accountability, and the Weight of Covering

Man must cover his wife.
This is not cultural, it is a divine order.
God established a structure from the beginning:

God → Man → Woman → Child

Not in value.
Not in worth.
But in *responsibility*.

Because of this design, **the man carries the greater accountability in the household**. He is the covering, the priest, the watchman, and the spiritual guard of his marriage. When he fails to cover, the door opens. When he stays silent, the enemy speaks. When he hides, confusion enters the home.

Where I Was Wrong and Where I Was Not

Regarding my second marriage to Tiffany, I will speak plainly.

Did I handle the phone call wisely?
No.

Did I sin spiritually?
No, I do not believe I did.

From a *religious perspective*, people will label anything as sin if it violates their personal codes. Religion will condemn a man over appearances, assumptions, or misunderstandings.

But Jesus looks at the *heart*, not the optics.

This situation was no different from the Pharisees trying to accuse Jesus of sin when there was none.
Religion threw stones.
Christ extended truth and grace.

So yes, my wife felt betrayed.
Yes, she believed I committed adultery because of a phone call.
But this accusation aligns more with **Pharisaical judgment** than with the heart of Christ.

Christ does not condemn for appearances.
Christ examines intent, integrity, and truth.

Where I Take Responsibility

I fully recognize the area where *I failed*:

I should have told her.

Not because the call was sinful,
not because the interaction was inappropriate,
but because **transparency protects trust**.

If I had simply said:

"Honey, a woman I used to know from Canada called and wished me a happy birthday."

That would have cut the enemy off at the knees.
It would have proven that I was not hiding anything.

It would have covered my wife with communication, clarity, and leadership.

As the famous cliché goes, **"I should have nipped it in the bud."** This would have killed the accusation.

My mistake was not informing her.
The mistake was silence.
The mistake was hesitation.

That is where Adam fell.
And that is where I fell.

But Does That Justify the Destruction of a Marriage?

No.
I do not agree, and I do not believe Christ agrees, that this mistake should have cost me my marriage.

Religion would condemn a man for this.
Christ would correct a man, not crucify him for it.

Religion excommunicates.
Christ restores.
Religion kills.
Christ gives life.

There is a vast difference.

What I Leave in God's Hands

Whether God opens Tiffany's eyes, that is His work, not mine.
I release that to Him.

But what I do know is this:

427

- I will not condemn myself.

- I will not live under false guilt.

- I will learn from what happened.

- I will never repeat the same mistake.

If I marry again, and a similar situation happens, I'll say:

**"Honey, a female acquaintance reached out to wish me
a happy birthday
and I'm telling you immediately."**

Not because it's a sin
but because it is wisdom.

Not because I fear accusation
but because **covering begins with communication.**

Prophetic Truth Moving Forward

This was not a **sin** issue.
It was a **sense** issue.
A **common-sense issue** that I overlooked.

But I learned.

And I will not walk blind into the same trap again.

This is the power of repentance:
not self-condemnation,
but **correction, growth, and transformation.**

**Hindsight is 20/20.
But wisdom is using hindsight to change future
decisions.**

And that, I will carry into every relationship from this day forward.

Prophetic Commentary: Trust, Forgiveness, and the Real Meaning of Adultery

Was she wrong to snoop on my phone?

Yes, in the Word of God, trust is not optional in a marriage. If a husband and wife do not trust one another, the foundation of the covenant is already fractured.

Spying, snooping, and secret investigations are symptoms of more profound insecurity and broken trust. Just as I should have been transparent, **she should have trusted**.

And because both sides committed an error, those two failures **cancel each other out**.
The only matter left to judge is the **accusation of adultery**.

Did a text message equal adultery?

Some religious circles accuse anything *emotional* or *innocent* of being adultery, but Jesus' words in Matthew were **hyperbole**, not literal commands to gouge out eyes or cut off hands.

**"If your right eye causes you to sin, pluck it out…"
(Matthew 5:29)
"If your right hand causes you to sin, cut it off…"
(Matthew 5:30)**

Jesus was emphasizing the *severity* of sin, not giving physical instructions.

So if someone interprets His words **literally**, then yes, even a phone call or a text could be labeled as adultery.

But that interpretation falls apart because Jesus clearly used exaggeration to make a point.

He was not commanding mutilation. He was calling for discipline and purity of heart.

By that standard, the text message was **not adultery** in Christ's eyes.

Moses and Divorce: What Does It Really Mean?

When Moses permitted divorce, it was not because God endorsed it.
It was because people were **hard-hearted and demanded it**.

Moses allowed divorce **because they pressured him**, just as God sometimes "gives people over" to their own desires **(Romans 1:24).**

But God's heart has never changed:

"I hate divorce."
— Malachi 2:16

God hates divorce, not because He hates divorced people
But divorce breaks the covenant, wounds souls, and destroys families.

Forgiveness is the heart of God.
Forgiveness is the center of Christianity.
Forgiveness is why Christ died.

So the real question becomes:

Was there repentance?
Was there humility?
Was there a contrite spirit?

Forgiveness in a marriage is tied to the **heart posture** of the one who sinned, not just the action itself.

Should forgiveness be given in cases of real adultery?

You stated it correctly:

- If a spouse **committed actual adultery,**

- But comes with a **contrite heart,**

- Takes **responsibility,**

- And sincerely asks for forgiveness,

Then, yes, forgiveness should be extended, because that is how Christ forgives us.

"If we confess our sins, He is faithful and just to forgive us."
1 John 1:9

But if someone commits adultery, refuses repentance, shows no remorse, and continues in sin, then **that person condemns the marriage**, not the spouse who was hurt.

In that case:

- Forgiveness as a spiritual release is still required (for personal freedom)

- But reconciliation is not commanded

- And divorce becomes a permitted option, not a sin

Jesus Himself taught that *sexual immorality* was the one clear biblical reason for divorce **(Matthew 19:9).**

In my Case

I did not commit physical adultery.
I did not engage in an affair.
I did not defile the marriage bed.

My error was a communication issue, not a moral one.
Her error was one of **distrust**, not righteousness.

We both made mistakes, but **neither justified the destruction of the marriage in** the heart of Christ.

Religion would condemn you.
Christ would correct you.

Religion looks at appearances.
Christ looks at intent.

Religion punishes.
Christ restores.

"Adultery in Scripture What It *Really* Means"

1. Physical Adultery (The Biblical Definition)

In Scripture, adultery refers **primarily and explicitly** to sexual unfaithfulness within marriage. The Hebrew word *na'aph* and the Greek word *moichao* both mean:

"to have sexual relations with someone who is not your spouse."

This is the core biblical meaning, not texting, not emotional misunderstanding, not accidental communication.

---

2. Heart-Level Adultery (Jesus' Teaching)

Jesus expanded the definition not to condemn, but to expose the *inner motive*:

"Anyone who looks at a woman with lust has already committed adultery in his heart."
— Matthew 5:28

This is *not* physical adultery.
This is *moral intention*, a sin of the heart, not an act of betrayal.

Christ's point wasn't to redefine adultery, but to show that:

- sin begins internally

- temptation must be resisted

- lust destroys purity

- holiness starts in the mind

---

3. Hyperbole, Not Literal Commands

Jesus used **hyperbole**, intentional exaggeration, to make His teaching unforgettable:

**"If your eye causes you to sin, pluck it out...
If your hand causes you to sin, cut it off..."**
(Matthew 5:29–30)

Jesus was not commanding self-mutilation.
He was saying:
"Deal decisively with anything that leads you into temptation."

To interpret His words literally is to misunderstand His method.

---

4. What Adultery Is *Not*

According to Scripture:

433

- A birthday call is not adultery

- A text message is not adultery

- A misunderstanding is not adultery

- Suspicion is not adultery

- Fear is not adultery

Adultery requires **sexual sin**, intent, or lust — not innocent communication.

---

5. God's Heart on Adultery

Adultery wounds deeply because it breaks covenant.
But even then, God's response is always:

- **Repentance**

- **Restoration**

- **Healing**

- **Grace**

If a sinner comes with a **contrite heart**, Scripture teaches that forgiveness must follow.

PASTORAL BREAKDOWN OF MATTHEW 5 & MATTHEW 19

Matthew 5 — Jesus Addresses the Heart

In the Sermon on the Mount, Jesus goes after the *root* of sin:

- Lust = adultery in the heart

- Anger = murder in the heart

This is **moral intensification**, not legal redefinition.

Key Pastoral Takeaways

- Jesus exposes inward motives

- Jesus calls believers to purity

- Hyperbole (eye/hand) emphasizes seriousness, not literal action

- Jesus is showing that holiness begins long before physical action

Matthew 5 deals with **internal morality**, not marital law.

Matthew 19 — Jesus Addresses Divorce

The Pharisees tried to trap Jesus with a legal trick:

"Is it lawful for a man to divorce his wife for *any reason*?"

Jews of that era divorced their wives over:

- bad cooking

- aging appearance

- arguments

- trivial offenses

Jesus rejects this entire system.

Key Teachings from Matthew 19

1. **Marriage is God's design, not man's convenience**
   "What God has joined together, let no man separate."

2. **Moses permitted divorce because of "hard hearts," not because God approved.**

3. **The only marital sin Jesus identifies as grounds for divorce is sexual immorality (porneia).**
   This word refers to actual sexual betrayal — not assumptions, not misunderstandings, not paranoia.

4. **Christ prioritizes healing, forgiveness, and restoration whenever possible.**

To summarize:

- **Matthew 5** → purity of heart

- **Matthew 19** → covenant of marriage

Jesus honors both — but they are not the same issue.

A PROPHETIC WORD: MARRIAGES DESTROYED BY SUSPICION

There is a spirit moving through homes today — a spirit not of God, but of fear.
It whispers in the night.
It stirs insecurity.
It magnifies small things into mountains.
And it destroys marriages long before sin ever enters the picture.

This is the **spirit of suspicion**.

Suspicion:

- questions without evidence

- assumes without facts

- accuses without truth

- destroys without cause

Suspicion is a counterfeit of discernment.
Discernment comes from the Holy Spirit.
Suspicion comes from fear, wounds, and the enemy.

And the Lord says:

**"Where suspicion reigns, love cannot grow.
Where accusation replaces communication, the
serpent has already entered."**

Many marriages today are not destroyed by adultery —
but by the **fear of adultery**,
the **assumption of wrongdoing**,
and the **mistrust that suffocates intimacy**.

Suspicion is the serpent's whisper:

- "He's hiding something."

- "She's lying."

- "You know you can't trust them."

Accusation is the devil's native language (Revelation
12:10).
Where suspicion rules, Satan builds a home.

But the Lord is calling marriages back to:

- **truth**

- **communication**

- **grace**

- **forgiveness**

- **transparency**

Suspicion destroys.
Love restores.

Accusation kills.
Trust resurrects.

A marriage built on fear will crumble.
A marriage built on grace will endure.

And the Spirit of God says:

"Rebuke the spirit of suspicion.
Silence the voice of accusation.
Restore the covenant of trust.
For what I have joined together,
let no spirit tear apart."

Tiffany's Perspective — A Heart Trying to Protect Itself

To fully understand the moment, you must also understand Tiffany's heart.

She wasn't a woman looking to accuse.
She wasn't a wife hoping to find fault.
She was a woman who had lived through her own battles, her own fears, and her own history.
Her instinct wasn't to destroy, it was to protect.

And when a woman has been wounded before, even long before the marriage, every shadow looks like danger, and every unknown looks like betrayal.

What She Saw Through Her Eyes

From Tiffany's perspective, the phone call wasn't "just a birthday greeting."
It was a crack in the wall.
A hidden detail.
A missing piece.

In her heart, secrecy meant risk.
Silence meant danger.
A woman from the past meant the possibility of hurt.

So when she found the number, her reaction wasn't born out of malice
it was born out of fear.

Fear of abandonment.
Fear of betrayal.
Fear of not being enough.
Fear of repeating old wounds.

To her, the world had taught one lesson:
"If you don't guard your heart, someone will break it."

So she guarded intently, maybe too intently.
And in guarding herself, she began interpreting every motive through the lens of her own past pain, not through the truth of the moment.

Why She Searched Your Phone

Was it right to snoop?
Biblically, no trust is the foundation of marriage.

But emotionally, fear often convinces people to check what trust should cover.

To Tiffany, searching your phone wasn't an act of betrayal.
it was an act of self-protection.

She wasn't hoping to find wrongdoing.
She was hoping to prove that she was safe.

But when a heart is afraid, even innocence can look dangerous.
Even light can look like shadows.
Even a birthday call can feel like a threat.

When Hurt Meets Silence

When Tiffany saw the call, her fear collided with your silence
and the collision felt like betrayal.

Not because you betrayed her in action,
but because you didn't guard her heart with information
that could have calmed her fears.

To you, it meant nothing.
To her, it meant everything.

Your silence created a space where her insecurities began to scream.

And when her fear got loud enough, reason became quiet.

That is how misunderstanding becomes accusation.
That is how fear becomes certainty.
That is how suspicion becomes "proof."

In her mind, the story formed instantly:

- "Why didn't he tell me?"

- "What else is he hiding?"

- "Has this happened before?"

- "Does this mean something deeper?"

The truth didn't matter —
the fear did.

The Accusation: What It Felt Like to Her

In her heart, she wasn't trying to condemn you with Scripture.

440

She wasn't trying to weaponize religion.
She wasn't trying to act like a Pharisee.

She was trying to make sense of her pain.

And sometimes, when a heart is scared, it uses the Bible
not as guidance
but as a shield.

Her accusation wasn't theological.
it was emotional.

It wasn't based on doctrine.
it was based on fear.

It wasn't about your action
it was about her reaction.

She interpreted the call through the lens of insecurity, not
Scripture.

What She Needed But Didn't Know How to Ask For

If she could have expressed it clearly, her heart may have
said:

"I just needed to feel safe.
I needed to know you were honest with me.
I needed to know I was enough,
and that no one else had a piece of you."

Her accusation of adultery came from a place that wasn't
trying to punish you
it was trying to protect herself from repeating a past she
never healed from.

She wasn't looking for a reason to leave
she was looking for a reason to trust.

She didn't find the reassurance she needed in the moment.

A Compassionate Closing

This does not excuse her decision.
It does not justify the divorce.
It does not make the accusation right.

But it *does* explain the heart behind it.

Tiffany reacted as a woman who desperately wanted security,
and in the absence of information,
her fear wrote its own story.

Understanding her perspective does not change your truth.
it simply reveals the depth of her wound.

And sometimes, the most extraordinary compassion we can show someone
is not to agree with their reaction,
but to understand their pain.

Reflection: "What I Wish She Knew and What I Learned"

There are moments in life when you look back, not with regret, but with clarity.
Moments where you wish understanding could travel backwards in time.
Moments where you realize that two people can be in the same marriage but live with two very different fears.

This is one of those moments.

What I Wish She Knew

I wish she knew that the phone call meant nothing.
Not a temptation.
Not a spark from the past.
Not a secret desire.

I wish she knew that my heart never drifted, not even for a
moment.
My loyalty wasn't divided.
My intentions weren't hidden.
My integrity wasn't compromised.

I wish she knew that the silence wasn't secrecy
it was an oversight.
A failure of communication, not a failure of character.

I wish she knew that I wanted to protect her heart,
not hurt it,
not confuse it,
not shake its foundation.

I wish she knew that I didn't tell her because I didn't see
the moment as dangerous
but had I known the fear it triggered in her,
I would have spoken up instantly.

I wish she knew that I wasn't choosing another woman's
call over hers
I simply didn't see it as a threat in the first place.

I wish she knew that her worth to me was never in
question,
that she never had to compete with a voice from my past,
that she was enough
more than enough.

I wish she knew that trust could have healed us,
That forgiveness could have restored us,
that communication could have saved us.

And most of all,
I wish she knew that Christ would never have condemned
me the way fear did.

What I Learned

I learned that silence can be loud.
That's what seems small to one heart can feel enormous to
another.

I learned that trust is fragile.
not because love is weak,
but because wounds from past seasons still bleed into new
ones.

I learned that transparency is protection.
Not just for the marriage,
but for the peace of the home.

I learned that fear interprets shadows as truth,
and insecurity turns coincidences into conclusions.

I learned that even innocent actions need clarity,
because clarity guards the heart.

I learned that marriage is not just two people loving each
other
It is two people learning from each other.

I learned that it's possible to be right in action
but wrong in communication.

I learned that leadership in marriage means
going the extra mile to ensure your spouse feels safe,
even when you believe the situation is harmless.

I learned that forgiveness is the hinge of covenant
and without it, nothing stands.

I learned that religion destroys with accusation,
but Christ restores with understanding.

I learned that what happened to me was not the end
it was preparation.

Preparation for the man I will be.
Preparation for the husband I will become.
Preparation for a love grounded in communication, grace,
and spiritual covering.

A Closing Thought

If I could go back, I would speak sooner.
Listen deeper.
Explain better.
Protect her heart before fear had a chance to speak.

But I also know this:

God uses even broken moments to build stronger men.

And I walk forward now not with bitterness,
but with wisdom
the kind of wisdom that only pain can teach
and only grace can heal.

How This Changed the Way I Love

There are moments in life that don't just change your
circumstances
they change *you*.
They carve new wisdom into your spirit.
They sharpen your discernment.
They soften your heart.

They reshape your understanding of what love truly requires.

This experience did exactly that.

It didn't destroy me.
It didn't embitter me.
It didn't make me cynical.
It made me wiser.
More intentional.
More transparent.
More mature in how I give and protect love.

It changed the way I love in ways I never expected.

---

1. I Love With More Communication

I learned that love doesn't hide
not because it is guilty,
but because it is considerate.

Now I over-communicate, not out of fear,
but out of respect.

If something happens that could be misunderstood,
I bring it to light first.

Not because I owe explanations
but because love chooses clarity.

Transparency is not a burden.
It is a gift I give to protect the heart of someone I value.

---

2. I Love With More Awareness

I learned that love must be aware of another person's wounds.

Not all battles come from the present
some come from the ghosts of the past.

So now, when someone flinches emotionally,
I don't react to the surface
I look deeper.

I see the history behind the emotion.
I hear the fear behind the words.
I recognize the insecurity behind the reaction.

Love that understands wounds
is love that knows how to heal.

---

3. I Love With More Compassion

I learned that a person can overreact and still be worthy of
compassion.
That hurt people sometimes respond from fear,
not from mistrust.
That misunderstanding doesn't make someone the enemy.

I don't judge as quickly anymore.
I don't assume someone's reaction tells the whole story.
I look for the heart behind the behavior.

Compassion softens conflict
and strengthens the connection.

---

4. I Love With More Patience

This experience taught me that relationships require
patience
not the passive kind,
but the kind that actively chooses grace.

I'm slower to anger now.
Slower to take offense.
Slower to assume the worst.

Because I learned that assumptions burn bridges,
but patience builds them.

Love isn't rushed.
Love listens.
Love gives space.
Love takes its time.

5. I Love With More Integrity

I learned that integrity in love is not just about avoiding sin
it's about avoiding confusion.

It's not just about being faithful
It's about being eligible.

Not just loyal
but consistent.

Integrity is not only what you do when no one is watching,
it's what you willingly show when someone *is*.

I now love with a level of openness.
that leaves no room for shadows.

6. I Love With More Spiritual Covering

This experience reminded me of the divine order of
protection in a marriage.

A husband is not just a partner.
he is a covering.

He guards,
he prays,
he communicates,
he leads with humility and transparency.

I now understand more deeply
That covering is *not* control
It is a responsibility.

It is the role Christ models with His Bride.

---

7. I Love With More Intentionality

I don't live casually with love anymore.
I don't take relationships lightly.
I don't assume trust
I cultivate it.

I am intentional with my words,
my time,
my communication,
my emotional presence.

I love with purpose,
not impulse.

I love with intention,
not assumption.

I love with clarity,
not confusion.

A Final Thought

This chapter of my life didn't merely teach me a lesson
it reshaped the man I am becoming.

It taught me that love grows best in the soil of:

- communication

- trust

- transparency

- spiritual covering

- compassion

- intentionality

And if I ever love again,
I will love better
not because I failed,
but because I *learned*.

Because wisdom grows where wounds once lived,
and love becomes stronger when truth refines it.

What I Hope For in My Next Marriage

When I think about the future, I don't think about repeating the past.
I think about building something new
something whole,
something healed,
something rooted in grace
and guarded by wisdom.

I don't hope for perfection.
I don't hope for a flawless life or a flawless partner.
I hope for something **real**.

Something God-written.
Something Christ-centered.
Something where two people choose each other every day
with commitment, kindness, and clarity.

This is what I hope for in my next marriage.

1. A Marriage Built on Trust, Not Fear

I hope for a relationship where trust isn't fragile,
where love isn't questioned,
and where honesty is a natural language not a forced
discipline.

I hope for a home where:

- no one feels the need to snoop

- no one feels afraid of secrets

- no one imagines betrayal in shadows

- no one interprets silence as guilt

I want trust to be the foundation,
not suspicion.
The default,
not the exception.

---

2. A Marriage of Clear, Gentle Communication

I want a marriage where communication is effortless,
not a battlefield.

Where conversations aren't loaded with assumptions,
or weighed down by fear,
or strained by insecurity.

I want a relationship where we can say:

"Here's what happened today,"
without fear of misinterpretation.

Where we share openly
not because we're hiding something,
but because we value transparency.

Communication is the first covering of a marriage,
and I want a love protected by clarity.

---

3. A Marriage of Healing, Not Punishment

I hope for a marriage where mistakes are treated with
mercy,
not judgment.

Where two imperfect people choose grace
because Christ extended grace to them first.

Where misunderstandings don't escalate into accusations.
Where hurt leads to conversation,
not condemnation.

I want a relationship where we fight *for* each other,
not against each other.

Where forgiveness is the first response,
not the last resort.

---

4. A Marriage Where We Know Each Other Deeply

I hope for a woman who wants to understand my heart,
not just my actions.

Someone who can say:

"Tell me how you feel,
not just what happened."

And I will understand her the same way.

I want to know her fears,
her wounds,
her hopes,

her history,
her triggers,
her joys.

Because love grows strongest
where understanding runs deepest.

---

5. A Marriage That Honors the Order of God

I hope for a relationship built on the divine order:

God → Husband → Wife → Home

Not a hierarchy of value,
but hierarchy of responsibility.

I hope for a marriage where I can take my role as covering
seriously —
where I can lead gently,
serve humbly,
protect spiritually,
and love sacrificially.

And I hope for a wife who embraces her role with joy,
knowing she is cherished, not controlled;
honored, not overshadowed.

This is a partnership under Christ,
not over each other.

---

6. A Marriage Filled With Peace, Joy, and Friendship

I want laughter in the home.
Lightness.
Friendship.
Ease.

I hope for a companion
someone who's not just a wife,
but a friend,
a confidant,
a teammate in the storms,
and a partner in the victories.

I want a relationship where we enjoy each other,
not just endure each other.

A marriage where peace is normal
and chaos is temporary.

Where joy is daily
and conflict is rare.

---

7. A Marriage Protected by Christ at the Center

Most of all,
I hope for a marriage where Christ isn't an accessory
He is the cornerstone.

Where prayer isn't a formality
it is oxygen.

Where worship is shared.
Where Scripture shapes our decisions.
Where grace flows freely.
Where humility reigns.
Where Christ binds us closer
than emotions ever could.

I don't want a marriage built on feelings
or fear
or assumptions.

I want a covenant built on faith.

A Closing Prayer Wrapped Inside the Hope

I pray for a love that is:

- healed

- whole

- mature

- trustworthy

- transparent

- gentle

- faithful

- spiritually anchored

A love that reflects Christ and His Church.
A love that grows stronger with time.
A love that survives storms because it was built on the Rock.

I hope for a marriage where we choose grace over accusation,
communication over silence,
trust over fear,
and truth over insecurity.

I hope for a marriage where love looks like Jesus.

And when that day comes
I will love better,
lead better,
serve better,
and protect better
because of everything this chapter taught me.

Prophetic Commentary: The Fall of Adam and the Crisis of Modern Marriage

The Spirit of God is exposing a crisis in our generation a crisis rooted in the same failure that took place in Eden. What destroyed Adam's covering over his home is the same force destroying marriages today: men stepping back while women stand alone.

Eve was deceived, but Adam was silent.
Eve reached, but Adam watched.
Eve fell, but Adam followed.

And the Lord says:
"The sin of silence has returned."

Today, many husbands have surrendered their spiritual authority. Men no longer guard the gates of their homes. They no longer cover their wives in prayer. They no longer lead their families into righteousness. The same passivity that opened the door to the serpent in Eden is opening the door to destruction in marriages around the world.

The Prophetic Parallel

Just as Adam abandoned his post, modern husbands:

- **Abandon spiritual leadership**

- **Abandon intercession**

- **Abandon responsibility**

- **Abandon accountability**

- **Abandon the role God gave them as the head, the priest, and the protector of the home**

And when the covering collapses, the enemy enters.

Where men fail to lead, the serpent begins to preach.
Where men fail to guard, deception begins to grow.
Where men fail to stand, families begin to fall.

This is not a word of condemnation but a call to repentance and realignment.

God Is Restoring Covenant Headship

The Lord is calling men back to the mantle Adam dropped.

"Awake, O sleeper, and rise from the dead, and Christ will shine on you."
— Ephesians 5:14

This is a prophetic call for husbands to rise:

- Rise into priesthood

- Rise into responsibility

- Rise into sacrificial love

- Rise into spiritual warfare

- Rise into the role Christ modeled with His Bride, the Church

A husband cannot blame his wife for what he refused to cover.
A man cannot complain about what he refused to confront.
Adam blamed Eve but God confronted Adam.

And God is still confronting Adam today.

Women Are Not the Enemy — Lack of Covering Is

Eve fell because she stood alone in a moment she should never have faced without her covering. The enemy has always targeted the unprotected.

The prophetic warning is this:

When a woman is left uncovered, the serpent comes to whisper.
When a man abandons his post, the enemy fills the silence.

But when a husband stands in his God-given authority, the atmosphere changes:

- Temptation loses its grip

- Confusion loses its voice

- Division loses its foothold

- The serpent loses access

The strength of a home is not in the perfection of the wife, but in the covering of the husband.

A Prophetic Call to Husbands Today

The Lord is calling men to return to the altar and take back what Adam dropped. Husbands must become:

- Intercessors — standing between their home and the attack of the enemy

- Watchmen — guarding the gates from spiritual infiltration

- Teachers — leading their family in the Word

- Warriors — protecting their marriage from compromise

- Servant-leaders — loving their wives as Christ loved the Church

The voice of God is thundering over a generation of passive men:
"Take your place. Cover your home. Stand in the gap."

When Men Surrender Their Authority: How Evil Gains Power

From the beginning of time, every story of destruction in Scripture has one common thread:

Evil gains power when a man surrenders his God-given authority.

A woman does not become evil on her own.
A man becomes vulnerable to evil through:

- lack of spiritual knowledge

- lack of conviction

- lack of leadership

- weakness

- worldliness

- ignoring the voice of God

Even godly men — men chosen, anointed, or empowered by God — fell into destruction when they gave their authority away.

The story is not about women being inherently evil.
The real issue is men forfeiting the spiritual covering God commanded them to carry.

Where there is no headship,
sin grows.
Where there is no spiritual guard,
manipulation thrives.
Where a man lays down his authority,
evil picks it up.

Scripture gives several sobering examples.

Samson and Delilah — Strength Without Discernment

Samson was not an ordinary man.

- He was chosen before birth.

- He was anointed with supernatural strength.

- He carried divine purpose as a judge over Israel.

But his downfall came through one weakness:
he gave a woman influence God never intended her to carry.

The Philistines paid Delilah to discover the secret of his strength.
She pressed him day after day.
Samson resisted physically,
but spiritually he was already compromised.

When he surrendered the truth,
he surrendered his calling.

Delilah did not defeat him —
Samson's lack of spiritual discernment did.

She shaved his hair while he slept.
The Philistines captured him,
gouged out his eyes,
and his season as a judge came to an end.

Samson fell because he laid down his authority in the lap of a woman who had no covenant with God.

Ahab and Jezebel — The Weak King and the Ambitious Queen

Ahab was King of Israel,
but he ruled with no strength, no conviction, and no spiritual backbone.

Jezebel, on the other hand, was:

- strong-willed

- manipulative

- intelligent

- politically driven

- deeply involved in Baal worship

Ahab surrendered his authority,
and she picked it up.

Jezebel:

- murdered God's prophets

- manipulated legal systems

- orchestrated Naboth's death

- led Israel into idolatry

- openly defied the Word of God

Ahab didn't become corrupt because of Jezebel
he became corrupt because he refused to lead.

When the man refuses to lead with righteousness,
evil leads in his place.

Herod, Herodias, and Salome Lust, Pride, and
Manipulation

Herod's downfall began long before the beheading of John
the Baptist.

He married Herodias unlawfully.
John called it out publicly.
Herodias was furious and held a deep grudge.

At Herod's birthday feast, her daughter Salome danced,
and Herod overcome with lust and pride made a foolish
vow:

"Ask me whatever you want, and I will give it to you."

Salome went to her mother,
and Herodias seized the moment.

She demanded John's head.
Herod complied.

Not because Herodias had divine authority
but because Herod surrendered his moral authority.

When a man refuses to stand for righteousness,
evil manipulates his weakness.

The Pattern Is Clear

A woman becomes powerful
dangerously powerful
when a man:

- surrenders his spiritual covering

- lays down his role

- ignores God's voice

- seeks approval instead of obedience

- gives emotional control to someone outside of
  God's order

Women in Scripture were not born evil.
Their power became destructive because a man refused to
stand in his God-given place.

Why This Matters for Today

Even now, in the modern world,
women do not gain ungodly power by themselves.

They gain it because men:

- are passive

- are spiritually blind

- are emotionally driven

- seek validation over vision

- surrender leadership

- ignore warnings

- prioritize peace over truth

The moment a man gives a woman the role God gave him,
confusion enters the home.

The spiritual headship shifts.
Authority becomes inverted.
And the result is:

- manipulation

- emotional control

- moral compromise

- spiritual blindness

- destruction of purpose

It is not about women being evil.
It is about men refusing to be who God commanded them to be.

A woman becomes powerful through one thing only:
a man laying down his authority.

The Conclusion

This is not an insult to women
it is an indictment of weak men.

Every biblical downfall involving a woman begins with the same mistake:

A man surrendered what God gave him to protect.

God gives authority to the man
not to dominate,
but to guard,
to lead,
to protect,
to discern,
to reject evil,
and to keep the household aligned with heaven.

When man drops the mantle,
evil picks it up.

And that truth is not just biblical
it is visible in the lives of men today.

A Prophetic Promise

For every man who returns to his proper position, God will restore what the enemy has broken. He will heal marriages. He will mend wounds. He will silence serpents. He will rebuild homes on the foundation of covenant order.

What Adam lost, Christ restores.
What Adam dropped, Christ lifts.
What Adam failed to cover, Christ redeems.

This is the hour for men to rise
not as tyrants,
not as dictators,
but as Christ-like husbands who carry the cross, not the crown.

When men return to the mantle, marriages return to Eden.

Prayer for Forgiveness in Marriage

Father God,

Thank you for teaching me that forgiveness is the bridge between broken hearts.
Thank You for reminding me that even when love fails, grace still stands.

Lord, teach husbands and wives to forgive as You forgive
to remember that forgiveness is not condoning sin, but
conquering it with mercy.

Heal every marriage that has been torn apart by pride,
pain, or misunderstanding.
Let Your Spirit of reconciliation move through homes
again.

Remind every couple that marriage is not a contract of
convenience but a covenant of commitment.

Let forgiveness flow where bitterness once lived.

And let every heart remember that Your love covers a
multitude of sins.

In Jesus' name,
Amen.

Chapter Twelve – The Church at the Crossroads (Expanded Edition)

Every age comes to a turning point, a moment when the
people of God must choose between comfort and
conviction. The ancient prophets stood in that moment.
The apostles stood in that moment. And now, so do we.

The Church has come to a crossroads.

We have built cathedrals of glass and light, but lost the fire
that once made fishermen fearless. We've learned how to
brand our message but forgotten how to bear our cross.

We speak the name of Jesus, but too often we package Him for convenience rather than reverence.

It is not that the Church has ceased to believe, but that it has learned to think safely.

The Modern Pharisee

In the days of Jesus, the Pharisees were not villains in their own eyes; they were protectors of purity, guardians of tradition, experts in the letter of the Law. But over time, they became blind to the Spirit that gave that Law life.

Today's Church faces the same danger. We exalt structure over substance, form over fire. We confuse the preservation of an institution with the presence of God.

Religion, when stripped of compassion, becomes idolatry dressed in righteousness.

"Having a form of godliness, but denying the power thereof." — 2 Timothy 3:5

If Jesus walked among our sanctuaries today, He might again overturn tables not of merchants, but of ministers selling grace like it were merchandise.

Faith in the Age of Platforms

The modern age has given every believer a pulpit, but not every pulpit preaches Christ.
Our phones have become the new temples: our followers, our congregation.

Many have traded revelation for relevance. The crowd's applause has replaced the Spirit's whisper. In the rush to be seen, we have forgotten how to be still.

There was a time when revival meant people kneeling in tears. Now it means trending hashtags and stage lights. But the Spirit of God does not live in algorithms. He lives in the altar of the heart.

"Not by might, nor by power, but by My Spirit, saith the Lord of hosts." — Zechariah 4:6

The Church at the crossroads must decide: will we be influencers or intercessors? Performers or prophets?

The Day I Walked Out of a Church

There was a well-known church in our neighborhood a big name, a big crowd, a big reputation.
They were on television every Sunday.
People talked about them like they were the spiritual hub of the community.

My wife, at the time, knew many who went there coworkers, friends, acquaintances from social gatherings.
So one weekend, she suggested we visit.
I agreed.

We walked in, found our seats, and settled in like any couple looking for a place to worship.
But what happened next revealed everything I needed to know.

The Auction in the House of God

The pastor stepped up for the offering, nothing unusual there.
But instead of a prayerful moment of giving, the sanctuary turned into an auction house.

A man stood up and offered $25.
The pastor shouted, "Do I hear 40?"

Another stood and offered $40.
Again he called, "Do I hear 50?"

Then $50.
Then $75.
Then $100.
Then $200.
Then $300.

It was no longer an offering —
it was bidding.

It felt like the house of God had become a marketplace,
a stage,
a spectacle of financial competition.

And not one person walked out.

The Sermon That Exposed the Truth

After the "auction" settled, the pastor began his sermon.

He was maybe five minutes in when he shifted to the topic of Adam and Eve — the very section of this book concerning my first marriage.

He proclaimed that Adam and Eve were equal in their guilt,
equal in their role, equal in responsibility.
He preached it with confidence.
He preached it like doctrine.
He preached it from a worldly lens, not a biblical one.

My spirit was disturbed.
I knew what Scripture said.
I knew Adam bore the covenant responsibility.
I knew federal headship isn't cultural it's a divine order.

So I took my wife's hand
and quietly led her out of the church.

Her face was puzzled, almost embarrassed.
She whispered, "Why are we leaving? What did we do?"

When we reached the car, I pulled out the Scriptures and
showed her truth.
I showed her where the pastor had twisted the Word.
I showed her why what he said was wrong — not just
theologically, but spiritually.

She understood.
And we never went back.

Why We Left — And Why No One Else Did

What stunned me most wasn't the pastor
it was the crowd.

Hundreds of Christians sat there cheering on an auction.
Hundreds nodded at false teaching.
Hundreds remained blind to manipulation and error.

We were the only two people who walked out.

That moment revealed just how biblically illiterate many
believers are.

Not because they lack intelligence,
but because they have been fed a worldly gospel,
a watered-down theology,
and a seminary-trained religion divorced from the Holy Spirit.

And *that* is one of the reasons I'm writing this book.
to shine light on what has become of the church culture.

The Problem with Modern Seminaries

Most pastors don't become pastors because they are drenched in the Holy Spirit.
Most go to seminary because they want a career
a path,
a position,
a paycheck.

Seminaries today are often more worldly institutions than spiritual ones:

- They teach from a secular academic lens.

- They strip the supernatural from Scripture.

- They reduce the Word to theories, philosophies, and historical debates.

- They produce polished speakers, but not Spirit-led shepherds.

This isn't true of *every* seminary,
nor of *every* pastor.
I have met some Spirit-filled men who went through those institutions and remained holy, humble, and faithful to God's voice.

But they are the exception.
not the rule.

Just as Constantine blended political power with
Christianity,
modern seminaries blend earthly wisdom with divine truth.
They produce ministers trained in the world's system,
but not in the Holy Spirit's fire.

And that combination
worldly education plus spiritual authority
is dangerous.

Because when pastors preach from human wisdom
instead of divine revelation,
error becomes doctrine,
pride becomes leadership,
and manipulation becomes ministry.

Why This Story Matters in This Book

That day in the church during my first marriage
was more than an uncomfortable visit
it was a revelation.

It showed me:

- how easily people accept false teaching

- how crowds can be entertained but not transformed

- how some pastors use the pulpit for profit, not truth

- how far the church has drifted from the Spirit-led
  example of Christ

- how religion replaces revelation when the world
  trains men

And it proved to me that many believers do not know the
Word
and because of that, they cannot recognize deception.

This book exists to confront that darkness, expose that deception, and call believers back to truth.

Because if the church doesn't awaken,
if pastors don't return to Spirit-led teaching,
and if believers don't learn the Word for themselves,
we will continue to see churches full of people
and empty of truth.

The Seven Churches: Then and Now

When the Apostle John was exiled on the island of Patmos, he received a revelation that still speaks to us today. The risen Christ dictated letters to **seven churches in Asia Minor** — each one representing both a historical congregation and a spiritual condition that still exists within the modern Church.

Ephesus — The Church That Lost Its First Love

"Nevertheless, I have somewhat against thee, because thou hast left thy first love." — Revelation 2:4

Ephesus was strong in doctrine but weak in devotion. They knew how to expose false teachers but had forgotten intimacy with Christ.
So too, many modern believers can quote Scripture but cannot weep in His presence. Our orthodoxy has outgrown our intimacy.

Smyrna — The Persecuted Church

"Be thou faithful unto death, and I will give thee a crown of life." — Revelation 2:10

Smyrna had no rebuke, only encouragement. They suffered in silence yet stayed faithful. They are the underground churches of today, the persecuted, the unheard, the faithful remnant.

Their message to us: faith that costs nothing accomplishes nothing.

Pergamum — The Compromised Church

"Thou hast there them that hold the doctrine of Balaam." — Revelation 2:14

Pergamum lived in a pagan city and began blending truth with error. The Church today has its own Pergamum, where the message is softened to attract the crowd, and the cross is replaced with comfort.

Thyatira — The Corrupted Church

"Thou sufferest that woman Jezebel... to teach and to seduce my servants." — Revelation 2:20

Thyatira tolerated false prophets who corrupted grace with immorality. The same spirit works today when morality is mocked, and holiness is labeled hate.

God's love does not cancel His standard; it fulfills it.

Sardis — The Dead Church

"Thou hast a name that thou livest, and art dead." — Revelation 3:1

Sardis looked alive but was spiritually dead, the perfect description of the performance-driven Church. Crowds, lights, and sound cannot resurrect what only the Spirit can.

Philadelphia — The Faithful Church

"I have set before thee an open door, and no man can shut it." — Revelation 3:8

Philadelphia remained faithful despite little strength. They represent the quiet believers who walk in humility yet hold fast to truth.
They are the praying mothers, the hidden intercessors, the ones who love Christ more than reputation.

Laodicea — The Lukewarm Church

"Because thou art lukewarm... I will spue thee out of my mouth." — Revelation 3:16

Laodicea was rich and self-satisfied but blind to its poverty. It is the modern Western Church, wealthy, busy, and self-congratulatory, but devoid of repentance.
Jesus still knocks at this door, not to enter a building, but to enter hearts.

The Crossroads Moment

John's vision is not just ancient prophecy; it is present reality.
Every believer must ask: Which church am I?

The Spirit is still speaking: return to your first love, hold fast to truth, strengthen what remains, and open the door to Christ again.

The Church now stands where Israel once stood, called to choose between revival and ruin, truth and tradition, power and purity.

Reflection — Standing at the Crossroads With God

The Church is no stranger to crossroads. Scripture itself is a history of holy intersections — moments where God's people had to choose between the broad road of comfort and the narrow path of conviction. Israel faced it. The prophets faced it. The disciples faced it. And now, in our generation, the weight of that choice rests upon us.

We stand in sanctuaries filled with light, yet our hearts often flicker with shadows. We preach about transformation yet fear the kind of surrender that would transform *us*. We have learned to speak of Jesus, but not always to walk with Him. The ancient fire that once turned fishermen into apostles has been traded for a faith that offends no one and changes nothing.

And so the Spirit calls again:
"Awake thou that sleepest, and arise from the dead, and Christ shall give thee light." — Ephesians 5:14

Not to condemn us, but to restore us.

A Mirror Held to the Modern Church

The seven letters in Revelation are not merely history; they are a mirror. John did not record them for first-century congregations alone, but for every believer who would ever drift, doubt, compromise, or grow cold.

Each church reveals a condition that still breathes in us:

- **Ephesus warns us that doctrine without devotion becomes a lifeless religion.**

- **Smyrna reminds us that true faith is proven in fire, not in comfort.**

- **Pergamum exposes how easily we blend holiness with culture until the line disappears.**

- **Thyatira unmasks the subtle seduction of a gospel designed to please the flesh.**

- **Sardis confronts the tragedy of looking alive while being spiritually comatose.**

- **Philadelphia inspires us that small strength can carry great faithfulness.**

- **Laodicea convicts us that the most dangerous spiritual state is not rebellion, but lukewarmness.**

The letters diagnose not churches long gone, but hearts still beating. And in every letter, Christ gives the same invitation:
"He that hath an ear, let him hear what the Spirit saith unto the churches."

This is not nostalgia; it is a wake-up call.

The Crossroads Before Us

The crossroads today are no less dramatic than they were for the early Church. Ours is a choice between image and identity, between influence and intercession, between being a church that performs and a church that *prevails*.

We have platforms, but not always prayer lives.
We have ministries, but not always mercy.
We have buildings, but not always brokenness.

The danger is not that the Church will stop gathering.
The danger is that it will gather without God.

When Jesus stands at the door and knocks, as He did in Laodicea, it is a tragic sign: those called by His name have somehow locked Him out.

But His knock is also hope.
It means He has not given up on His bride.
It means revival starts not with an event, but with a door opened from the inside.

A Call to Personal Renewal

Before the Church can choose the right road, each believer must. Revival does not begin with crowds; it begins with individuals who respond to the whisper of the Spirit:

- Return to your first love.

- Strengthen what remains.

- Hold fast to truth.

- Reject compromise.

- Open the door to Christ again.

The real crossroads is not corporate, it's personal.
The Lord is not merely asking, *"What is the Church becoming?"*
He is asking, **"What are *you* becoming?"**

When Joshua stood before the people of Israel and said, **"Choose this day whom ye will serve,"** **he did not speak as a committee but as a man whose mind was settled:**
"As for me and my house, we will serve the Lord."

So must we.

A Prayer at the Crossroads

Lord Jesus,
Bring Your Church back to the place where faith is more precious than applause and obedience more important than opinion.
Break our confidence in platforms and restore our dependence on prayer.
Deliver us from lukewarmness, revive our first love, and cleanse our hearts from the idols we have baptized.
Open our eyes to the condition of our own souls.
Give us ears to hear Your Spirit, courage to choose truth, and humility to walk the narrow road.
May we be a Philadelphia in a Laodicean age, faithful, steadfast, surrendered.
And may Your fire fall again upon a people who choose conviction over comfort and Christ over everything.
Amen.

Closing Reflection

The Church is not dying, it's being purified.
God is stripping away everything that cannot stand in His presence. Titles, trends, and trophies will burn like straw in the fire of His holiness.
What will remain are hearts that tremble, hands that serve, and lips that still whisper: *"Here I am, Lord."*

Prayer

Lord, we stand at the crossroads. Give us eyes to see beyond the noise and hearts that burn for truth. Tear down

our idols of comfort and control. Teach us again the power
of simplicity, the beauty of obedience.
May Your Church rise, not as a monument to man, but as
a living body filled with Your Spirit.
Revive the altar. Rekindle the flame.
In Jesus' name, Amen.

The Priesthood of Every Believer

One of the greatest deceptions of religious history is the
idea that man needs another man to reach God.
For centuries, priests have stood between the people and
the Presence not as intercessors of compassion, but as
gatekeepers of grace.
The faithful were taught that access to God must come
through the Church, through confessionals, through
sacraments, through men clothed in holy garments.

But the veil was torn.
When Christ gave up His spirit on the cross, **the curtain
that separated man from God was ripped from top to
bottom,** not by human hands, but by divine declaration.

*"Having therefore, brethren, boldness to enter into the
holiest by the blood of Jesus…"* — Hebrews 10:19

That moment marked the end of the age of earthly
mediators.
No priest, no pope, no pastor can now stand between the
soul and its Creator.
There is only one High Priest who intercedes forever,
Jesus Christ.

*"For there is one God, and one mediator between God
and men, the man Christ Jesus."* — 1 Timothy 2:5

The Call to Personal Relationship

The tragedy of modern faith, particularly within the Catholic system, is that many have traded personal relationships for **institutional dependence.**
They wait for a priest to read the Word instead of opening it themselves.
They confess to men rather than communing directly with God.
They ask saints for favor while ignoring the One who already gave them access to the throne of grace.

"Let us therefore come boldly unto the throne of grace, that we may obtain mercy." — Hebrews 4:16

The Word of God was never meant to be chained to a pulpit or translated only by clergy.
Jesus came to make **disciples**, not dependents.
He came to fill every believer with His Spirit so that each heart could become a temple, each voice a prayer, each life a ministry.

No one can pray on your behalf better than the Spirit who dwells within you.
And no one can interpret Scripture more faithfully than the Author who lives in your heart.

The same Spirit who inspired the apostles now dwells in the believer who kneels beside their bed and opens the Word for themselves.

Breaking the Chains of Dependence

For generations, Catholics have been taught that holiness is conferred through sacraments, confession, baptism, and communion controlled by the Church.

But holiness is not a ritual; it is a relationship.
It is not earned by repetition, but born through revelation.

God never desired a people who rely on priests to hear Him.
He desires people who hear Him personally, daily, intimately.

That is why Jesus said,

"My sheep hear My voice, and I know them, and they follow Me." — **John 10:27**

The true Church is not a hierarchy; it is a household, a living body where every member is called, anointed, and equipped.
When we depend on others to pray for us, read for us, and believe for us, we remain children in faith.
But when we take ownership of our walk with God, we grow into sons and daughters who reflect His glory in the world.

This is not rebellion against leadership; it is the restoration of liberty.
Christ freed the Church from priestly control so that the Spirit could fill every believer with priestly power.

"Ye are a chosen generation, a royal priesthood, a holy nation..." — **1 Peter 2:9**

The Spirit of God does not dwell behind the altars of institutions.
He dwells in the hearts of His people.
And when believers begin to pray directly, study intensely, and live boldly, the fire that once fell in Acts will fall again.

Reflection: The Return of the Lie

The greatest battle a believer faces often begins **after** discovering the truth. When someone truly finds God and begins to walk in His light, the darkness they escaped doesn't simply disappear; it waits. The demon returns.

But this time, he doesn't come roaring; he comes whispering.
He says, *"You're not worthy."*
He says, *"It's too hard to live holy."*
He says, *"You were happier before."*
These are the same lies he's told since the garden — the same deception that separated humanity from God in the beginning.

And yet, the Word of God exposes every lie. Scripture is not merely a book of blessings; it is a **manual for warfare**. Paul wrote,

"For we wrestle not against flesh and blood, but against principalities, against powers, against the rulers of the darkness of this world, against spiritual wickedness in high places."
— Ephesians 6:12

When you begin to understand that spiritual warfare is real, not just around you, but within you, your eyes open to the conflict that spans nations, hearts, and souls. Wars, disease, division, and temptation all trace their roots to sin.

I think of my mother, now ninety. Her strength has been my example, but her age reminds me that time is fragile. I have often feared life without her, yet I rest in the promise of Christ:

"I will never leave thee, nor forsake thee."
— *Hebrews 13:5*

That promise silences fear. I no longer dread death, for Christ has defeated it. But victory in Christ does not mean neglecting the body. The Word teaches us that our bodies are **temples of the Holy Spirit (1 Corinthians 6:19-20).** When the mind and body are disciplined, the soul thrives. A sick soul often begins with a neglected spirit.

This brings to mind Steve's struggle, his sickness, and how the frailty of the flesh can mirror the weight of sin. Whether illness comes from inheritance or habit, it reminds us that sin, left unhealed, eventually manifests as destruction. Yet healing is found in obedience. James wrote:

"Confess your faults one to another, and pray one for another, that ye may be healed."
— *James 5:16*

Disease may be physical, but the deeper infection is spiritual. The Bible declares that **sin is the root of death**. From Adam's failure in Eden to our own, death entered when humanity believed a lie. Satan told Eve, *"You will not surely die... you will be like God."* (**Genesis 3:4–5**) And in that moment, mankind traded divine order for pride.

But Jesus came to restore what Adam lost.

The Temptation of Christ

After His baptism, Jesus was led by the Spirit into the wilderness not by accident, but by purpose. For forty days, He fasted, alone, hungry, and weak in the body. That's when Satan came not during strength, but in weakness.

He tempted Christ three times:

1. **The Temptation of the Flesh:**
   "If you are the Son of God, command these stones to become bread."
   — *Matthew 4:3*
   Satan attacked His hunger, just as he attacks ours. But Jesus replied,

"It is written, Man shall not live by bread alone, but by every word that proceedeth out of the mouth of God."
— *Matthew 4:4*
Christ showed that obedience is nourishment greater than food.

2. **The Temptation of Pride:**
   Satan took Him to the pinnacle of the Temple and said,
   "Cast yourself down, for it is written: He shall give His angels charge over you."
   — *Matthew 4:6*
   Here, Satan used Scripture out of context just as false teachers do today. But Jesus answered,

"It is written again, Thou shalt not tempt the Lord thy God."
— *Matthew 4:7*

3. **The Temptation of Power:**
   Finally, the devil offered Him all the kingdoms of the world if He would bow down and worship him.
   — *Matthew 4:8–9*
   Jesus replied,

"Get thee hence, Satan: for it is written, Thou shalt worship the Lord thy God, and him only shalt thou serve."
— *Matthew 4:10*

Three temptations: flesh, pride, and power, the same that ensnare humanity still.

But Jesus stood firm, proving that **the Word of God is the ultimate weapon** against deception.

The devil left Him, but notice this: *"he departed from Him for a season."* (**Luke 4:13**) meaning, he would return. Even Jesus was not free from Satan's taunts. The enemy came again through Judas, through Peter's denial, through the crowd's hatred, and through the loneliness of the cross.

If Satan dared to attack the Son of God, he would surely come for us.
But take heart, for Jesus has already won the war.

"Be of good cheer; I have overcome the world."
— John 16:33

Closing Prayer

Heavenly Father,
Teach us to recognize the enemy's lies.
Strengthen our minds and bodies to stand firm in Your truth.
When Satan whispers that we are unworthy, remind us that Christ has made us whole.
When fear grips us, fill us with faith.
When our families falter, restore divine order: God first, then love, then service.
May we live not by bread, but by every word that comes from Your mouth.
And may we, like Jesus, overcome the tempter by the power of Your Word.
In Jesus' name, Amen.

Spiritual Warfare and the Modern Church

When we look at today's church, we see that the same spirit that tempted Jesus in the wilderness now creeps within religion itself. The temptations of the flesh, pride, and power, the very ones that Satan used against the Son of God, are the same snares he uses to corrupt the body of Christ.

The Temptation of the Flesh — Comfort Over Conviction

Many churches have chosen comfort over conviction. The gospel has been softened, and sermons have become entertainment instead of transformation. Satan whispers, *"Give them what they want to hear."* And so the Word that once called men to repentance now promises them only blessings and prosperity.

Paul warned us of this in his letter to Timothy:

"For the time will come when they will not endure sound doctrine; but after their own lusts shall they heap to themselves teachers, having itching ears." *— 2 Timothy 4:3*

The modern church too often feeds the flesh instead of the soul. We no longer fast; we feast. We no longer weep; we perform. We no longer carry the cross; we decorate it.

When Jesus said, *"If any man will come after me, let him deny himself, and take up his cross daily, and follow me"* **(Luke 9:23),** He meant surrender, not comfort. Yet many congregations now follow personalities rather than Christ.

The Temptation of Pride — Pastors on Pedestals

Satan tempted Jesus to throw Himself from the temple to prove His divinity before men. Pride was the snare. Today, that same pride has infected the pulpit. Many pastors have been placed on pedestals meant only for Christ. The church that was once the body has become a stage, and the servant has become the celebrity.

Jesus said,

"The greatest among you shall be your servant." *— Matthew 23:11*

But we have forgotten this. Some pastors now act as though they alone hear from God, creating spiritual dependency rather than discipleship.
The early church was a fellowship, a family where all believers shared in ministry and prayer. The Spirit was poured out on **all flesh**, not just the clergy. **(Acts 2:17)**

The problem today is that many Christians have surrendered their divine calling to the personality behind the pulpit. They no longer seek God's voice for themselves. They wait for a man to speak for them.

But Jesus tore the veil from top to bottom so that *no man* would stand between God and His people. **(Matthew 27:51)**
When we place a pastor where only Christ should be, we rebuild the very wall that Jesus died to destroy.

The Temptation of the Flesh — The Silent Sin of Fornication

There is a sin that the modern church refuses to touch, not because Scripture is unclear, but because pastors fear the faces of the people more than they fear the holiness of God.
It is the sin of **fornication**.

We preach loudly against pornography because it is a convenient enemy, a sin tied to screens, hidden in shadows, and easy to condemn without confronting the lifestyles sitting openly in the pews. Pornography is indeed wicked; it corrupts the imagination, poisons desire, and trains the heart to entertain lust. Jesus warned clearly:

"Whosoever looketh on a woman to lust after her hath committed adultery with her already in his heart."
— Matthew 5:28

But Jesus was addressing the **furnace of the mind**, the danger of nurturing thoughts that eventually lead to action. His command to **"gouge out your eye"** or **"cut off your hand"** was not literal, but a divine warning:
Do not feed what will later destroy you.

Pornography **feeds the imagination**.
Fornication **fulfills it**.

One corrupts the thoughts.
The other corrupts the body.

One stains the conscience.
The other crosses the line God clearly forbids.

The Apostle James said:

"When lust hath conceived, it bringeth forth sin: and sin, when it is finished, bringeth forth death."
— James 1:15

Pornography is the *conception* of sin…
Fornication is the *birth* of it. And the birth of it brings forth death.

Why Pastors Avoid the Topic

Today's churches will preach entire series about overcoming pornography, but remain eerily silent on fornication, cohabitation, and sex before marriage. Why?

Because confronting fornication means confronting the lifestyles of half the congregation:

• couples living together,
• boyfriends and girlfriends sleeping together,
• Christians sharing homes without sharing covenant,
• young adults who treat purity like an outdated tradition.

If the pastor preaches against fornication, he risks losing tithers, members, families, and influence.
So instead, he attacks the *surface sin* of pornography while ignoring the deeper rebellion hidden in everyday life.

Porn is an easier sermon.
Fornication is a dangerous one.

Many pastors have chosen **crowd preservation over spiritual purification**.
They avoid the topic not because Scripture is unclear, but because Scripture is unwelcome.

Paul wrote to the Corinthians with fearlessness:

"Flee fornication."
— 1 Corinthians 6:18

He did not say to negotiate with it.
He did not say manage it.
He said **flee,** run, escape.

490

But today the church has replaced that command with:

"God understands."
"We love each other."
"We're committed in our hearts."
"Marriage is just a piece of paper."

And so pulpits remain silent, while the body of Christ grows weak under the weight of tolerated sin.

Pornography vs. Fornication — A Necessary Distinction

Pornography is wicked. It destroys marriages, twists desires, and contaminates the mind. But pornography, by itself, is **not** the same as fornication.

Fornication is a **sexual union outside of marriage**. It is a sin committed with the body, and Scripture speaks with frightening clarity about it:

"Every sin that a man doeth is without the body; but he that committeth fornication sinneth against his own body."
— 1 Corinthians 6:18

Fornication is not just a sin of the mind; it is a sin of the flesh, the very act that Scripture calls a spiritual crime against one's own body, the temple of the Holy Spirit.

David's sin with Bathsheba did not begin on the rooftop; it started in the imagination.
He saw.
He considered.
He entertained.
Then he acted.

Jesus condemned the **entertaining** of lust.
Scripture condemns the **consummation** of it.

491

Pornography is the gateway.
Fornication is the grave.

Why the Church Must Speak Again

A married person who watches pornography sins because they violate the covenant of their marriage in mind and heart. But fornication is a direct violation of God's design for sexuality and covenant. It leads to death, not physical, but spiritual death, the slow dulling of conscience and loss of spiritual authority.

And yet…
I have rarely heard a pastor preach against it.

Not once have many believers heard a clear message calling them to holiness, purity, and sexual obedience. The culture celebrates fornication and the Church, in silence, affirms it.

Silence is not compassion.
Silence is surrender.

Holiness cannot return to the Church until the Church returns to holiness.
And holiness begins with honoring God in the body in sexuality, in covenant, and in obedience to His Word.

The Church does not need more polished sermons.
It needs more prophetic courage.

It needs a voice willing to say:

**"Thus saith the Lord:
Flee fornication.
Live in holiness.
Honor God with your body."**

Until we confront the sin we refuse to name, revival will always be one step beyond our reach.

Prophetic Warning — The Hidden Sin That Devours a Generation

The Lord is speaking to His Church with urgency:
Fornication is the silent destroyer of destinies.
It is the sin that steals spiritual authority, dims discernment, and cracks the foundation of a believer's walk with God.

Throughout Scripture, sexual sin is never treated lightly. It is never minimized. It is never brushed aside. It is always met with divine warnings because it carries more profound consequences than the eyes can see.

"For this is the will of God, even your sanctification, that ye should abstain from fornication."
— 1 Thessalonians 4:3

Fornication is not merely a private act; it is a spiritual agreement.
It merges bodies, but it also merges souls.
It creates soul ties that chain the heart, cloud the mind, and drag believers into spiritual numbness.

The prophetic warning is this:

If the Church does not confront fornication, fornication will confront the Church.
If pastors remain silent, judgment will speak louder.
If holiness is not restored, power cannot return.

The Holy Spirit is sounding the alarm:

- Fornication opens doors that prayer alone cannot close.

- Fornication weakens spiritual authority faster than compromise, distraction, or unbelief.

493

- Fornication turns worship into performance and prayer into routine.

- Fornication drains anointing, invites confusion, and breeds spiritual instability.

It is not possible to walk in the fullness of God's power while living in what God calls sin.

This is why revival tarries.
This is why churches feel empty even when the seats are full.
This is why worship feels emotional but not transformational.

The Lord is warning His people:

**"Come out from among them, and be ye separate…
and I will receive you."**
— 2 Corinthians 6:17

A Church that refuses to be separate cannot be Spirit-filled.
Revival demands repentance.
Holiness precedes power.

Redemption and Restoration — The God Who Makes Us New

But the prophetic warning is not the end of the story.
Because the same God who exposes sin is the God who restores sinners.
The same God who calls us out also calls us home.

No sin is greater than God's mercy.
No stain is too deep for the blood of Jesus.

Fornication may break the soul, but Jesus heals the brokenhearted.

Sexual sin may shackle the mind, but Jesus sets captives free.
Shame may whisper **"You're unclean,"** but the cross declares **"You are forgiven."**

**"If we confess our sins, He is faithful and just to forgive us our sins,
and to cleanse us from all unrighteousness."**
— 1 John 1:9

Restoration is not a second chance; it is a new beginning.

How God Restores the Broken

1. He cleanses the heart.
The blood of Jesus removes every stain — not just the guilt, but the residue.

2. He renews the mind.
Where lust once lived, purity can reign.
Where confusion once clouded, clarity can return.

3. He breaks soul ties.
God severs unhealthy spiritual bonds and restores the heart to wholeness.

4. He gives back dignity.
Shame loses its voice when grace takes its place.
Your past does not define you
you are defined by the One who redeemed you.

5. He restores purpose and anointing.
The same power that raised Christ from the dead resurrects purity, holiness, and spiritual authority.

God does not merely fix broken things, He makes them new.

"Behold, I make all things new."
— Revelation 21:5

Closing Prayer — Purity, Power, and Return

Heavenly Father,
You who see every heart and heal every wound—
we come before You with humility and repentance.

Forgive us for tolerating what You call sin.
Forgive us for choosing comfort over conviction, silence over truth,
and compromise over holiness.

Lord, purify Your Church.
Purify our bodies, our minds, our desires, and our motives.
Break every chain of fornication, every soul tie, every secret struggle,
and every hidden sin that drains our spiritual strength.

Wash us in the blood of Jesus.
Restore purity where it was lost.
Restore innocence where it was stolen.
Restore holiness where it was abandoned.

Give pastors courage to preach the truth without fear.
Give leaders boldness to confront sin in love.
Give the congregation hearts that hunger for righteousness.

Let the fire of the Holy Spirit burn again in us
not the fire of performance,
but the fire of purity, surrender, and obedience.

Create in us a clean heart, O God.
Renew a right spirit within us.
Make us a people marked by holiness,
empowered by Your Spirit,
and devoted to Christ above all.

We choose Jesus.
We choose holiness.
We choose the narrow road.
We choose Your presence over our pleasure,
Your truth over our comfort,
You will over our flesh.

**In the mighty name of Jesus Christ,
Amen.**

**Subchapter: Holiness and Sexual Purity — The
Forgotten Fire**

Holiness is not a suggestion.
Holiness is not a cultural option.
Holiness is not an outdated doctrine from a stricter
generation.

Holiness is the **heartbeat of God**.

**"Be ye holy; for I am holy."
— 1 Peter 1:16**

But in a world that worships pleasure, holiness has
become the narrow road few want to walk.
Sexual purity has become a sermon few want to hear.
And fornication has become a lifestyle many Christians
treat as normal.

Yet from Genesis to Revelation, sexual purity is treated
with the utmost seriousness.
Not because God is restrictive, but because God is
protective.

He knows that nothing destroys the soul, fractures relationships, and erodes spiritual authority faster than unrestrained sexual sin.

Holiness Is Not About Perfection — It Is About Alignment

This is the part so many people don't understand. Christians think they have to be sinless to know God or to walk with him. This is not true. God doesn't expect us to be sinless; we are all sinners and fall short of the Glory of God. Acknowledge God in all your ways, give reference to him every chance you get, even when you think it doesn't matter. The small things add up.

To walk in holiness is to walk in agreement with God. It is to surrender desires that wage war against the soul. It is to guard the heart like a treasure chest, because God has placed His Spirit inside it.

Holiness is not about legalism.
Holiness is about **belonging**.

Belonging to Christ means our bodies are no longer our own.
They are temples.
They are vessels.
They are altars.

**"Know ye not that your body is the temple of the Holy Ghost…
and ye are not your own?"
— 1 Corinthians 6:19**

Holiness is not merely morality;
it is worship.

The War for Purity

The enemy knows that if he cannot destroy a believer's soul, he will attack their purity.
If he cannot stop their calling, he will weaken their consecration.
If he cannot steal their salvation, he will steal their authority.

Sexual sin brings shame, confusion, soul ties, spiritual dullness, and emotional fragmentation.
It is not simply "behavior."
It is spiritual warfare.

And the Church must rise again with clarity, conviction, and compassion to proclaim:

Purity is not old-fashioned.
Purity is powerful.
Purity is freedom.
Purity is worship.

The narrow road is not the painful road—it is the protected road.

Holiness is not a prison; it is a promise.
A promise that God's presence rests on those who walk in His ways.

Prophetic Call to Pastors — Preach the Whole Truth Again

The Spirit of the Lord is calling pastors, leaders, and shepherds back to the **full counsel** of God.
Not the comfortable parts.
Not the popular parts.
Not the parts that keep the seats full and the budgets stable.

The whole truth.
Especially the truth about sexual sin.

The prophetic word for pastors is this:

"If you do not warn them, their blood will be on your hands."
— Ezekiel 3:18

Many pulpits today preach blessing without repentance, grace without surrender, love without holiness.

But God did not call pastors to be motivational speakers. He called them to be watchmen.

A watchman who refuses to sound the alarm is not compassionate—he is compromised.

This generation does not need more positivity from the pulpit.
It needs **purity** from the pulpit.
It needs warnings spoken in love, truth spoken in boldness, and holiness preached without apology.

The Spirit is saying:

- Preach against fornication.

- Preach against sexual immorality.

- Preach against cohabitation.

- Preach against adultery.

- Preach against the sins that cripple the soul and quench the Spirit.

Do not fear their faces.
Do not fear their reactions.
Do not fear losing members.

Fear only this:
What happens to the sheep if you refuse to feed them the truth?

The Church will never walk in power until pastors walk in purity.
And pastors will never walk in purity until they return to preaching holiness without hesitation.

God is raising up a remnant of bold shepherds—men and women who fear God more than applause, who speak truth in love, who call sin what God calls sin, and who lead the Church back into the fire of holiness.

Companion Prayer for Young Adults — Purity, Identity, and Covenant

Father,
In the name of Jesus, I lift up every young man and young woman living in a world that glorifies lust and mocks holiness.
Give them strength where they feel weak.
Give them clarity where they feel confused.
Give them an identity where the world offers imitation.

Lord, guard their eyes.
Guard their hearts.

Guard their bodies.
Break every chain of pornography, fornication, soul ties, and secret struggles.
Let them know that purity is not punishment.
it is power.
It is peace.
It is a purpose.

Teach them to honor You with their bodies.
Teach them to value covenant more than convenience.
Teach them to wait with hope, not frustration.
To stand with conviction, not compromise.
To choose holiness, not the applause of culture.

Let the Holy Spirit become their strength.
Let the Word become their anchor.
Let Jesus become their desire.

And for every young adult who has fallen, remind them:

Grace is greater.
Mercy is stronger.
Restoration is real.
You still have a future.
You still have a calling.
You still have worth.

Purify them.
Restore them.
Empower them.
Set them apart as vessels of honor for Your kingdom. In Jesus' mighty name,
Amen.

Follow-Up Teaching: Soul Ties — When the Body Creates Bonds, the Spirit Must Break

The modern Church has forgotten a spiritual truth that the early believers understood well:
Sex is not merely physical. It is covenantal.
It is spiritual. It is binding.

Every sexual union creates a **soul tie** an invisible spiritual bond that links two hearts, two bodies, two destinies, and two histories together.

This is why God created sex to be the seal of marriage, not the substitute for it.
Sex unites, binds, fuses, and intertwines.
It is covenant glue.

When sexual intimacy occurs outside of marriage, the soul ties created bring:

- emotional confusion

- spiritual heaviness

- obsessive attachment

- loss of identity

- difficulty letting go

- guilt that lingers

- memories that haunt

- spiritual fragmentation

Soul ties are not superstition.
They are Scripture.

"The two shall become one flesh."
— Genesis 2:24, Matthew 19:5, Ephesians 5:31

One flesh is not poetic language — it is spiritual reality.

Why Soul Ties Are So Dangerous

Because they connect you to the spirit, trauma, wounds, habits, and demons of another person.

If you unite yourself with a broken person, you inherit their brokenness.
If you unite yourself with a lustful person, you inherit their captivity.
If you unite yourself with a confused person, you inherit their instability.

The world sees "casual sex,"
but the spirit realm sees **covenant**.

Soul ties:

- dilute spiritual discernment

- make it hard to hear God's voice

- cloud decision-making

- bind people to toxic relationships

- weaken prayer life

- invite spiritual warfare

- and reopen doors God tried to close

Many believers wonder why they cannot move forward spiritually.
The answer is simple:

Your spirit is still tied to someone God never approved for your life.

How Soul Ties Are Broken

They are not broken by time.
They are not broken by distance.
New relationships do not break them.
They are not broken by ignoring the past.

Soul ties are broken by:

1. Confession and repentance
Admitting the sin and renouncing the connection.

2. Breaking the agreement
Speaking aloud:
"I break every soul tie formed with _____ in Jesus' name."

3. Renouncing emotional attachment
Letting the Holy Spirit sever the invisible bond.

4. Choosing holiness moving forward
Closing the door permanently.

5. Allowing God to restore the heart
He heals what sin has entangled.

Soul ties keep many believers stuck in cycles they do not understand.
But when they are severed, the soul becomes free, the mind becomes clear, and spiritual strength returns.

The Spiritual Cost of Cohabitation — When Convenience Becomes a Covenant

Cohabitation, living together outside of marriage, has become so common in society that many Christians treat it as acceptable, harmless, even practical.

But cohabitation is not a lifestyle decision.
It is a spiritual decision.
And it carries consequences far more serious than most realize.

The Church often avoids this topic because it touches the lives of many couples sitting quietly in the pews. But God has not changed His mind:

Sexual union belongs inside the covenant, never outside it.

Why Cohabitation Is Spiritually Destructive

1. It creates a marriage-like bond without God's blessing.

The couple receives the benefits of marriage without the covering of marriage.

God does not honor a relationship built in disobedience.

2. It establishes sexual sin as the foundation of the relationship.

If the foundation is sin, the structure is unstable from the start.

3. It creates destructive soul ties long before the covenant.

4. It produces spiritual vulnerability.

No matter how happy the home looks, the spiritual realm sees a house built on sand.

5. It stunts spiritual growth.

Couples cohabiting almost always experience:

- weakened conviction

- inability to hear God clearly

- lack of peace

- hidden guilt

- emotional instability

- internal spiritual warfare

6. It invites the enemy into the relationship.

What God does not cover, Satan will occupy.

7. It trains the heart for future instability.
Cohabitation is built on convenience, not covenant.
Convenience relationships produce convenience breakups.

The Lie of Cohabitation

Culture says:

- "We love each other."

- "We're preparing for marriage."

- "We're saving money."

- "It's just practical."

- "God understands."

But Scripture says:

"Flee fornication." — 1 Corinthians 6:18
"Abstain from sexual immorality." — 1 Thessalonians 4:3
"Let marriage be held in honor." — Hebrews 13:4

Cohabitation is not preparation.
Cohabitation is an imitation of a counterfeit covenant.

It offers intimacy without holiness, companionship without commitment, and pleasure without responsibility.

The Spiritual Cost Is Higher Than You Think

Cohabitation:

- kills spiritual authority

- erodes conviction

- creates cycles of sin

- blocks the flow of the Holy Spirit

- disrupts God's direction

- steals future marital peace

- postpones spiritual maturity

- opens the door to heartbreak, deception, and bitterness

God cannot bless what He has commanded us to flee.

But God will bless the couple who humbles themselves, repents, and chooses the path of holiness.

He restores.
He forgives.
He redeems.
He rebuilds.

He breaks chains and rewrites stories.

Restoration Pathway for Couples Living Together — Returning to Covenant

God's heart is not to condemn couples living together; His heart is to **restore** them.
He does not expose sin to shame us.
He exposes sin to **heal** us.

Many couples who cohabit genuinely love each other, desire a future together, and believe they are doing what makes sense. But spiritual restoration requires more than good intentions it requires **alignment** with God's design.

Below is a clear, biblical pathway of restoration for any couple living together outside of marriage:

---

1. Acknowledge the Sin

Restoration always begins with truth.

"He that covereth his sins shall not prosper..."
— Proverbs 28:13

God cannot heal what we hide.
The couple must acknowledge that:

- cohabitation is a sin

- Fornication is a sin

- The lifestyle must change

Honesty before God opens the door to healing.

---

2. Repent Together

Repentance is not an apology it is a **turning**.

The couple must:

- repent individually

- repent as a unit

- renounce the sexual behavior

- renounce the spiritual agreement they have made

Repentance breaks the enemy's legal rights.

---

3. Realign Their Living Situation

There are several ways couples can realign:

Option A: Separate living quarters until marriage.
Option B: Live in the same home but in separate rooms AND abstain from sex (a temporary and difficult but viable option for those who cannot separate financially).

Option C: Pursue a covenant marriage quickly if God has confirmed the relationship.

God honors the couple who moves toward holiness.

---

4. Break Soul Ties

Both partners must break all unhealthy soul ties from past partners and from each other (in the sinful context). A new bond can form later under God's blessing.

---

5. Enter Covenant the Right Way

Marriage welcomes God into the relationship.

Covenant restores:

- peace
- harmony
- spiritual authority
- protection
- clarity
- blessing

When a couple chooses God's way, God rebuilds what sin damaged.

God does not withhold blessings from those who return to Him.

Prayer to Break Soul Ties

In the name of Jesus Christ,
I renounce every ungodly soul tie formed through sexual
sin, emotional attachment, or disobedience.
I break every bond connecting me to anyone who is not my
spouse or ordained by God for my life.

I command every spiritual chain to be broken.
Every unhealthy attachment must be severed.
Every emotional dependency needs to be released.
Every memory that binds me to be healed.

I declare that my mind, my body, my soul, and my spirit
belong to Jesus Christ alone.
No past partner has power over my emotions, desires,
identity, or future.
I am free from every spiritual residue, every emotional
entanglement, every demonic foothold, and every invisible
rope tying me to my past.

Holy Spirit, fill every empty place in me.
Restore my purity.
Restore my wholeness.
Restore my identity.

In Jesus' mighty name,
Amen.

Deliverance-Style Declaration for Spiritual Cleansing

Speak this aloud with authority:

**"By the blood of Jesus, I reclaim my body as the
temple of the Holy Spirit.
Every spirit of lust, fornication, confusion, shame, and
addiction has no place in me."**

"I break every chain of sexual sin.
I break every generational curse of sexual immorality.

I rebuke every demonic influence that entered through pornography, fornication, or ungodly relationships."

"I close every door I opened through sin.
I cancel every assignment of the enemy against my purity.
I uproot every seed planted by lust, trauma, manipulation, or temptation."

"My mind is renewed.
My body is cleansed.
My spirit is restored.
I walk in holiness, purity, clarity, and spiritual authority."

"Whom the Son sets free is free indeed.
I am free.
I am forgiven.
I am restored.
I am consecrated.
I belong to Jesus."

Amen.

Teaching on Sexual Purity in Marriage — Holiness Within the Covenant

Sexual purity does not end at the wedding altar.
it begins **anew** there.

Marriage does not make lust disappear.
Marriage does not eliminate temptation.
Marriage does not automatically purify the heart.

Sexual purity in marriage is the ongoing commitment to honor God, honor your spouse, and honor the covenant.

1. Marriage Is a Covenant, Not a Contract

Contracts can be broken.
Covenants are consecrated.

A covenant marriage invites God into the union and makes the couple **one flesh** under God's protection.

2. Purity Protects Intimacy

Purity is not prudish.
Purity creates deeper:

- trust

- intimacy

- unity

- emotional connection

- spiritual strength

Impurity destroys these things.

3. Guarding the Marriage Bed

Scripture commands:

"Marriage is honorable... and the bed undefiled."
— Hebrews 13:4

This means:

- no pornography

- no fantasy with others

- no adulterous thoughts

- no emotional affairs

- no opening the marriage to outside influences

The marriage bed is a sacred altar.

4. Holiness Strengthens Communication

Couples who guard their purity communicate:

- more honestly
- more humbly
- more intimately
- more compassionately

Impurity creates distance, secrecy, and shame.

5. Purity Is a Weapon Against the Enemy

Satan attacks marriages through:

- lust
- secrecy
- boredom
- resentment
- unmet needs
- comparison
- temptation

Purity protects the marriage against these assaults.

6. Purity Requires Discipline and Surrender

Holiness in marriage requires:

- prayer together
- confession when necessary

- accountability

- boundaries with others

- forgiveness

- renewing the mind

- choosing love daily

Marriage thrives when God is first.

7. Purity Makes Intimacy Worship

Sex in marriage is not dirty; it is divine.
It is not shameful, it is sacred.
It is not casual, it is a covenant.

When a married couple guards their purity, their intimacy becomes:

- worship

- unity

- healing

- bonding

- spiritual renewal

- the expression of two becoming one

Sexual purity in marriage honors the God who created desire, designed intimacy, and blessed the union.

Covenant Steps for Couples Preparing for Marriage A Guide to Holy Foundation

Marriage is not built on romance, compatibility, finances, or even love alone.
Marriage is built on a **covenant**.
A covenant relationship must begin on a covenant foundation.

Here are the essential steps for couples preparing for a God-ordained marriage:

---

1. Establish Spiritual Alignment

Before you plan a wedding, ensure you are united in spirit.

Ask:

- Do we pray together?
- Do we worship together?
- Do we study the Word together?
- Do our callings align?
- Do we lead each other toward holiness?

Spiritual alignment determines long-term stability.

---

2. Renounce Past Soul Ties

Every past romantic or sexual connection must be broken.

Unbroken soul ties become:

- emotional interference
- spiritual baggage
- jealousy
- insecurity
- hidden temptation

A clean covenant requires a cleansed soul.

---

3. Pursue Purity and Abstinence Until Marriage

Abstaining is not punishment.
It is preparation.
It is an honor.
It is obedience.

Purity clears the spiritual atmosphere and blesses the home.

---

4. Seek Godly Counsel

A covenant marriage needs seasoned voices:

- pastors

- mentors

- married believers who walk in integrity

Wise counsel exposes blind spots before they become battles.

---

5. Deal With Generational Patterns

Address patterns such as:

- divorce

- infidelity

- abuse

- addiction

- manipulation

- father or mother wounds

Whatever is not confronted will be repeated.

---

6. Establish Healthy Boundaries

Set boundaries with:

- co-workers
- friends
- former partners
- social media
- emotional "safe spaces" outside the relationship

Boundaries protect unity.

---

7. Invite God Into Every Part of the Relationship

Not just the spiritual side, but:

- communication
- finances
- conflict
- intimacy
- decision-making

Marriage is strongest when God is central.

---

8. Enter Marriage With a Covenant Mindset

Marriage is not temporary.
It is not an experiment.
It is not trial-based; it is not like buying a car, you don't get a test drive before you buy it. Meaning, you don't base your marriage on sexual performance.

It is:

- sacrificial

- holy

- sacred

- binding

- unbreakable under God

A covenant marriage is built to last because God Himself holds it together.

Prayer for Married Couples to Restore Intimacy

Heavenly Father,
In the name of Jesus, I lift our marriage before You.
Touch our hearts.
Heal our wounds.
Restore our emotional, spiritual, and physical intimacy.

Remove every wall that years of pain have built.
Remove every memory that hinders closeness.
Remove every lie of the enemy that whispers division.

Lord, purify our desire for one another.
Let love flow freely.
Let forgiveness be complete.
Let every broken place be mended by Your hand.

Where passion has faded, rekindle it.
Where communication has failed, rebuild it.
Where trust has been wounded, restore it.

Let our intimacy become holy again.
Free from shame, comparison, fear, or resentment.
Let our unity reflect the unity of Christ and the Church.

Bless our marriage.
Bless our covenant.
Bless our home.

In Jesus' mighty name,
Amen.

Prophetic Exhortation for Men — Rise Into Your Calling

Men of God,
the Spirit is calling you higher.

You are not called to be passive, silent, or spiritually absent.
You are called to be:

- protectors

- priests of your home

- providers

- leaders

- intercessors

- warriors

- men of purity

- men of integrity

- men of prayer

You are called to carry the weight of spiritual authority—not as dictators, but as servants.

The Lord says:

"Rise, O mighty man of valor."

Break the chains of lust.
Break the chains of generational sin.
Break the chains of apathy.

Your family depends on your obedience.
Your wife depends on your leadership.
Your children depend on your example.
Heaven depends on your holiness.
Hell fears your awakening.

Stand up.
Take your place.
Walk in righteousness.
Lead with humility.
Fight for your family.
Serve with love.

This is not the hour for weak men.
This is the hour for holy warriors.

The Temptation of Power — Kingdoms Instead of Crosses

Finally, Satan showed Jesus all the kingdoms of the world and offered them in exchange for worship.
And the tragedy of the modern church is that many have accepted that offer.
Power has replaced purity. Politics has replaced prayer. The pulpit has become a platform for influence rather than intercession.

We have seen it before when Constantine used the cross to unify Rome, when popes crowned kings, and when governments used religion to control hearts. The pattern has not changed; it has only evolved.

Jesus refused the kingdoms of the world, yet today many churches seek them. They build empires instead of altars. They chase followers instead of souls. They crave applause instead of anointing.

"What shall it profit a man, if he shall gain the whole world, and lose his own soul?"
— *Mark 8:36*

The true kingdom of God is not of this world. **(John 18:36)** When religion seeks earthly power, it loses heavenly authority.

The True Church — A Body, Not a Throne

The church Jesus built was never meant to be a monument. It was meant to be a movement of a living body where every believer serves, preaches, prays, and ministers.
Paul said:

"Now ye are the body of Christ, and members in particular."
— *1 Corinthians 12:27*

Every part matters. Every member is called. The Spirit gives gifts to all, not just pastors, prophets, or bishops. When only one man speaks, the rest of the body grows silent. And when the body stops talking, the world stops hearing the gospel.

That is why revival doesn't begin on the platform; it starts in the pew.
It begins in the heart of the ordinary believer who decides to live as Christ's hands and feet.

Closing Reflection and Prayer

Heavenly Father,
We see how the enemy has deceived not only individuals but also Your church.
Forgive us for exalting men where only Christ should reign.
Forgive us for loving comfort more than conviction, and power more than purity.
Raise up a generation of believers who will speak truth even when pulpits fall silent.
Restore the church to be a body again, every member filled with the Spirit, every heart surrendered to Christ, every home an altar of prayer.
Let pastors lead in humility, congregations rise in ministry, and Your Son be the only head of the church.

In Jesus' name, Amen.

Epilogue

The Living Christ

I've come to see that the most significant evidence of Christ alive today isn't found in stained glass or sermons, it's found in **changed lives**.

There is no greater miracle than watching a person turn from darkness to light, from sin to salvation. I've seen it with my own eyes, the moment when conviction breaks through pride, when tears of repentance wash away years of pain, and when a once cold heart comes alive again.

That's when you know God is real. That's when you know the Spirit is moving.

"My brothers, if anyone among you wanders from the truth and someone brings him back, let him know that whoever brings back a sinner from his wandering will save his soul from death and will cover a multitude of sins."
— **James 5:19–20**

There is **power in ministry,** not the ministry of titles or stages, but the ministry of compassion and courage. Every time we share the Gospel with someone who's lost, we are continuing the work Jesus began. And that work was never confined to the four walls of a church.

Ministry Beyond the Walls

Jesus did His ministry in the streets, the fields, and the homes of ordinary people. He ate with tax collectors, spoke with outcasts, and laid hands on lepers. He was not a spectator. He was a servant.

He didn't wait for people to come to Him in a temple; He went to them where they lived.

Today, too many churches have forgotten that. Sunday mornings have become performances, with rows of spectators listening to one man preach while the congregation sits quietly and calls it "worship." But the Bible says otherwise:

"Be doers of the word, and not hearers only, deceiving yourselves."
— James 1:22

God didn't call us to be listeners; He called us to be *laborers.*
Faith isn't a show; it's a service.

Every believer is called to ministry. You don't need a pulpit to preach, just a heart that's willing. The real work of the Church happens on Monday through Saturday in workplaces, neighborhoods, prisons, and hospitals, wherever the hurting need hope.

The Church Must Awaken

The Church today must rise from comfort and reclaim its purpose. Too much emphasis has been placed on the preacher's personality rather than on the Presence. The focus has to return to God alone.

For too long, the Church has traded its spiritual authority for worldly approval. When the government begins to dictate what truth can be spoken, faith becomes compromised.

In 1954, under **President Lyndon B. Johnson**, the **501(c)(3)** tax-exempt status was introduced, allowing churches to avoid taxes only if they remained silent on certain political matters. What seemed like a benefit became a form of bondage.

When the state can silence the Church, the light of truth begins to dim.
The Gospel must never be filtered through fear of losing funding.

The pulpit should be the one place in the world where truth is spoken boldly, not politically, but **biblically**. The Church must be free to speak out on moral issues of life, righteousness, justice, and sin without fear of penalty.

Jesus Himself confronted both religious and political powers. His message was spiritual, but it had earthly consequences because it challenged corruption and injustice. That's why both the temple and the empire conspired to crucify Him.

The Church must follow His example not by aligning with parties, but by standing for *principles.*
Vote by **godly conviction**, not cultural convenience.
Support leaders who defend truth, protect life, and honor God's Word.

If you must align with a party, align with the party that defends the life of the unborn and the sanctity of life. Align with the party of free speech. Not the party of Lyndon B Johnson, who offered the bail of Satan with tax exemption to quiet the church.

I encourage churches to no longer file for tax-exempt status and to be free from Government control. Exercise your free speech and do as Jesus commanded us to do, render unto Caesar what is Caesar's and render unto God what is God's.

Silence has never been the calling of the Church. Truth must be spoken even when it costs us. Especially then.

The Church of Jesus Christ was never meant to slumber under the comfort of culture. It was meant to **stand as a light in darkness**, a voice crying out in the wilderness, a city set upon a hill that cannot be hidden **(Matthew 5:14).** But somewhere along the way, the flame grew dim.

Too many pulpits have traded the **Presence of God** for the popularity of men. Too many preachers have pursued applause rather than anointing. The modern Church has become a stage for performance instead of a sanctuary for repentance.
The focus must return to **God alone,** not the preacher, not the personality, not the platform, but the **power and presence of the Holy Spirit**.

"Awake thou that sleepest, and arise from the dead, and Christ shall give thee light."
— *Ephesians 5:14*

From Authority to Approval

For too long, the Church has traded its divine authority for worldly approval.
Once, prophets confronted kings; now, pastors seek their approval.
Once, truth thundered from pulpits; now, it is whispered through fear of offense.

The Lord said through the prophet Isaiah:

"Cry aloud, spare not, lift up thy voice like a trumpet, and show my people their transgression."
— *Isaiah 58:1*

But instead of sounding the trumpet, many have muted it.

What appeared to be a blessing was in fact a **bribe from Babylon**.
It was Satan's subtle bargain: *"I will give you comfort, if you give me your voice."*

Jesus warned,

"No man can serve two masters... Ye cannot serve God and mammon."
— *Matthew 6:24*

The 501(c)(3) status became the golden chain that bound the pulpit to the state.
When the government dictates what truth can be spoken, **faith becomes compromised**. The same spirit that told the apostles, *"Do not speak in this name anymore,"* now whispers through policy and fear.

But Peter and John replied:

**"Whether it be right in the sight of God to hearken unto you more than unto God, judge ye.
For we cannot but speak the things which we have seen and heard."**
— *Acts 4:19–20*

That is the courage the Church must rediscover.

Render Unto Caesar, But Speak for God

Jesus Himself confronted both **religious and political powers**. His message was spiritual, yet it carried earthly consequences because it threatened corruption, greed, and injustice. The Pharisees wanted to silence Him. Rome wanted to crucify Him.

Both religion and government united against truth, and they still do.

When asked whether to pay taxes, Jesus answered,

"Render therefore unto Caesar the things which are Caesar's; and unto God the things that are God's."
— Matthew 22:21

That means we honor lawful authority, but **we do not surrender our divine authority**.
Render Caesar his coin but never your conscience.

The Church must not be afraid to speak about life, righteousness, and sin.
To remain silent about abortion, corruption, sexual perversion, and deception is to join hands with darkness.
The Gospel is not political, but it **is moral**, and morality will always clash with politics when the world walks in sin.

The Church and the Crossroads of Courage

The early disciples faced prison, exile, and death for proclaiming the truth. Yet their courage turned the world upside down.

"These that have turned the world upside down are come hither also."
— Acts 17:6

Compare that to the comfort of today's padded pews, polished sermons, and pulpits afraid of offending donors.
The modern Church often fears losing funding more than losing the fire of the Holy Spirit.

But a Church afraid to speak the truth is already dead.
Silence in the face of sin is not humility; it is **complicity**.

"If the watchman sees the sword coming and does not blow the trumpet to warn the people... I will hold the

watchman accountable for their blood."
— *Ezekiel 33:6*

It is time for pastors to become prophets again.
It is time for pulpits to thunder again.
It is time for the Church to wake from its sleep.

The Cost of Freedom and the Call to Speak

Freedom is never free. The cross itself was the cost of truth.
Jesus was not crucified for performing miracles. He was crucified for **speaking the truth** that exposed hypocrisy and corruption.

The Church that bears His name must follow His example.
Not by aligning with parties, but by aligning with **principles**, the principles of life, righteousness, and truth.

Vote by **godly conviction**, not **cultural convenience**.
Support leaders who defend the unborn, protect speech, and honor the Word of God.
Do not fear the loss of tax exemption; fear the loss of truth.

Do not support the party of Lyndon B Johnson that offered the bribe of Satan to keep the churches quiet. I encourage the churches not to take the bribe of Satan; instead, **"Render therefore unto Caesar the things which are Caesar's; and unto God the things that are God's."**
— *Matthew 22:21*

Let the Church once again declare:

"We must obey God rather than men."
— *Acts 5:29*

If a church must choose between freedom and faith, let it choose faith.

If it must choose between silence and truth, let it speak, even at high cost.

A Call to the Sleeping Bride

The Church is the Bride of Christ, but too often she has fallen asleep in the lap of Delilah, comforted by the world that seeks to destroy her strength. Like Samson, she has had her hair, the symbol of her covenant, cut by compromise. But God is calling her to awaken again.

"Let us rejoice and be glad and give Him glory! For the wedding of the Lamb has come, and His bride has made herself ready."
— *Revelation 19:7*

The sleeping Bride must awaken, wash her garments in righteousness, and rise to meet her Bridegroom.
She must preach again. She must prophesy again. She must pray again.

Silence has never been the calling of the Church.
Truth must be spoken even when it costs us.
Especially then.

Revival Beyond the Walls: The Power of God in the Streets

"A call to awaken the Church beyond its walls."

The Power of God Cannot Be Contained.

The power of God is not confined to four walls.
Buildings, pulpits, or stained glass cannot contain it.
The power of God is alive in the streets, in the prisons, in the shelters, and in the places where hope has been forgotten.

We gather in church to **refuel**, not to **retreat**.
We meet to encourage one another, but the real test of our faith begins when we step outside those doors.
The Gospel was never meant to be trapped inside a sanctuary.
It was meant to be carried to the hungry, the addicted, the abandoned, the cold, and the forgotten.

"Go ye into all the world, and preach the gospel to every creature." — **Mark 16:15**

That is where Jesus went to the forgotten places.
He healed the broken, fed the hungry, and comforted the lost.
And that is where He still waits for His Church to follow.

A Challenge to the Comfortable Church

We can gather for a few hours every Sunday, and we should, but the mission doesn't end there.
The Church that gathers only, but never goes, becomes a museum of memories rather than a movement of miracles.

It's time for believers to rise from their seats, shake off complacency, and become the hands and feet of Christ.
Jesus didn't preach from behind a pulpit.
He preached on mountainsides, from fishing boats, and in the marketplaces.
He touched lepers, ate with sinners, and defended the condemned.
He went where the religious refused to go.

"For I was hungry and you gave Me food; I was thirsty, and you gave Me drink; I was a stranger, and you took Me in." — **Matthew 25:35**

It's time for pastors to get uncomfortable.
It's time for the Church to step down from its platform and walk with the people.
It's time for sermons to turn into service.

Hope in the Darkness

My favorite word in the Bible is **Hope** not because it sounds poetic, but because I've lived it.
I learned the meaning of hope when I was down to nothing, when the lights were out, when I was taking cold baths by candlelight, when I had no answers, no strength, and no one to turn to.

But in that silence, God spoke.
Not through thunder or earthquake, but through a whisper that said, *"You're not done yet."*
That whisper ignited the fire of hope within me, the same hope that I now carry to others.

The same God who met me in my darkness is calling His Church to meet others in theirs.
We are called to bring light into places where candles have long since burned out.

"The people who sat in darkness have seen a great light." — **Matthew 4:16**

Faith in Action

It's time to move beyond attendance into **action**.
God never called us to be spectators; He called us to be servants.

Stand up when others sit down.
Feed the hungry, visit the sick, clothe the poor, comfort the lonely.

The true Church is not measured by attendance, but by **impact**.
Every soul we touch is a sermon.
Every act of compassion is a worship service.
Every prayer we whisper over a stranger is a testimony.

Let the people of God rise not in pride, but in purpose.
Let pastors step out from behind pulpits and into the pain of their communities.
Let believers walk into neighborhoods, shelters, and hospitals and declare, *"There is still hope."*

"The harvest truly is great, but the labourers are few."
— Luke 10:2

Revival in the Streets

The power of God is found in motion, not in walls.
We are His vessels, and revival begins when we carry His Spirit to where it's most needed.

The streets are God's sanctuary.
The broken are His congregation.
The forgotten are His priority.

We are not called to build kingdoms; we are called to build bridges.
We are not called to grow audiences; we are called to grow disciples.

534

"Then the Lord said to the servant, Go out into the highways and hedges, and compel them to come in, that My house may be filled." — Luke 14:23

We must go to the streets, the neighborhoods, and the homes where pain lives, for that is where Jesus still walks.

The Spiritual Root of Disease and the Battle for the Lost

Every physical struggle has a deeper spiritual root. Scripture teaches that iniquity can pass "to the third and fourth generation" **(Exodus 34:7),** and many of the wounds we carry today are spiritual diseases inherited from the brokenness of those before us. I know this truth personally. For years, I wrestled with a deep, invisible pain I could not explain until God revealed it: a spirit of rejection.

I was adopted. My biological mother abandoned me. And whether a person realizes it or not, abandonment opens the door to a spiritual wound that can follow a person for decades. At a ministry retreat, beinhealth.com, the Holy Spirit exposed what had been tormenting me all my life. It wasn't just emotion; it was a spiritual assignment against my identity and calling.

This is the same battle consuming so many in our world today. People in addiction are not merely making bad choices; they are lost souls numbing spiritual wounds. They reach for drugs to bury loneliness, emptiness, and unhealed pain. The addiction isn't the root; it is the symptom. The real battle is spiritual.

This is why God called me into ministry:
To reach the broken, the addicted, the forgotten, and to expose how the enemy uses drugs as a weapon to destroy lives.

I see the same battle that was in my life, and now I see it in other people's lives. The drugs are not the true enemy; they are the chains the enemy uses to choke out their purpose. Even after addicts become clean, the enemy will not simply walk away. Jesus Himself warned that when an unclean spirit leaves a person, it seeks to return with seven more **(Matthew 12:43–45).** This is biblical warfare, spiritual reality, and foundational truth.

The retreat is not just a detox. It is deliverance, equipping her with the knowledge and spiritual armor to defeat an enemy that will try again.

Drugs are ripping apart our nation. They are destroying minds, fragmenting families, and eroding the moral and spiritual fabric of America. Drive through any city, and you will see the evidence: homelessness, addiction, despair, and people wandering like sheep without a shepherd. These are not "problems." These are souls. Lost, wounded, spiritually starved souls who need prayer, compassion, and the truth of God.

But instead, culture encourages selfishness. Especially around Christmas, the season is meant to reflect the generosity of Christ. People rush through stores, obsessed with gifts, distracted by busyness, and blind to the suffering at their feet. We forget that this season is not about consumption; it is about compassion.

Christmas is also the time when the suicide rate climbs higher. Why? Because the lonely feel lonelier. The rejected feel forgotten. Those with no family feel the weight of emptiness more deeply than at any other time of year.

If you have a family to sit with during the holidays, you are profoundly blessed, and you should thank God. Because many do not. They are on the streets. They are isolated. They are lost.

And they are there for a reason: they do not yet know God, and they are waiting for someone who *does* to see them, reach them, and remind them that they matter.

A Call to Action

So I challenge you this day:
Be uncomfortable for God.
Stand up until your feet ache.
Serve until your heart is spent.
Go where others won't.
Speak to the forgotten, the broken, the addicted, the rejected.

Jesus didn't wait for people to come to Him. He went to them.
He called fishermen from boats, tax collectors from tables, and sinners from despair.
He said, *"Follow Me."*
And they did not go into a temple, but into the world.

If we are truly His followers, then we must walk where He walked.
We must move beyond the four walls and into the fields, the alleys, the shelters, and the streets.
That's where revival lives.
That's where miracles happen.
That's where the power of God still moves.

"The harvest truly is great, but the labourers are few."
— Luke 10:2

Closing Prayer for Revival

Heavenly Father, stir our hearts again.
Tear down the walls of fear and comfort that keep us silent.

Send us into the streets, into the dark corners, into the broken places of this world.
Let us be Your hands, Your feet, Your voice, and Your light.
Anoint our steps and fill our mouths with hope.
Revive Your Church, Lord, not in buildings, but in hearts.
And may we never again be content inside the walls.
In Jesus' name, Amen.

AMEN

Closing Prayer — A Cry for Awakening

Father in Heaven,
Awaken Your Church from slumber.
Break the chains of compromise that bind the pulpit and silence the prophets.
Give Your people boldness to speak truth without fear of man or loss of favor.
Let every pastor be a watchman, every believer a warrior, every church a beacon of truth.
May we render to Caesar what is his, but never give him what belongs to You, our voice, our faith, our conviction.
Let the sleeping Bride arise, clothed in fire, fearless before kings,
Proclaiming once more: **"Jesus Christ is Lord."**
Amen.

The Living Christ in Us

The same Christ who walked the shores of Galilee now walks through us. Every act of love, every soul saved, every truth spoken in courage, that's Christ still alive in the world.

He lives through ministry.
He moves through mercy.
He reigns through righteousness.

The world doesn't need more religion; it needs more reflection of Him.

When believers stop watching and start working, the Spirit of God begins to flow again. And when the Church stops hiding and starts helping, the Kingdom advances like wildfire.

That's the Church Jesus died to create, not a monument, but a movement.

Closing Words

I've seen God's power in many forms in nature, in prayer, in Scripture, but nowhere more powerfully than in a heart that turns back to Him. When a sinner repents, heaven rejoices. When one soul returns, the Kingdom expands.

That's the living Christ still redeeming, calling, saving.

He doesn't live behind the altar. He lives inside every believer willing to say, **"Here I am, Lord, send me."**

And suppose the Church ever rediscovers that truth. In that case, if believers rise to *do* the Word instead of merely *hearing* it, the fire of revival will sweep the earth again, not through religion, but through relationship.

Because Jesus is not dead, and His work is not done. He lives through every one of us who dares to believe, to speak, and to serve.

Epilogue/Summary

"Religion killed Him, but love raised Him."

In *Religion Killed Jesus*, author **James LeCroy** takes readers on a journey through history, scripture, and personal revelation to uncover one of the most uncomfortable truths in all of faith: that the same human systems built to honor God have often betrayed Him.

From the crucifixion of Christ to the corruption of early power, from the burning of prophets to the modern church's complacency, LeCroy traces the repeating pattern of religion choosing control over compassion.

Yet this book is not a condemnation; it's a call to awakening.

Through personal testimony, biblical insight, and spiritual reflection, *Religion Killed Jesus* invites readers to rediscover the living Christ outside the walls of organized religion. It challenges believers to trade routine for relationships, fear for faith, and ritual for the raw power of grace.

LeCroy reminds us that the Gospel was never meant to be bound by politics, institutions, or titles, but to be lived through love, truth, and the transforming power of the Holy Spirit.

This is not a book about losing faith.
It's about finding it again in its purest, most potent form.

"Be doers of the Word, and not hearers only."
— James 1:22

Author's Note

James LeCroy lives in Raleigh, North Carolina, where he writes, studies, and reflects on faith, history, and truth. When not at home, he often retreats to the mountains or the coastal places where he says he feels **"closest to the heartbeat of God."**

James is a student of Scripture, a lifelong seeker of truth, and a minister who has witnessed firsthand the transforming power of grace. His writings blend historical insight with spiritual conviction, calling readers to a deeper walk with Christ, not bound by religion but set free by relationship.

"The greatest proof that Jesus lives is not in our churches, but in changed hearts." *James LeCroy.*

Dedication

This book is lovingly dedicated to **Archie Morris**, my late friend from Chesterfield, Virginia, whose faith, wisdom, and unwavering belief in God shaped my understanding of truth. His life and friendship were a testimony to the quiet strength of the Holy Spirit.

To **my mother, Irene LeCroy**, the one who has stood by me through every storm and season of life, the only person who has truly loved me without condition. Her loyalty, faith, and love have been my foundation and my constant reminder of God's grace in human form.

To **Charlie Kirk**, a modern-day disciple of Christ who has boldly spoken truth in the face of darkness and cultural opposition. His courage to stand against evil inspires this generation to do the same.
May his unwavering devotion to righteousness remind us all what it means to be a faithful witness for Jesus Christ.
#WeAreCharlieKirk

And finally, this book is dedicated to the calling God placed on my life through **Living Stones Spiritual House Ministries**, inspired by 1 Peter 2:4-5, *through my brother in Christ,* **Doug.** Doug and I met through a mutual friend at Beach Church in Myrtle Beach. beachchurch.org

"As you come to Him, the living stone rejected by humans but chosen by God and precious to Him, you also, like living stones, are being built into a spiritual house to be a holy priesthood."

Through **LivingStonesSpiritualHouse.org**, I strive to continue that work, ministering beyond walls, reaching the lost, and teaching believers to become the living stones of God's spiritual house.

If you need someone to talk to about your spiritual life or need to know more about the power of God, please call my Living Stones spiritual retreat hotline at **800-865-7822**, and someone will talk with you.

Spiritual Support and Guidance
If you find yourself in need of someone to talk to about your spiritual journey or if you desire to learn more about the transformative power of God, you are not alone. The Living Stones Spiritual Retreat Hotline is available for you. By calling **800-865-7822**, you will be connected with someone ready to listen, support, and walk with you in

your search for faith and truth. No matter where you are on your journey, compassionate guidance and prayerful encouragement are just a phone call away.

I also dedicate this work to my creative journey through writing and media, including my first published book, **ElvisIsAlive.org**, available on Amazon, a work of fiction that carries a powerful message from God, and my **YouTube channel, RunFitness.com**, a ministry of health and spiritual endurance.

My vision is to continue traveling across the United States and soon overseas to share the message of **faith, fitness, and the fullness of life** that comes from walking daily with Christ.

If you or anyone you know is suffering from a disease, mental anguish, depression, drug addiction, divorce, suicidal thoughts, demonic oppression, anything, please get in touch with Beinhealth.com at:

Main Campus

4178 Crest Highway
Thomaston, Georgia 30286
Phone: M-F, 8:30am - 5:00pm

706.646.2074
800.453.5775
Contact

Please ask for Jamie and mention that James LeCroy referred you.

May this book, and every project that flows from it, honor the One who lives forever
Jesus Christ, the Living Stone.

www.ingramcontent.com/pod-product-compliance
Lightning Source LLC
Chambersburg PA
CBHW070337090426
42733CB00009B/1213